WOMEN'S ROLES IN SEVENTEENTH-CENTURY AMERICA

WOMEN'S ROLES IN SEVENTEENTH-CENTURY AMERICA

Merril D. Smith

Women's Roles in American History

GREENWOOD PRESS
Westport, Connecticut • London

Library of Congress Cataloging-in-Publication Data

Smith, Merril D., 1956–
    Women's roles in seventeenth-century America / by Merril D. Smith.
        p.cm. — (Women's roles in American history, 1553-507X)
    Includes bibliographical references and index.
    ISBN 978-0-313-33976-9 (alk. paper)
        1. Women—United States—History—17th century. 2. Women—United
States—Social conditions—17th century. 3. Social role—United States—
History—17th century. 4. United States—Social conditions—17th
century. I. Title.
    HQ1416.S63 2008
    305.40973'09032—dc22   2008010078

British Library Cataloguing in Publication Data is available.

Library of Congress Catalog Card Number: 2008010078

ISBN: 978-0-313-33976-9
ISSN: 1553-507X

First published in 2008

Greenwood Press, 88 Post Road West, Westport, CT 06881
An imprint of Greenwood Publishing Group, Inc.
www.greenwood.com

Printed in the United States of America

∞™

The paper used in this book complies with the
Permanent Paper Standard issued by the National
Information Standards Organization (Z39.48–1984).

10   9   8   7   6   5   4   3   2   1

For my mother
Sylvia L. Schreiber
And my daughters
Megan J. Smith and Sheryl C. Smith

Contents

Series Foreword

Women's history is still being reclaimed. The geographical and chronological scope of the Women's Roles through History series contributes to our understanding of the many facets of women's lives. Indeed, with this series, a content-rich survey of women's lives through history and around the world is available for the first time for high school students to the general public.

The impetus for the series came from the success of Greenwood's 1999 reference *Women's Roles in Ancient Civilizations*, edited by Bella Vivante. Librarians noted the need for new treatments of women's history, and women's roles are an important part of the history curriculum in every era. Thus, this series intensely covers women's roles in Europe and the United States, with volumes by the century or by era, and one volume each is devoted to the major populated areas of the globe—Africa, the Middle East, Asia, and Latin America and the Caribbean.

Each volume provides essay chapters on major topics such as:

- family life
- marriage and childbearing
- religion
- public life
- lives of ordinary women
- women and the economy
- political status
- legal status
- arts

Country and regional differences are discussed as necessary.
   Other elements include

- introduction, providing historical context
- chronology
- glossary
- bibliography
- period illustrations

The volumes, written by historians, offer sound scholarship in an accessible manner. A wealth of disparate material is conveniently synthesized in one source. As well, the insight provided into daily life, which readers find intriguing, further helps to bring knowledge of women's struggles, duties, contributions, pleasures, and more to a wide audience.

Acknowledgments

The writing of a book is never a solo effort. I owe thanks to the many people who have inspired, admired, encouraged, and helped me with this project. Sarah Colwell, my first editor for this volume at Greenwood, helped me get off to a good start. Wendi Schnaufer, who took over for Sarah, has been a wonderful editor. She has encouraged and prodded, but she understands that "real life" sometimes interferes with the best-laid plans. I look forward to working with her again.

My mother, Sylvia Schreiber, and my daughters, Megan and Sheryl, to whom I've dedicated this book, have helped me to understand my role—and theirs—as twenty-first-century women. I have learned so much about being a daughter, a mother, and a wife from them. My mom has taught me valuable lessons about parenting, working outside of the home while managing a household, and cooking without recipes using a little of this and that—a skill I've tried to pass on to my daughters. Both daughters have helped with this book by reading portions, helping to look for illustrations, and ignoring the clutter of books and papers I leave all over the house. My daughters are all that I could wish for, and I write this despite having gone through the college application process, boyfriend/girlfriend issues, and general teenage angst. They have taught me important lessons about being a mother. From them I have also learned that somehow it is possible to talk to several people online, surf the Web, listen to music, pretend to listen to your mother, do homework, and somehow get good grades. In addition, I have learned that Stephen Sondheim is indeed a god, and that chocolate is an essential key to happiness.

Else L. Hambleton has truly been a wonderful friend. She has read and commented on all of the chapters at some point, and she has even read some of them while on vacation. I cannot express my thanks and appreciation strongly enough, but I owe her at least one dinner. Besides being my "designated reader," she has been a friend who understands about being a wife and mother in the present, as well as in the seventeenth century. Thanks to phones and the Internet we can discuss husbands, children, recipes, travel plans, and our history projects. Although I wish we lived closer to one another, it's probably good that we don't—because we would spend all of our time talking and eating!

Doug, my husband of almost thirty years, has been supportive and patient, as I've worked on yet another book. He has watched me work through weekends, holidays, and long past my normal bedtime. Somehow all this fun has not inspired him to write, but that's good, because this house could not handle two writers, I fear.

Finally, thanks to friends who are always willing to listen to me complain and vent: Debby Mosley-Duffy, Stephanie Scanlon, Ann Hayes, Beth Kohler, and Guy Pridy. You don't know how much that means to me when I'm sitting here alone with my computer.

Introduction

Women's Roles in Seventeenth-Century America describes, examines, and analyzes the lives of women and girls in the British North American colonies of the seventeenth century. In writing *Women's Roles in Seventeenth-Century America*, I hope to achieve two goals. The first is to examine how seventeenth-century attitudes, perceptions, and beliefs about women affected and shaped their lives. Common beliefs about the weakness of women's bodies and minds must have had an effect on many women, while the restrictions placed on women regarding such things as attending college or speaking in public prevented many women from entering careers or even expressing their views.

The other goal of this volume is to demonstrate how significant women were in shaping the world around them. Despite restrictions and prohibitions, some women did step outside of their usual roles to publish their work, to express religious beliefs, and to initiate court suits. Yet within their typical roles as wives and mothers, women were also important, as the early Chesapeake settlers found when there were few women in the settlement to cook, mend, and do laundry. The phrase "women's roles" is somewhat misleading because it implies fixed positions and responsibilities for women, when, in fact, women's roles in the seventeenth century were fluid and overlapping, as I suspect they have been in most periods of history. Not only were most women wives and mothers, but also at times, many of them were immigrants, church members or heretics, accused witches, court participants, teachers, servants, businesswomen, farmers, poets, and warriors—among other roles.

Although both religious and secular leaders frequently viewed women as beings who needed to be closely watched and controlled because of their perceived lustful natures and weak self-control, many women bravely adapted to new lives and circumstances in the British North American colonies, sometimes placing themselves in hazardous situations, while, in many cases, also bearing children and running households. Some women, such as Puritan Anne Hutchinson and Quaker Mary Dyer, dared to speak in public; others, such as Indian captive Hannah Duston, physically confronted enemies. Some women, such as Puritan Anne Bradstreet, expressed themselves through poetry, and a few women, such as African Mary Johnson, were able to establish successful lives and raise families, despite being captured in Africa and transported to Virginia as slaves. Most women, however, toiled anonymously, lost to the historical record unless their names were recorded in court papers, ship records, church minutes, or in someone's diary or letter. Other sources, such as advice books, medical treatises, and popular ballads, provide some indication of how women were perceived in the seventeenth century.

Women's Roles in Seventeenth-Century America considers the lives of white, black, and Native American women between 1600 and 1700. The lives of these groups of women intersected because economics, religion, social forces, and politics all combined to induce and promote European colonization and the growth of slavery and the slave trade during this time period. Some of these movements or forces existed before 1600, or were the result of long-standing conditions, such as rivalries between European nations, which encouraged these powers to conquer new lands and increase their treasuries by establishing colonies. Others were the result of colonization. The success of tobacco as a cash crop in Virginia and Maryland, for example, led to the need for more laborers, which eventually led to the importation of thousands of men and women from Africa, and the institutionalization of chattel slavery in the English colonies, and later the United States.

The seventeenth century was a time of enormous change, conflict, and confusion in the western world. It was an age marked by both great advances in scientific thought and by the continuation of superstitious beliefs. It was a period of religious conflict and of attempts to create religious havens. It was an era when European powers fought each other, as well as the indigenous inhabitants, to establish permanent colonies in the Americas, including the settlements that would eventually form the United States of America. Finally, it was during this century that slavery became firmly rooted in North America.

These revolutions in political, religious, and scientific thought and the modification of political and geographical boundaries had an enormous effect on women throughout the world. Women were transported around the globe, sometimes by choice and sometimes through coercion and slavery. Because only women give birth, some facets of their lives and their roles have remained the same throughout the centuries, and it might first appear that their roles have remained static. Indeed, the roles of most European women in the early modern period revolved around children and the household. Nevertheless, the events taking place in the wider world beyond the family and household were significant to women in the seventeenth century—even if they themselves were sometimes unaware of many of the events shaping their lives.

Non-European women, as well, were affected by the tumultuous events of the seventeenth century. The launch of new trade routes and the establishment of colonies by Europeans had a direct effect on the lifestyles and roles of indigenous women, sometimes changing them in significant ways. Moreover, thousands of Native Americans died because they had no immunity to the diseases brought by Europeans. Thus, even the indigenous women of the Americas who did not come into direct contact with Europeans found their lives transformed because villages, kinship connections, and cultural identities and traditions vanished. For African women, who were brought across the Atlantic Ocean against their will, the New World was a place where they were forced to take on new identities and new roles, usually as servants or slaves of white masters. Separated from their families and the language and culture of their homelands, these women had to learn to adapt to a new language, culture, and identity.

In contrast, white European women had more to say about their immigration across the Atlantic. Most arrived by their own choice (or by the choice of their husbands or fathers), although some may have been forced by circumstances in England or other nations to make the decision to leave the country of their birth. Some were free, and some were indentured servants, who had to live through and fulfill their contracts before they could marry. Most European women undoubtedly expected to live and work as housewives in a fashion similar to the way in which they had lived or wished to live in their homes across the sea. For many of these women, life was probably disappointing and scary, as well as arduous.

A brief overview of seventeenth-century Europe then will help to explain some of the forces that shaped the settlements in North America and women's roles there.[1] Western Europe at this time was composed of many nations and city-states, nominally Christian, although some were Catholic and some Protestant. The non-Christian population frequently faced persecution, and Jews were not accorded the same rights as Christians. Indeed, they were persecuted, tortured, and sometimes executed, along with others who were considered to be heretics. The Muslim Moors were driven out of Spain following the fall of Granada in 1492, but the

Ottoman Turks conquered Hungary and much of Eastern Europe, and they threatened areas of Western Europe, as well.

Christians, however, were not a single, united group. Factions, rebellions, and even wars developed as supporters attempted to put either Protestant or Catholic monarchs on the various thrones throughout Europe. In England, Henry VIII became the first head of the Church of England in 1531, when he broke with the Catholic Church in Rome to divorce Catherine of Aragon and marry Anne Boleyn (who was executed in 1536). His successor, the young Edward VI, son of Henry's third wife, Jane Seymour, was also Protestant. When Edward died without leaving an heir, his Catholic sister Mary became queen in 1553, and once again England was Catholic. Mary, too, died without an heir, and her sister, Elizabeth I, who was Protestant, became queen of England in 1558. It was during Elizabeth's reign that English colonization efforts began, first in Ireland, then in Virginia with the unsuccessful settlement of Roanoke in 1587.

England remained a Protestant country after Elizabeth's reign ended with her death in 1603, but there were still attempts from within to bring it back to Catholicism, as well as political threats from the Catholic nations of France and Spain. There were also those within England who believed the country was not Protestant enough. By the seventeenth century, many of them were so unhappy with the state of affairs in England that they decided to leave. Members of the Separatist Protestant group, now known as the Pilgrims, left their home in Scrooby, England, to travel to and live in the Netherlands. They settled in Amsterdam first, and then in the city of Leiden in 1609. Finally, some of them sailed across the Atlantic to settle in Plymouth, Massachusetts, in 1620. Members of another group, the Puritans, who believed the Church of England needed to be purified and made less like the Church of Rome, also eventually decided to leave England where they were being persecuted, as the Church of England moved closer towards Roman Catholicism under Charles I and William Laud (Archbishop of Canterbury, 1633–1645). Many Puritans fled England in the Great Migration (c. 1630–1642), some of them settling in New England to establish a model religious settlement there.

England was undergoing political disputes, as well as religious ones, during the reign of Charles I. Eventually Royalist forces faced off against Parliamentary forces, in what is known as the English Civil War (1642–1649). Parliamentary forces finally captured King Charles I, and he was beheaded in 1649, and his son, the future Charles II, went into exile. Oliver Cromwell, who had gained recognition for his leadership of the army and actively supported the trial and execution of Charles I, became Lord Protector of England in 1653, and England became a Puritan state. Cromwell died in 1658, and his son, Richard, was unable to hold the Protectorate together. The monarchy was restored in 1660 after Cromwell's death, and Charles II became King of England.[2]

Life in England changed following Charles II's restoration to the throne. The strict morality of the Puritan interregnum did not disappear entirely, but life at Court was decidedly looser For one thing, Charles II openly kept several mistresses, one of them the actress Nell Gwynne. In addition, the London theaters, which had been closed under Cromwell's rule, reopened, and women began to appear on the stage.[3] Other amusements, such as sports and dancing, were also popular. Charles rewarded some of his supporters with grants of land in British North America.

Religious and political upheavals occurred elsewhere in Europe, too. The Thirty Years War (1618–1649) disrupted many towns and people throughout much of continental Europe. During this period of social upheaval when community bonds were broken and economic, political, and religious changes were taking place, many blamed witches for their misfortunes. This was particularly true in the areas most affected by the Thirty Years War, notably parts of what would now be considered Germany, northern France, and Switzerland, where hundreds of witches—mostly women—were tortured and executed. The turmoil of war also sent inhabitants fleeing for a safe haven, and some sought it in North America. The "new world" thus became a religious haven for Catholics, Puritans, Quakers, French Huguenots, Jews, and other groups at various times and places.

For European powers, however, the primary motivation for establishing colonies was to make money. Originally seeking new routes to the riches of the East, the European monarchs and their advisors eventually determined that the route to wealth and power—as well as gaining new strongholds for Catholicism or Protestantism—lay in acquiring as much territory as possible in the new world. Mostly they either ignored or attempted to conquer the inhabitants who already lived there. The Spanish conquistadores both raped the native women of the civilizations they encountered and took them as wives, creating a significant mixed-race population known as *mestizos*. Although European adventurers did not find gold, they did find profit in fish, furs, sugarcane, and tobacco—and in the trade and trafficking of African slaves.

By 1619, one million Africans had been captured and transported to the Americas, most of them going to the West Indies, Brazil, and other parts of the Spanish Americas. The Portuguese explorers of the fifteenth century brought gold and slaves back to Portugal from Western Africa in 1441, thus beginning the European trade in African slaves. The Portuguese built forts on the coast to hold slaves captured inland. The Dutch later took over the forts, as they gained dominance over the slave trade in the seventeenth century. In 1672, England chartered the Royal Africa

Company, thus officially starting the country's involvement in the slave trade. James, Duke of York, later King James II, was the principal shareholder. The company's power declined when James was deposed from the throne in 1688. In 1712, the slave trade became open to all. By the mid-eighteenth century, England dominated the trade in human bodies from Africa.[4]

Besides war, religious fervor, and adventure, what motivated European men and women to leave their homes and journey across the Atlantic Ocean? Many sought to better their economic condition and to acquire land. In England, the law of primogenitor meant that many estates went to the first-born sons. The enclosure of formerly common grazing lands and a growth in the population increased the number of those without land and the unemployed. Those without the money to afford transportation and the expenses involved in settling across the sea found that they could be transported as indentured servants. Because young men and women were used to hiring themselves out as servants and contracting to live with and to work for an employer for a particular period of time within England, they did not find it strange to extend this type of service to the colonies. Thus, the system of indentured servitude was easily transferred and adapted to conditions in the English settlements in America.

The governments and trading companies attempting to establish permanent settlements of Europeans soon realized that in order to make their colonies successful, they would need to provide wives for their settlers. Once in the American colonies, however, the new immigrants, male and female, faced lives far different from the ones they had in Europe. For one thing, the first European settlers lived in a wilderness in frontier conditions, far from European "civilization." They had to build houses, find food, and coexist with the native inhabitants. The tobacco economy of the Chesapeake led to a demand for first servants, and then slaves, and an emphasis on getting rich over everything else. Moreover, there was an imbalance of men and women in this area. In the Chesapeake colonies of Virginia and Maryland, white men outnumbered white women by approximately six to one in the first few decades of settlement. (This imbalance was true of the British West Indies, as well, where the emphasis was on growing sugar.) This sex rate imbalance had a great effect on the demographics of the region. It meant that nearly all white women married if they lived past servitude in this fever-producing region. The high mortality rate and the lack of family ties and religious authorities led to a high rate of premarital sex, which was tolerated, as long as the couple married and the community did not have to support illegitimate children.

Furthermore, women's status in the seventeenth-century British colonies may have differed from their status in England. In some areas, women may have had more control over their lives during the early years of settlement. Knowing that they would probably die before their children reached maturity, husbands in the early Chesapeake colonies trusted that their wives would make the right decisions about their properties and businesses in order to ensure the future of their offspring.[5]

In contrast, the New England colonies had a more equal sex ratio, and most people lived in family groups. Governed strictly by Puritans during the seventeenth century, the authorities in these colonies prosecuted men and women for engaging in premarital sex, even if they married before a baby was born. In fact, couples whose babies were born too soon after the wedding had to pay fines and perform acts of penance. Although the courts tried both men and women when they were married to each other, judges usually treated pregnant single women more harshly than their partners. Yet it was also easier for a woman to get a divorce in New England than in either England or the other colonies. In part this was because marriage was a civil contract, rather than a sacrament under the Puritans, but it was also because Puritans considered the family to be essential for maintaining order within their society. If a husband abandoned his wife and family, his wife might be left destitute and forced to seek both help and solace from another man, as women were popularly considered to be weak and lustful. Thus, a divorce could actually help to make a household more stable.

Households were the foundation of society. According to seventeenth-century English thought, fathers were like sovereigns ruling over their families. In fact, the seventeenth-century English philosopher Thomas Hobbes called the family "a little monarchy." Other theorists of the time mostly agreed with this idea, but Sir Robert Filmer in his *Patriarcha* (1642) made the analogy between fathers and kings even more explicit: "as the Father over one family, so the King, as Father over many families, extends his care to preserve, feed, clothe, instruct and defend the whole commonwealth."[6] This vision of political authority and natural law maintained that the authority of the state came from the monarch and emanated downwards. Similarly, in a well-ordered society, the power of the family ideally rested with the father. Family and state complemented each other: an orderly society depended on well-maintained and functioning families.

In the American colonies, where controls and strong institutional support did not exist as they did in England, especially in the early years of settlement, laws were quickly enacted to make the head of the household legally bound to supervise and control the members of the household. Throughout the early colonies, these laws attempted to ensure that children and servants were supervised, educated, and controlled. For instance, a 1632 Virginia law required masters to teach their servants and children to read the catechism, or to send them to church so that they could learn there. Laws passed in several New England colonies required fathers to make sure that their children and servants learned to read English and were educated in some occupation, trade, or "calling." In all of the early colonies, fathers or masters could be fined if their children or servants were caught misbehaving or acting in a disorderly manner. As well, a husband was responsible for his wife's behavior and maintenance, as marriage subsumed her legal identity under coverture.

Although it would appear then that women held no place of value within this patriarchal society, in fact, they were essential to its existence, most importantly because they were necessary for its reproduction. In addition to their roles as wives and mothers, women took care of the house and household by cooking, preserving food, sewing, spinning, tending gardens, taking care of sick or injured members of the household, and many other tasks.

Although most white women worked at domestic tasks of some sort, the actual work any one woman did was subject to a number of factors. Lured by the idyllic images of the colonies painted by promoters trying to encourage settlement, female servants expected to perform only household chores in their New World homes, as they generally did in England. Their expectations did not match the reality of their situations, however, as female servants in the Chesapeake colonies frequently worked in the tobacco fields, especially in the early years of the colonies. Because in England, agricultural work was generally considered to be "men's work," it went against established norms when white women had to work in the fields.

Yet English observers did not understand the labor systems and gender roles of the Native Americans they encountered. They commented frequently about the drudgery of Indian women who had to work in the fields, and considered Indian men to be lazy, since they hunted, as English gentlemen did for sport. African women who were brought to the colonies, however, were treated differently, especially toward the end of the seventeenth century, and they were given agricultural work to do, as well as household tasks. As colonial society stabilized, and slavery became entrenched in the southern colonies, race became an important social category, although gender distinctions remained important.[7]

As the seventeenth century closed, conditions for European settlers and native-born colonials were much different than they had been earlier in the century. In 1700, the population of the English colonies was about 250,000. Conditions in the Chesapeake colonies had changed so that the gender ratio was about equal, and slavery and racial codes were entrenched in the society. In New England, the strict values and the sense of mission that the first generation had felt were no longer so apparent.

Boston was the largest city in the English colonies, but by the mid-eighteenth century, Philadelphia would overtake it and continue to grow.

Although readers should be aware that England's colonies included the highly profitable West Indies, and that Spain and France controlled much of what is now the United States of America, this volume focuses mainly on the British North American colonies, specifically the area that became the first thirteen states of the United States of America. Chapter 1 discusses women's roles within the family and household and how women's experiences in the various colonies differed. Anglo-Americans expected white women to marry and have families. Men, women, and children were supposed to live in households. Usually a man was the head of the household, but sometimes a widow took charge of a household after the death of her husband. Because of their power, wealthy widows were often respected—and feared. This chapter also explores the similarities and differences between the lives and roles of white women, Native American women, and African women in the seventeenth-century British colonies.

Chapter 2 considers women and the law. Single women and widows could own land and conduct business, but under English Common Law, married women had no legal identity—they were "covered" by their husbands. Nevertheless, they did come before the court as witnesses and defendants, and as widows, they went to court to settle their estates and guardianship issues. This chapter also examines the way in which the various colonies handled divorce and prosecuted fornication, bastardy, and rape.

Chapter 3 looks at women and immigration. European women immigrated to the Americas as servants, as part of family groups, and to escape religious persecution. African women were brought by force as servants and slaves. Both groups faced new situations, as well as arduous passages across the seas. Women's work is the subject of Chapter 4. All colonial women worked within the home, preparing food, sewing, taking care of children, and making household goods, such as candles and clothing. Some women also ran their own businesses, farms, or acted as midwives or teachers. English observers were appalled by Native American women doing the agricultural work in their communities, but eventually decided it was acceptable for African women to work in the fields of their colonial masters. I discuss women and religion in Chapter 5. Religion was a significant issue in colonial America. Puritans, for example, arrived with a sense of mission and tried to prevent sin in their "city on a hill." Although Puritans expected women to attend church and become members, they did not want women to speak in public or explain religious doctrine. Women who did so were accused of being troublemakers, or even witches. Quakers, Jews, and Catholic women also tried to find religious havens in the British North American colonies. English Protestants fought

French and Spanish Catholics for territory and souls, and both Protestants and Catholics tried to convert Native Americans. Chapter 6 examines women's role in war. Some women during this time became real-life "warrior women," as opposed to those celebrated in popular ballads of the time. Colonial Americans faced many wars with Native Americans, with devastating effects on both societies. After Metacom's Rebellion (King Philip's War) in 1676, hundreds of captured Native Americans were sold into bondage. This war and the succeeding conflicts also traumatized New England colonists in numerous ways. A good many of the accused and accusers in the Salem Witchcraft crisis of 1692 had some connection to the Maine frontier and the Indian wars. Several of the young female accusers, for example, had been orphaned and lived as servants in other people's homes. Some women became captives of Indians, and the captivity narrative became a genre of colonial literature. In addition, contests between European powers spilled over into the new world colonies. As well, women took part in colonial insurrections, such as Bacon's Rebellion in Virginia (1676). Women's education and involvement in literature and the arts is the focus of Chapter 7. Puritans believed that women should be educated—at least enough to read the Bible—but many other women did not read or write. Still, most women did receive an education in the arts of housewifery. Few women (or men) in colonial America had the time or training to pursue literary endeavors, but some women, such as Anne Bradstreet, did write and publish poetry. Other women expressed their creativity through such activities as embroidery.

NOTES

1. Women's roles in Europe during this time are covered in Meg Lota Brown and Kari Boyd McBride, *Women's Roles in the Renaissance* (Westport, CT: Greenwood Press, 2005).

2. There are many books about the English Civil War. See for example, Ann Hughes, *The Causes of the English Civil War*, 2nd ed. (New York: St. Martin's Press, 1998), and Peter Gaunt, *The English Civil War: The Essential Readings* (Oxford: Blackwell, 2001).

3. For the closing of theaters, see "An Ordinance for the Suppression of All Stage-playes and Interludes, Renascence Edition," transcribed by R. S. Bear, University of Oregon, May 2003. Available at: http://hdl.handle.net/1794/80.

4. For more on the Royal African Company, see William A. Pettigrew, "Free to Enslave: Politics and the Escalation of Britain's Transatlantic Slave Trade, 1688–1714, *William and Mary Quarterly* 64 (January 2007): 3–38. For an overview of the Atlantic slave trade, see the Web site of the PBS series "The Terrible Transformation." Available at: http://www.pbs.org/wgbh/aia/part1/narrative.html.

5. Lois Green Carr and Lorena S. Walsh, "The Planter's Wife: The Experience of White Women in Seventeenth-Century Maryland," in *A Heritage of Her Own: Toward a New Social History of American Women,* ed. Nancy F. Cott and Elizabeth H. Pleck (New York: Simon and Schuster, 1979).

6. For a detailed discussion on Filmer and Filmerian theory, see Mary Beth Norton, *Founding Mothers and Fathers: Gendered Power and the Forming of American Society* (New York: Vintage Books, 1996). *Patriarcha* can be found online at *Patriarcha or the Natural Power of Kings by the Learned Sir Robert Filmer* [1680], http://www.constitution.org/eng/patriarcha.htm.

7. Kathleen M. Brown, *Good Wives, Nasty Wenches, and Anxious Patriarchs: Gender, Race, and Power in Colonial Virginia* (Chapel Hill: University of North Carolina Press, 1996).

SUGGESTED READING

Brown, Kathleen M. *Good Wives, Nasty Wenches, and Anxious Patriarchs: Gender, Race, and Power in Colonial Virginia.* Chapel Hill: University of North Carolina Press, 1996.

Carr, Lois Green, and Lorena S. Walsh. "The Planter's Wife: The Experience of White Women in Seventeenth-Century Maryland." In *A Heritage of Her Own: Toward a New Social History of American Women,* ed. Nancy F. Cott and Elizabeth H. Pleck, 25–57. New York: Simon and Schuster, 1979.

Norton, Mary Beth. *Founding Mothers and Fathers: Gendered Power and the Forming of American Society.* New York: Vintage Books, 1996.

Smith, Merril D., ed. *Sex and Sexuality in Early America.* New York: New York University Press, 1998.

Chronology

1603	Death of Elizabeth I, Queen of England; King James VI of Scotland becomes James I of England.
1604	King James of England condemns tobacco use as a "vile custom" in *A Counterblaste to Tobacco*.
1607	Jamestown, Virginia, colony founded. This is the first permanent English settlement in North America. In December, John Smith is brought before Powhatan, chief of the Powhatan. Smith believes that Powhatan's daughter, Pocahontas, saved his life.
1608	First French settlement in Quebec founded by French explorer Samuel de Champlain.
1613	Pocahontas and Virginia colonist John Rolfe marry. Pocahontas is now known as Rebecca.
1617	Pocahontas dies in England before she can return home.
1619	African slaves brought to Jamestown on a Dutch ship. They may not have been the first slaves to arrive.
	The Virginia House of Burgesses meets for the first time.
1620	Pilgrims arrive at Plymouth, Massachusetts, on *The Mayflower*; forty-one adult men sign the Mayflower Compact.
1621	Ninety young women arrive in Virginia to become brides of the male settlers.

1622	An attack by the Powhatan tribe kills 347 Virginia settlers and sparks a war between Native Americans and the English colonists.
1624	Dutch establish New Netherland (New York).
	John Smith publishes his *General History of Virginia, New England, and the Summer Isles.*
	Thomas Morton sets up a maypole at Merry Mount (now Quincy, Massachusetts). Plymouth colonists are appalled by Morton and his followers drinking, dancing, and engaging in lewd behavior with Indian women.
	George Fox, founder of the Society of Friends (Quakers), is born in Drayton-in-the-Clay, England.
1625	Virginia becomes a royal colony because of the mismanagement of the Virginia Company.
	Charles I becomes King of England.
1630	Boston, Massachusetts, founded.
1630s	The Puritan Great Migration: thousands of Puritans flee persecution in England and settle in the Massachusetts Bay Colony.
1631	John Smith dies in England.
1632	Charles I grants charter to Lord Baltimore for a colony that will become Maryland (named after Queen Henrietta Maria).
1633	William Laud becomes Archbishop of Canterbury, a position he holds until his execution by Puritans in 1645.
1634	Puritan midwife and later dissident Anne Hutchinson arrives in Massachusetts.
1635	Colonists from Massachusetts settle Connecticut.
1636	Roger Williams establishes Rhode Island after being banished from Massachusetts.
1637	Pequot War.
	Harvard College founded in Massachusetts.
1638	Anne Hutchinson expelled from Massachusetts Bay Colony and excommunicated from the church. She settles in Rhode Island.
	Swedish colonists settle in Delaware.
1639–1649	English Civil War.
1642	Montreal, Canada, founded.

1643	Ann Radcliffe Mowlson funds first scholarship at Harvard University.
1648	Margaret Brent (1601–1671) denied the right to vote in the Maryland General Assembly.
1649	Charles I of England is executed. England is declared a commonwealth and Oliver Cromwell is appointed Lord Protector for life.
1650	Puritan Anne Bradstreet's first volume of poetry, *The Tenth Muse Lately Sprung Up in America*, published in London.
1654	The first Jewish settlers arrived in New Amsterdam (present-day New York City) after fleeing Brazil on the *St. Catherine*.
1658	Oliver Cromwell dies.
1660	Charles II restored to the throne of England after death of Oliver Cromwell. The Anglican Church becomes the state church.
1660	Quaker Mary Dyer executed.
1662	The Halfway Covenant is adopted in some Massachusetts churches permitting children to be baptized, even if their parents have not become members of the church.
1663	Puritan writer and minister Cotton Mather is born in Massachusetts.
	Virginia courts rule that children born to slave mothers are slaves.
1664	The Dutch surrender New Netherland to the English, who name the colony New York.
1664	Law passed in Maryland makes slaves for life. Virginia adopts a similar act in 1667.
1665	Great Plague in London kills 75,000 people.
1667	Publication of John Milton's epic poem *Paradise Lost*.
1669	Revolt of the Long Swede, an attempt to return colony of New Sweden back to Swedish control.
1672	England charters the Royal African Company, officially starting the English slave trade.
1675	Metacom's Rebellion (or King Philip's War) begins. Six hundred New England colonists and 3,000 Native Americans die in this conflict.

1676	Bacon's Rebellion, led by Nathaniel Bacon, begins. Bacon burns Jamestown down. Bacon dies in October 1676.
1677	Women in Marblehead, Massachusetts, attack and kill Indian prisoners.
1681	William Penn receives a charter for Pennsylvania from Charles II.
1682	Publication of Mary Rowlandson's captivity narrative.
1685	James II becomes King of England.
	New England colonies consolidated into Dominion of New England under Governor Edmund Andros.
1687	Governor Andros orders Boston's Old South Meeting House to be converted to an Anglican Church.
1688	Glorious Revolution. James II forced to leave throne in favor of his daughter, Mary, and her husband, William, Prince of Orange.
1689	Leisler's Rebellion in New York. Jacob Leisler is executed.
	William and Mary crowned King and Queen of England.
	Governor Andros is jailed by colonists, then sent back to England.
1691	Massachusetts granted a new charter.
1692	Salem Witchcraft crisis. Many suspected witches are arrested and imprisoned.
1693	College of William and Mary founded in Virginia.
1697	Massachusetts General Assembly expresses regret for actions taken during the Salem Witchcraft crisis. Compensation is offered to families of those wrongly accused.
	Hannah Duston is captured by Indians in Haverhill, Massachusetts. She escapes, killing ten Indians and returning with their scalps.
1699	Capital of Virginia moves to Williamsburg.

1

---∞∞∞---

Women and the Family

The primary role of most seventeenth-century white women in America was that of wife and mother. Indeed, most women's lives centered on the household and family. Whether mistress of a well-to-do household or wife of a poor man, a woman's physical domain generally encompassed the house and garden, but excluded the outlying fields, wharves, and mills, except during times of necessity. Daughters and female servants, as well as wives, spent most of their time within the borders of the house and garden, learning about and assisting with household chores. Over the centuries, bearing and caring for children, cooking, and taking care of the home have been the usual activities for many women throughout the world, but colonial American women and men identified these duties, along with being pious, modest, and helpful, with being a good wife—and good wives, subordinate and obedient to their husbands—were necessary for preserving and sustaining families and the social order.

The image of the "good wife," a chaste, pious mother and wife who was obedient to her spouse and who dedicated her life to domestic pursuits, remained the ideal expression of white womanhood throughout the seventeenth century. In Puritan New England, the good wife was often compared to Bathsheba, the mother of Solomon who "looketh well to the ways of her household, and eateth not the bread of idleness."[1] The growing number of advice books and social commentaries published in England during this time, such as Richard Brathwaite's *The English Gentlewoman* (1631), also maintained that good wives—wives who knew their place within the household—were necessary for maintaining social order in the community. In contrast, women who committed adultery, or who were considered flirtatious, aggressive, or "unruly," overstepped their bounds and were often considered a threat to their communities.

The ideology of the early modern world depicted women as seductive, lust-filled creatures. They were the "daughters of Eve." According to Judeo-Christian beliefs, Eve was made from Adam to be his companion and helpmeet, but she led him into temptation after being "beguiled" by the serpent to eat the forbidden fruit of the Tree of Knowledge. As a result, God cast Adam and Eve out of Paradise, the Garden of Eden, and as a symbol and reminder of their true natures, God declared women would suffer in childbirth and be ruled by their husbands. Many seventeenth-century Anglo-Americans took these Biblical injunctions literally. They believed that as descendants of Eve, women were weak and open to suggestion; they were easily beguiled, but they were also seductive and licentious. To keep them from tempting men, women needed to be bound by laws and traditions and placed under the subjugation of fathers or husbands. Marriage, then, was one way of putting women under male authority, thereby preventing them from inappropriate actions or behavior. Unruly women, women who questioned authority or challenged community standards, harkened back to the image of "daughters of Eve" and needed to be punished or restrained.

Marriage, therefore, was the first step in family formation, and families were the source of strong communities. Yet, just as "wife" had a very specific connotation to seventeenth-century Anglo-Americans, so, too, did the terms "family" and "household." A family in seventeenth-century terms differed both from the older tradition of an extended family of grandparents, their children, their children's children, and various other kin living together, and the more modern examples of a nuclear family composed simply of parents and their children. To English colonists in America, a family meant all of the people living in a household and subject to the authority of one person. The head of the household was generally the husband/father, although widows headed some families. If a widow remarried, however, then her husband became the new head of the household, as her husband's identity, wealth, and position subsumed hers. Households usually included a husband, his wife, and their unmarried children, but it might also include any children from a previous marriage or marriages, other dependent relatives, and servants. Young, unmarried people of both sexes were expected to live with families. Because of the demographic imbalances in the Chesapeake colonies during the early years of the settlement, some households there consisted mainly of male servants. Thus, members of a colonial family were not always related by blood or marriage, but all were supposed to be under the authority of its head.

Early modern beliefs and practices maintained that strong and stable families were necessary for keeping communities in order. As the father kept "the little commonwealth" in line, he also helped to prevent disruption in the community. Within the structure of the family, women had several roles: the first role was that of the wife, which encompassed the dual subroles of the chaste and domestic good wife and the husband's sexual companion. In addition, a wife sometimes served as her husband's assistant, taking over his duties if he was incapacitated or unavailable.[2] Next came the role of mother (since only married or widowed women were able to be "good" mothers), which was the self-sacrificing role through which women redeemed themselves. If a woman outlived her husband, then she was a widow, who might take charge of her husband's business affairs and property, as well as becoming head of the household. The family might also include the other female roles of daughters or servants, who would be taught the domestic arts and absorb the essential elements of being a good wife.

Despite English convictions and expectations, however, family life was not stable in the early years of settlement in Virginia and Maryland. For one thing, marriages there were usually brief due to the high mortality rate, and children were frequently left without one or both parents. The success of tobacco as a cash crop increased the need for laborers who could work in the fields, traditionally considered "men's work" in England. To address the need for laborers, many more men than women were transported to the Chesapeake as indentured servants, skewing the sex ratio. As a consequence of so many single men and women immigrating as indentured servants, marriages were often delayed in the Chesapeake, since servants could not marry unless someone paid the balance of their contract. (Immigration is discussed in more detail in Chapter 3.) This meant that both men and women tended to marry in their mid to late twenties. Yet if a woman survived and finished her period of servitude, then it was almost definite that she would marry. Thus, most women married, and because most of them did not have family in the New World, they had more freedom to choose to marry as they wished without parental interference. Because there were so many more men than women in the Chesapeake colonies, women who were widowed there almost always remarried.

However, the swampy terrain of the Chesapeake region produced "agues and fevers" in new immigrants, and many newcomers did not survive the "seasoning" process. Malaria, transmitted by the bite of mosquitoes, was the most likely cause of the chills and fevers affecting immigrants to the region. Malaria is a recurring disease that weakens the body and makes it more susceptible to diseases such as dysentery. Pregnant women were particularly vulnerable to malaria, making the hazards of childbirth even higher during this period in the Chesapeake colonies.[3] The sex ratio imbalance, combined with a high mortality rate and late marriage, meant that a native-born Anglo-American colony in the Chesapeake took time to establish, and life there remained frontier-like for a longer period than it did in New England.

The frontier conditions of the Chesapeake colonies were augmented by a scarcity of ministers and weak church authority. Consequently, institutional controls were not as strong there as they were in England or in other colonies. Yet, a traditional method of social control did exist—gossip. The small, cramped houses of colonial Americans, and the communal situations in which most people worked, made it difficult to keep secrets, but revelations about a person's words or behavior could have dire effects within seventeenth-century communities. In the early modern world, a person's reputation was particularly important. Men who were accused of unscrupulous business dealings or of being untrustworthy faced considerable obstacles in a society that did most of its business by oral agreement. In addition, men who were convicted of perjury or who were believed to be untruthful could not submit sworn statements in court. Therefore, the slander of a man usually involved a neighbor or business connection calling him a "knave" or "rogue" and accusing him of lying, cheating, or being a thief—words that might affect his business dealings with other men. In contrast, insults against women usually referred to their sexual conduct, and thus women were called "sluts," "whores," and other terms indicating sexual looseness. Since a woman's honor was connected to her sexual reputation, much more so than a man's, such terms and gossip were extremely harmful and might even prevent her from marrying—the one career choice for most white women. In both New England and the Chesapeake, neighborhood gossip helped to keep members of the community in order, although, in general, the effects of having a "bad reputation" were probably far worse for women in Puritan New England than they were for women in the early decades of settlement in the Chesapeake. Moreover, women in New England were more likely to face prosecution for sexual misbehavior than women in the Chesapeake.[4]

Despite the possibility of neighborhood disapproval, the number of early births following marriage suggests that without parental controls and supervision, women and men in the early Chesapeake frequently engaged in premarital sexual relations. Because they knew marriage would follow, free women did not have to be as concerned about pregnancy before marriage, and couples here were seldom prosecuted for conceiving a child before the wedding date. Moreover, English tradition long equated a betrothal as a contracted promise to marry. As such, this promise meant couples frequently believed it was permissible to engage in sexual relations once they were betrothed, but before the official wedding.

Some Anglo-American men and women may have followed this custom and engaged in premarital sexual relations with their intended spouse.

One Maryland example demonstrates a particularly open acceptance of premarital sexual relations. After courting Elizabeth Gary for a year, Robert Harwood convinced her to "lie with him" while they were out picking vegetables in her mother's garden. Apparently, Elizabeth Gary's mother and stepfather were not upset that the lovers had disappeared for quite a time because they appeared to be involved in a relationship that would lead to marriage. After their tryst, however, Elizabeth informed Robert that she did not want to marry him. Robert replied that she could not marry "any other man but him." To settle the matter, Peter Sharpe, Elizabeth's stepfather, prepared a contract giving Robert six weeks to convince Elizabeth to wed him. After that, he would have to stop harassing her. Moreover, for the six weeks of Robert's continued courtship, his visits would be chaperoned. Perhaps if Elizabeth had become pregnant, her parents might have been more anxious for her to marry, or at least for Robert to pay support.[5]

Servant women, however, faced a greater problem if they became pregnant. Yet without a reliable means of contraception, any seventeenth-century women who had sexual relations faced the possibility of becoming pregnant.[6] Unless someone bought her time, however, an expectant female servant would have the length of her indenture increased to make up for time missed due to pregnancy and birth. Some female servants ran away to hide a pregnancy. In the early years of the Chesapeake colonies, bastardy cases were prosecuted even when fornication cases were not because labor was valuable and masters wanted to be compensated for servants who were unable to work. Since they had to be supported, illegitimate children were generally taken from their mothers as soon as possible, and then they, too, were indentured, usually until they were twenty-one years old.

In contrast, fornication (sexual relations between any man, married or not, and an unmarried woman) was treated more harshly in the New England colonies, where strong Puritan beliefs about proper behavior were written into law right from the start of the Massachusetts Bay Colony. To act immorally was to break the covenant Puritans had with God and to tempt Him into destroying their "city on a hill." Puritans believed strongly in marriage, and their values demanded chastity and fidelity in both women and men. As a result, in the New England colonies stricter parental and societal controls kept illegitimate births at a lower rate. (Laws concerning bastardy, fornication, marriage, and divorce are covered in more detail in Chapter 2.)

Although Puritans believed that women were "daughters of Eve" and capable of tempting men with their bodies, they did not excuse men who were tempted, especially men who sought wickedness and deceived others. In his account of Plymouth Colony, William Bradford, Governor of Plymouth, recounted the conversation that Sarah, the wife of the disgraced minister John Lyford, had with a deacon and others after he was caught a second time sending letters to England that disparaged the settlement and the Separatists. Sarah's comments demonstrate her belief in an Old Testament God who would use the Indians to punish her and her husband for her spouse's deeds. She told the men that

> she feared some great judgment of God would fall upon them, and upon her, for her husbands cause; now that they were to remove, she feared to fall into the Indeans hands, and to be defiled by them, as he had defiled other women; ... [and] he had wronged her, as first he had a bastard by another before they were maried, and she having some inkling of some ill cariage that way, when he was a suitor to her, she tould him what she heard, and deneyd him; but she not certainly knowing the thing, other wise then by some darke and secrete muterings, he not only stifly denied it, but to satisfie her tooke a solemne oath ther was no shuch matter. Upon which she gave consente, and maried with him; but afterwards it was found true, and the bastard brought home to them. She then charged him with his oath, but he prayed pardon, and said he should els not have had her. And yet afterwards she could keep no maids but he would be medling with them, ... The woman being a grave matron and of good cariage all the while she was hear, and spoake these things out of the sorrow of her harte, sparingly, and yet with some further intimations.[7]

It was later revealed that Reverend Lyford had fled his parish in Ireland after he raped a woman while giving her premarital counseling. Although the colony had given Lyford several chances to make amends after officials learned of the letters, such wickedness could not be forgiven, and Lyford was banished from the colony.

Men and women in the seventeenth-century American colonies had expectations about the role of a wife and how she should behave, but as English women, wives had particular expectations, too, about their roles. Even though women might expect to obey a husband, they did not expect to be deceived, or to have their husbands engage in blatantly lewd behavior.

Most women throughout colonial America expected to marry and to someday have their own homes. This was not an unreasonable goal in the early colonies; since most adult, female colonists did marry, woman and wife were nearly synonymous terms. Unlike in England, land in the colonies was plentiful, and in the early years of settlement, at least, even a servant could expect to someday have his own farm or to be the wife of someone who owned his own farm. A woman's primary goal—and role—was to become a "good wife," a term that included being a good housekeeper, a sexual partner for her husband, as well as his helpmeet, and a loving and selfless mother. Under English law, a married woman was a *feme covert*, and her money and property belonged to her husband. In this patriarchal society, wives' identities were "covered" by their husbands. The noted English legal scholar Sir William Blackstone (1723–1780) described it this way in his *Commentaries on the Laws of England*:

> By marriage, the husband and wife are one person in law: that is, the very being or legal existence of the woman is suspended during the marriage, or at least is incorporated and consolidated into that of the husband: under whose wing, protection, and cover, she performs every thing; and is therefore called in our law-french a feme-covert; is said to be covert-baron, or under the protection and influence of her husband, her baron, or lord; and her condition during her marriage is called her coverture. Upon this principle, of an union of person in husband and wife, depend almost all the legal rights, duties, and disabilities, that either of them acquire by the marriage.[8]

Women were expected to obey their husbands, but that does not mean that wives were not valued or appreciated. Wives were not to be treated as servants or children. In a marriage manual published in 1712, Benjamin Wadsworth, Puritan minister and later President of Harvard College, outlined the duties of husbands and wives. Among other things, he advised them to love one another, to be patient and understanding, and to be faithful, but he also stated that: "Wives are part of the House and Family, and ought to be under the Husband's Government: they should *Obey their own Husbands.*" Yet he also noted, "Though the Husband is to rule his Family and his Wife, yet his Government of his Wife should not be with rigour, haughtiness, harshness severity; but with the greatest love, gentleness, kindness, tenderness that may be. Though he governs her, he must not treat her as a Servant, but as his own *flesh:* he must love her as himself.... On the other hand, Wives ought readily and chearfully to obey their Husbands: *Wives submit your selves to you own Husbands, be in subjection to them.*"[9]

Wives then had a specific place and role within marriage, but as well as being partners and helpmeets to their husbands, they were also valued for their role in the household, since they generally took care of household matters such as cooking, sewing, and doing laundry. Moreover, in New England, many women were educated so that they could read and discuss the Bible and educate their children. Cotton Mather's daughter, Katherin, even read Hebrew.[10] In England, and later in the colonies, wives were also engaged in the domestic production of butter and cheese, ale, and cloth and clothing from flax and wool. The sale of these goods brought additional income to family farms and helped to diversify the economy. (See Chapter 7 for more on education.)

Due to these popular beliefs about their roles, English women who arrived in the Chesapeake colonies as indentured servants were sometimes severely disappointed when they found themselves put to work in the tobacco fields instead of in the house and kitchen. Promotional tracts aimed at convincing more women to immigrate to Virginia and Maryland stated that they would be employed in "such domestique imployments and housewifery as in England, that is dressing victuals, righting up the house, milking, imployed about dayries, washing, sowing, etc." Yet most households in the early years of settlement lacked furniture and items of household production. In fact, colonial inventories for Virginia rarely show such items as spinning wheels or dairy equipment before 1640.[11]

Nevertheless, women who had little in England, and no hope of improving their lives there, still may have found the chance of becoming a planter's wife well worth the risks involved. Wives in England who had servants could use them to perform heavy or tiresome chores, such as laundry and spinning. In the Chesapeake, wives could put their servants to work in the fields so that they themselves would not have to work there. As long as tobacco prices remained high, the production of tobacco was paramount, and most of a planter's resources went there, rather than on his house, furnishings, or domestic comforts. However, a favorable market for tobacco also meant that even the wife of a poor planter might hope to see her condition improve so that she could afford servants to help her.

As well as creating families, marriage was a method used throughout the colonies to advance in status. In Virginia, this was of prime importance to the planter elite, who controlled the Council and Assembly and who were concerned that men of low status could become part of their select group. Men who were able to marry wealthy widows might gain a house, land, servants, and money, along with a wife. Samuel Mathews, for example, gained a considerable fortune and status as a result of his marriage to the wealthy Widow Piersey, ultimately, if briefly, becoming a governor of Virginia (1656–1660).[12] The colonial government therefore felt it necessary to regulate marriage almost from the beginning of the colony. In 1619, the Virginia Assembly passed an act requiring English women to get permission from their fathers or people who had power over them in order to marry.

Marriage laws and customs were somewhat different in the Middle Colonies. Under the Dutch law of New Netherlands, married women had more rights than did their English counterparts. The *usus* marriage contract, unlike coverture, permitted married women to keep their own legal identity, purchase and own property, and run businesses. Husbands and wives shared a partnership, even making out mutual wills. Married women in New Netherlands found their lives more restricted after the colony was taken over by the English in 1664 and became New York.

Because men were considered heads of the household, seventeenth-century Anglo-Americans believed it was part of the father's role to choose a spouse for his children, although the mother or guardians could take charge if the father was dead or not available. Fathers and guardians did not formally arrange marriages, but they did enter into negotiations with the parents of potential suitors. In England, authorities began to pass laws in the late sixteenth century to regularize marriage. Under these new edicts, clergymen were to officiate at marriage ceremonies. This was true in Virginia, as well.

In England, it was traditional for a man to give a woman a betrothal ring after the couple agreed to marry. The ring was worn on the woman's right hand, and it often had a message of love inscribed on its surface. During the wedding ceremony, the ring was transferred to the woman's left hand. Many Catholics and Anglicans in the colonies followed this custom, as well as the custom of signing a dowry contract before witnesses.[13]

In Maryland, and perhaps elsewhere, couples sometimes broke a coin in half as a pledge of betrothal. When Elizabeth Lockett, an unmarried, pregnant servant, went into labor in 1657, she swore, as she had done throughout her pregnancy, that Thomas Bright, a young planter, was the father. She noted that she and Bright "had betrothed themselves; they had broken a silver coin between them." Lockett and Bright each kept half as a token that they would marry.[14]

In colonial Maryland, Jesuit priests frequently officiated at both Catholic and Anglican weddings. They also sought to convert and have Native Americans marry within the church, and they demanded that their slaves be married. Marriage was considered a sacrament in the Catholic Church, and the marriage bonds could not be dissolved through divorce. Marriages were not supposed to take place at particular times of the year. An old verse refers to dates in the Christian calendar when couples were permitted to marry. Advent, for example, is the four-week period leading up to Christmas, and Low Sunday is the Sunday after Easter. "When Advent comes do thou refrain / Till Hillary set thee free again / Next Septuagesima saith thee nay / But when Low Sunday comes thou may / Yet at Rogation thou must tarrie / Till Trinitie shall bid thee marry." Thus, Catholics generally married right after Easter, in June, and in December. They often married on Sunday mornings.[15]

Anglican marriage rituals followed the Book of Common Prayer, but were quite similar to Catholic rituals. Puritans, intent upon purifying the Church of England, eliminated the rituals and sacraments of the Church. They did not follow the Book of Common Prayer, nor did they use rings. In New England, marriages were considered civil unions; therefore, magistrates performed the ceremonies, rather than ministers. This was true in

Marriage of Pocahontas, by John C. McRae. The marriage of Pocahontas and John Rolfe in 1614 was a diplomatic alliance, as well as a love match. This nineteenth-century painting presents an idealized vision of the couple's wedding. Courtesy of Library of Congress.

England and in other colonies during the Interregnum, when the Puritans were in power. In Maryland, however, whether a clergyman or a magistrate performed the wedding, couples wishing to marry were required by law to repeat the traditional wedding vows in front of two witnesses.[16]

In contrast, Friends, or Quakers, married before the members of their meeting without benefit of clergy or magistrate. Quakers required couples to appear before the Women's and Men's Meetings before they could marry. George Fox, the founder of Quakerism, outlined the process in his *Letters to Quakers on Marriage, 1660,* "And when any marriages is to be propounded, let it be laid before the women's meeting first. And after they have declared it there, if they do know any thing of the man or the woman, that it should not proceed so far as to the men's meeting, then let two or three women go to the mens' meeting...."[17]

Throughout the colonies, men and women who were free and of legal age did not have to have their parents' consent in order to marry, but they were expected to publicize their intent to marry by posting banns to prevent clandestine marriages. Race was not a consideration in early seventeenth-century marriage laws, although later, as slavery became codified, some colonies made interracial marriages illegal. A 1691 law passed in Virginia "for prevention of that abominable mixture and spurious issue which hereafter may encrease in this dominion ... whatsoever

English or other white man or woman being free shall intermarry with a negroe, mulatto, or Indian man or woman bond or free, shall within three months after such a marriage be banished and removed from this dominion forever." White women who gave birth to a bastard child fathered by a black man would be fined "fifteen pounds sterling." If she could not pay the fine, then she could be bound and sold as a servant; if she was already a servant, then her indenture would be extended.[18]

Parents generally selected prospective spouses for their financial situation, morals, and piety. They took the responsibility of overseeing their children's marriage prospects very seriously. Wealth, for instance, was not supposed to be the sole reason for marriage, but it was certainly a factor, and sometimes the desires of the young couple seemed to be the least important issue in the determination over whether a marriage should take place. In keeping with the tenets of their faith, however, Quakers expected to be guided by God in choosing whom and when to marry. Yet, as one historian has noted, "Like many other Englishmen, Friends attempted to marry virtuous, wealthy girls of good background."[19]

Although sons and daughters were seldom forced to marry someone, they were frequently persuaded to honor their parents' choice. Yet even young Puritan women dreamed of sweethearts—the teenage girls involved in the Salem witchcraft trials were reportedly involved in fortune telling about their future lovers—but romantic love was not considered to be a legitimate reason for marriage. The folly of disregarding the advice of older and wiser relatives and neighbors in favor of love became clear to observers in the case of Rachel Clinton of seventeenth-century Ipswich, Massachusetts. Rachel's parents were dead, and she used her inheritance to buy the freedom of an indentured servant, Laurence, whom she then married. This love match did not have a happy ending. Laurence kept company with other women, drank, and squandered Rachel's money. The magistrates would not allow her to divorce.[20]

Daughters were educated and trained to be good wives, but until they actually became wives, they were supposed to be guided by the advice of their parents. In this deferential society, it may have been very difficult to go against one's parents, or to even trust one's own judgment. It may be that some young women simply went along with their parents' choice for a spouse because it was too difficult for them to question their parents' authority.

Puritan parents took their duties seriously, and young men and women who went against their parents' wishes or who courted in secret faced prosecution and fines. In Essex County, Massachusetts, Matthew Stanley was ordered to pay a fine of 5 pounds in 1649 for "drawing away the affections of the daughter of John Tarbox his wife without liberty first obtained of her parents." Daniel Black was also fined 5 pounds in 1660 for "making love to the daughter of Edmund Bridges, without consent of her parents."[21]

Massachusetts's law also required parental consent for marriages. A magistrate could step in and act as a surrogate parent, if no parent was available to grant permission. The law required couples to post banns for three weeks before the wedding took place. In 1648, Thomas Rowlandson was fined 10 shillings because he married sixteen-year-old Martha Bradstreet without posting the banns for three weeks. The couple's marriage was annulled. Martha Bradstreet married William Beale seven years later.[22]

Nevertheless, English marriage manuals advised parents not to arrange their children's marriages because "tis the free-will offering of the heart, that can only unite and Graft their affections together." The free-will offering "is to be led by Love, not drawn by the Cords of Wedlock." The manuals further advised that couples should be of about the same age and social position.[23]

Once the wedding took place, parents customarily presented their offspring with gifts with which to begin their married lives. In fact, when they did not, it was remarked upon, and sometimes neighbors convinced the parents to bestow a gift on the new couple. Joseph Wickes, who attended the marriage of Thomas Hill, Jr., in Kent County, Maryland, in 1657, persuaded the elder Thomas Hill to deed to his son the heifer that Wickes owed him. After Hill agreed, the other guests contributed additional gifts to the couple.[24]

If wealth was not the prime reason to marry, neither was love, although husbands and wives were expected to love each other once they were married. We see brief glimpses of the love between husbands and wives in a few extant sources, most notably the poems of Anne Bradstreet (discussed in Chapter 8). Love was a necessary part of marriage, but too much love for one's spouse was not considered good either. Puritan men and women were frequently cautioned not to forget their love of God in their love of one another. In 1683, Mehitable Parkman of Salem, Massachusetts, wrote to her husband that an older neighbor "tells me often she fears that I love you more than god."[25] Mehitable worried about loving her spouse too much and imperiling her soul. Other Puritan women and men had the same fears.

Quakers, too, were cautioned to look for a spiritual love, or as William Penn referred to it, a "Union of Souls."[26] Although Friends considering marriage were advised to ponder on the religious unity between husband and wife, rather than allowing lustful thoughts to taint his or her motives, surviving letters and journals show young men and women were thinking of romance, as well. Quaker meetings even cautioned parents to draw up marriage contracts before the couple became too involved with one another.

Sexual compatibility, however, was also an important aspect of marriage. In fact, English colonists believed, as did many Europeans of the time, that mutual orgasm was necessary for conception to take place because both men and women produced "seed" at this time. The seeds came together to create life. English colonists read about these ideas in such books as Nicholas Culpepper's *Directory for Midwives*. That pleasure was key to reproduction is made clear by Culpepper in *The Complete Practice of Physick*, in which Culpepper explains that the seed emerges as "Her womb, skipping as it were for joy . . . powred forth in that pang of Pleasure."[27]

The writers of advice manuals were also clear about the importance of sexual pleasure. William Gouge, a Puritan minister, stressed the idea that sexual relations were a necessary part of wedlock in his sermons on marriage, which were published and circulated in both England and New England in a volume titled, *Of Domestic Duties*. Gouge explains in one section the difference between impotence and barrenness. He notes that impotence can be observed, but barrenness in only known because a woman does not bear any children, despite having sexual relations. Moreover, Gouge states that men who are impotent should not marry, since they can neither procreate, nor give satisfaction.

> Contrary to this manifestation of God's will do they sin, who conceal their impotency and join themselves in marriage, whereby they frustrate one main end of marriage, which is procreation of children; and do that wrong to the party whom they marry, as sufficient satisfaction can never be made.

Yet Gouge observes that this is not the case for barrenness, as there is always the possibility that a woman will conceive. Moreover, Gouge states that, "though procreation of children be one end of marriage, yet it is not the only end: and so inviolable is the marriage bond, that though it be made for children's sake, yet for want of children it may not be broken."[28] Therefore, husbands and wives were to take pleasure in sexual relations with one another, although officials throughout the colonies considered sexual relations outside of marriage, and indeed, any nonprocreative sex acts, as sinful and illegal. The birth of a child was evidence that a couple had a mutually satisfying sexual relationship, while not being able to consummate a marriage was grounds for divorce in New England. (See Chapter 2 for more on divorce.)

In giving birth, women fulfilled their other primary role, that of mother. Women who could not conceive often felt anguished and ashamed because they could not be mothers. In the seventeenth century, and through the eighteenth century in many areas, childbirth was a woman-centered event, filled with rituals. Childbirth united women, while separating them from men. During a birth, the women of the community, including a midwife, gathered and attended the mother-to-be, supporting her and comforting her in what often began as a party-like atmosphere where "groaning cakes" and other refreshments were served. (Midwives are discussed in more detail in Chapter 4.) Husbands were excluded from the birth, beyond sending for or actually going for the midwife and supplies, but occasionally ministers were summoned in extraordinary circumstances. Doctors, however, did not usually participate in births in the American colonies before the middle of the eighteenth century.

Both women and men expected labor, commonly called "travail," to be dangerous and painful. Mothers and infants frequently died in childbirth or soon after. After all, it was God's curse upon the daughters of Eve. However, it was also a time of great drama and a means of redemption. In surviving travail and giving birth to a healthy child, women were both tested by God and shown his mercy and love.[29]

Most women continued to work as usual throughout their pregnancies. However, afterward they were bound more firmly to their homes by the need to breastfeed their babies. During the Renaissance, breastfeeding had declined among the elite, as the breast became celebrated in poetry and art as an erotic symbol. Many men considered the breasts of their wives and mistresses to be their possessions. These men wanted access to the bodies of their spouses or lovers without worrying about competing with a baby. In England this view began to change in the seventeenth century, particularly among Protestants, who considered wet-nursing sinful and breastfeeding a duty of good mothers.

Most colonial women, however, did breastfeed their children. In doing so, they and others around them believed they literally gave of themselves, as medical texts of the time stated that breast milk was actually whitened blood. In fact, early modern people believed that it was the same blood that nourished the fetus, now directed to the breasts, where it could continue to feed the newborn child. French physician Jacques Guillemeau wrote "that every mother should nurse her owne child: because her milke which is nothing else, but the bloud whitened (of which he was made, and wherewith hee had been nourished the time hee staide in his Mothers wombe) will bee alwaies more naturall, and familiar unto him, that that of a stranger."[30] Breast milk was considered to be pure and wholesome, the opposite of menstrual blood, which early modern people considered unclean and repulsive. Mothers redeemed themselves by breastfeeding their babies. Puritan ministers extolled the virtues of mothers who did so and frequently used imagery comparing breastfeeding and maternal love with God's love nourishing true believers.

Usually after the baby was born, another mother would nurse the newborn at first, as even physicians believed colostrum, the fluid produced by mothers before their milk comes in, to be dangerous to babies. It is now known that colostrum is actually beneficial to infants. Since nearly all mothers in the colonies breastfed their babies, there were usually experienced women available in the community who could pass on advice and tips to the new mothers, such as how to treat sore breasts or cracked nipples, as well as take over nursing the newborn if the mother became ill or had difficulties with breastfeeding. Most colonial white women nursed their babies for approximately ten to sixteen months, with the interval between births averaging approximately every twenty-four to twenty-eight months. When it came time to wean them, some mothers went on "weaning journeys" without their babies to make sure they would not give in to their infant's cries and the urges of their own bodies and aching breasts. All in all, colonial women spent much of their lives pregnant, nursing babies, and caring for children.

In a poem written in 1659 as the preface to meditations for her children, the Puritan poet Anne Bradstreet recounts the joy and protectiveness she has felt in her children as they grew and matured. Using the theme of the mother bird whose babies leave the nest one by one, she expresses her feeling about motherhood and children. As well, she conveys the Puritan belief in the transience of life and the desire to be remembered.

I had eight birds hatcht in one nest,
Four Cocks were there, and Hens the rest.
I nurst them up with pain and care,
No cost nor labour did I spare
Till at the last they felt their wing,
Mounted the Trees and learned to sing.
. . . .
If birds could weep, then would my tears
Let others know what are my fears
Lest this my brood some harm should catch
And be surpris'd for want of watch
Whilst pecking corn and void of care
They fall un'wares in Fowler's snare;
Or whilst on trees they sit and sing
Some untoward boy at them do fling,
. . . .
Great was my pain when I you bred,
Great was my care when I you fed.
Long did I keep you soft and warm
And with my wings kept off all harm.
. . . .
When each of you shall in your nest
Among your young ones take your rest,

In chirping languages oft them tell
You had a Dame that lov'd you well,
That did what could be done for young
And nurst you up till you were strong
And 'fore she once would let you fly
She shew'd you joy and misery,
Taught what was good, and what was ill,
What would save life, and what would kill.
Thus gone, amongst you I may live,
And dead, yet speak and counsel give.
Farewell, my birds, farewell, adieu,
I happy am, if well with you.[31]

In general, if colonial women lived through successive pregnancies, perhaps spanning twenty years or so, they tended to outlive their husbands.
As widows, they might take over their husbands' farms and businesses, and
they took over sole responsibility for their minor children unless a guardian
was appointed. Under English common law, widows received one-third of
their husbands' real property, known as dower rights. Most of the English
colonies followed this tradition to some extent.

Yet the treatment of widows and legal provisions for them varied from
region to region. In the New England colonies, the courts tended to rule
on the merits of each case, and the behavior of a woman while she was
married could influence how she was treated when she was widowed. In
Plymouth Colony, a law passed in 1685 declared that the property of a
man who died intestate (without leaving a will) would only be granted to
his wife if she "hath not demerited the contrary by her wilful Absence or
Departure for her Husband or other notorious fact without reconciliation
to him in his life time."[32] Thus, the Plymouth courts could decide if the
widow was "worthy" of receiving a portion of her husband's estate. Moreover, legal codes throughout New England permitted justices to determine what a widow would receive from her husband's estate based on her
conduct as a wife.

In contrast, courts in the Chesapeake were much less likely to interfere
in the determining of a widow's portion. In fact, some historians have
suggested that in the early years of the Chesapeake colonies, planters may
have given their wives' more responsibility than was usual at the time.
Evidence from Charles County, Maryland, shows that almost one-fifth of
the men who left wills in the 1660s left everything to their wives—not just
the dower rights—trusting their wives to look after their children, even
though they knew their wives would probably remarry, as most Chesapeake area widows did. Men usually made their wives the executors of
their wills, but often they also appointed overseers to ensure that their
children received what they were due.

The inheritance laws of Virginia guaranteed that most widows there would be treated better than in either England or the other colonies. Under intestacy statutes, widows received a widow's dower of one-third if they had children, and one-half if the couple was childless. In addition, the widow received absolute interest in personal property—including slaves—as well as life interest in real estate. Husbands who did write wills could leave their widows more, but not less, than what was specified in the law.[33]

By the end of the seventeenth century, however, the courts in Virginia were less likely to grant widows the legal privileges they had given them earlier in the century. Authorities seemed to be more suspicious of households headed by women, and while earlier in the century women assumed authority to maintain stability in a household and community, toward the end of the century, this assumption of power often appeared to authorities as disruptive and a cause of disorder in the community. Local court justices seemed particularly concerned about the possible sexual misbehavior of widows and other women not under a male control.

Anxiety over rich, powerful, and independent widows can be seen in many fictional treatments written during the seventeenth century. Although the image of an independent and sexually voracious widow was not a new literary trope, it took on new life during the seventeenth century, when fictional treatments of Virginia widows began to appear. The title character of Aphra Behn's play, *The Widow Ranter: or the History of Bacon in Virginia* (1690), is a woman whose experiences to some extent mirror many of those of women who arrived in Virginia earlier in the century, only she is more outrageous. She travels to Virginia as a servant, but she manages to wed a wealthy planter, whom she outlives—and thus, inherits his wealth. The widow is depicted as an outspoken, drinking, cross-dressing woman. Many works written during the seventeenth century and early eighteenth century include Virginia widows as characters. These women are usually independent, sexually aggressive, and sometimes even cruel or violent.[34]

In reality, however, wealthy widows in Virginia may have fared best when they stayed within the socially approved role of dependent women. Although these women had wealth and independence, they often encountered rebellious servants and neighbors who were reluctant to have a woman exerting control over them. This was particularly true for women who did not have the wealth, resources, or knowledge of some of the high-ranking widows, who could more easily negotiate the boundaries between independence and dependence.[35]

Changing conditions and the growth of the colonies and institutions in the new world helped to adapt and alter the female roles of Anglo-Americans: daughter, wife, mother, and widow. In addition, the interaction of Europeans with the indigenous people of the Americas, as well as with Africans brought across the Atlantic, helped to define and transform female roles for all three groups. These transformations continued throughout the seventeenth century, as the American colonies grew in population, became more diverse, and spread beyond the initial coastal settlements, and as slavery became codified.

Several Native American societies lived along the Eastern coast in the seventeenth century when English settlers first established permanent colonies. Although they had distinct languages, and differences in political organization and family configurations, scholars have sometimes lumped them together as "Eastern Woodland Indians." There were some similarities within the various groups, however. Most of these Indian societies had a strong agricultural base controlled by the women, while the men lived more nomadic lives because they were hunters. Thus, there was a distinct sexual division of labor, but since women remained rooted to the land, communities were usually organized around them and their needs. In addition, women in these communities often controlled and distributed the food. Children usually received their family and kinship connections through their mothers, rather than through their fathers, as Europeans did. In some tribes, then, such as the Iroquois, it was the brother of a woman who became the most significant father figure for her child. The oldest women of each kinship line possessed much power and authority, but Iroquois society was based on principles of reciprocity. Therefore, there were also men who were powerful, and children were taught to respect their father and his kinship line, as well as their mother's.

The Iroquois lived in fortified towns consisting of anywhere from thirty to over one hundred longhouses surrounded by a palisade. The longhouses were made of saplings twisted together and covered with sheets of elm bark. On average, a longhouse was about one hundred feet long and slightly over twenty feet wide. Panels on the roof could be moved to let in sunlight and let out smoke. Inside, a corridor ran through the center with fireplaces at approximately every twenty feet. Bark-enclosed sleeping compartments for each family were set on raised platforms against the walls. A nuclear family lived in each "apartment" and shared the fire and meals with the family living across the fire from them, but all the families living in a longhouse were related through the female line.[36]

Thus, the longhouses were very different from the houses built by Europeans to house one family. Nevertheless, there were some similarities between Native American living quarters and those of European colonists. The households of colonists often included family members beyond the nuclear family, as well as servants and/or slaves. Many people slept in one room. In fact, several people were likely to share a single bed. A lack of privacy then was common to both Iroquois men and women and colonists. (For more on colonial houses, see Chapter 4.)

The lack of privacy made it difficult, but not impossible, for illicit sexual encounters to take place. Sarah Doolittle, a servant in New Haven, had or attempted to have sexual relations with more than one man. She noted that one time when she and John Thomas, Jr., tried to have sex in the house while everyone else was outside, "they lay down and he upon her naked body and attempted to penetrate her body." Thomas was unable to complete the act, however, "saying he was afraid." In another New Haven case from 1665, William Clark, a cooper, was in an outbuilding with a servant, Hannah Green, when "a noise affrighted him and made him run away and he then carried away in haste her petticoat instead of his britches."[37] In contrast, when the twenty-nine-year-old married gentleman Samuel Appleton raped the sixteen-year-old servant Priscilla Willson in a room at the old Iron Works in Lynn, Massachusetts, he was not deterred by the presence of another servant. Instead he simply pulled the curtains around the bed.[38]

Although modern-day readers might notice similarities in such things as a lack of privacy, most English people did not see similarities between their own society and that of the Native Americans they encountered. Many English observers, for example, criticized the work practices of Native Americans. Within Native American societies, men and women worked together to provide food the tribe needed to survive. Older men fished and younger men hunted, but women provided most of the nutritional needs of the tribe through the cultivation of maize, beans, and squash. In addition, they gathered berries, collected firewood, and made baskets in which to carry these items. English observers disapproved of women performing agricultural tasks, which were done by men in England, and they considered Native American men to be lazy. As George Percy, who was among the first group of soldier/colonists in Jamestown, commented, "I saw Bread made by their women which doe all their drugerie. The men takes their pleasure in hunting and their warres, which they are in continually one Kingdome against another."[39]

English settlers who came into contact with Native Americans also considered their matrilineal system to be suspicious, if not immoral and wrong. If women were not under the control of men, and were not accountable to them, then they were likely to be promiscuous. As evidence of their beliefs, Europeans noted that Indian women did not cover themselves in several layers of clothing, as did European women, and although Native American men and women did marry, they usually had had sexual relationships prior to marriage.

Marriage was important to many Native American societies because in addition to uniting a couple, it joined two clans. When a young man wanted to marry, he usually asked permission of the bride's parents. This was done through an intermediary, such as his own father or an uncle. Because clans were being united, other clan members were sometimes consulted about the wedding, and sometimes parents sought the opinion of a shaman. Women were seldom forced to marry someone they did not wish to wed. Divorces were usually easy to obtain; often couples simply agreed to divorce. In these matrilineal societies, the children remained with the mother if the parents divorced, since they were part of her clan.

Yet the ease with which Native Americans of this time and place divorced did not mean spousal compatibility was not important. Among the Micmac, for instance, who lived in what is now northern New England and Canada, couples were expected to abstain from having sexual relations with each other for their first year. This was to allow them to develop a loving relationship without sex, and to see whether they were compatible before they had children.

As with European women, motherhood was an important role for most Native American women. In contrast to European women, however, some Native American women with whom Europeans came into contact did not cry out in pain during childbirth. Many considered it a test of courage, similar to rituals male warriors underwent. However, some Anglo-Americans believed that Indian women did not feel pain during childbirth. To make sense of this, they concluded that Indian women were closer to nature, as Adam and Eve were before the Fall, and thus exempt from Eve's curse. Moreover, the English believed that Indian women were also more animal-like and savage than "civilized" European women.

Native American women generally nursed their babies far longer than did Anglo-American women. Often Native American mothers nursed their children for three to six years. This practice permitted mothers to provide their children with a nutritious, digestible, and portable diet when such food was not always available, thus improving each child's chance of survival. In addition, mothers usually abstained from sexual relations during this time to prevent another baby being born, as having two small children to care for could be difficult, especially if the mother had to carry both of them or food was scarce.

For the first year, many Native American babies were swaddled on a cradleboard and carried around by their mothers. This allowed the mothers to work in fields and yet attend to their babies' needs. The wooden boards were often decorated with paint, beads, and quills, and they expressed the hopes of the parents for their children. Although Anglo-American mothers did not use cradleboards, they also probably spent quite a bit of time carrying their babies around. In both cultures, babies usually slept in bed at night with their parents.

Vt Matronæ Dasamonquepeuc libe-   X.
ros gestant.

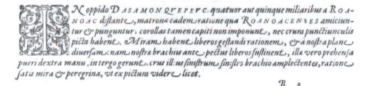

How the Chief Ladies of the Town of Dasamonquepeio Dress and Carry Their Children, 1590. Engraving by Theodor de Bry. Courtesy of Library of Congress.

African women brought to the American colonies were also likely to carry their babies around with them as they did their daily tasks. However, because they were generally either servants or slaves, they had to live their lives within the constraints placed upon them by their masters. Since they were forcibly removed from their homelands, African women lost all ties to their families, kinship networks, customs, and language. Large slave populations in the West Indies and in the later established colonies of South Carolina and Georgia permitted an African-based culture to become established within the slave population. In the Chesapeake colonies, however, the use of African men and women as a source of labor took some time to take hold. In fact, in the seventeenth century, an African woman might find herself the only African woman on a plantation there. However, as the pool of white indentured servants began to slow down in the late seventeenth century, and as economic conditions improved in England and opportunities for advancement in the colonies decreased, plantation owners began to depend more and more on black labor. Gradually, laws began to codify a system of chattel slavery, which had an enormous effect on African women's roles within the family. (Laws concerning race and slavery are discussed in more detail in Chapter 2.)

On plantations with few slaves, African women may not have been able to find husbands. Sometimes husbands and wives lived on separate plantations. In fact, as laws regarding slavery were enacted, slave marriages were outlawed altogether. Children usually remained with their mothers, but they could be sold or punished at the will of the master. In addition, slave women were subject to rape by their masters and other white men. Some men justified their actions by falling back on beliefs that Africans were lewd and savage, and that they had no sense of or belief in marriage or permanent relationships. In fact, some historians argue that by the eighteenth century, even the language referring to women had become racialized, and "wenches," which formerly referred to poor women and

Slave woman and child, undated. Courtesy of Library of Congress.

women suspected of sexual licentiousness, now referred almost solely to black women.[40]

By the eighteenth century, slavery was well established within the English colonies. The colonies themselves had moved beyond their shaky and idealistic beginnings. The early sex ratio imbalance in the Chesapeake became more even, changing women's roles and possibly giving them less authority. In New England, the early Puritan "city on the hill" gave way to a more diverse and commercialized society. As land became less available toward the end of the seventeenth century, many young men moved away or married women from other communities. The declining opportunities meant that larger numbers of New England women never married at all. The situation for poor women was even bleaker.

Yet by the middle of the eighteenth century, romantic love was beginning to assume more importance in courtship and marriage. More traditional beliefs about marriage and newer ideas sometimes collided and contributed to stresses within marriage. In addition, many young couples decided to engage in premarital sexuality to force their parents into letting them marry. Throughout the eighteenth century, the rate of premarital pregnancies rose. Thus, throughout the seventeenth century, women's primary role remained within the family; however, by the end of the century, family dynamics had changed in many areas as colonial society spread and became more diverse.

NOTES

1. Proverbs 31. The image of Bathsheba is discussed in Laurel Thatcher Ulrich, *Good Wives: Image and Reality in the Lives of Women in Northern New England, 1650–1750* (New York: Oxford University Press, 1982), chap. 1.

2. Ulrich coined the term "deputy husband" as a label for one of women's roles. Ulrich, *Good Wives*.

3. Lois Green Carr and Lorena S. Walsh, "The Planter's Wife: The Experience of White Women in Seventeenth-Century Maryland," in *A Heritage of Her Own: Toward a New Social History of American Women*, ed. Nancy F. Cott and Elizabeth H. Pleck (New York: Simon and Schuster, 1979), 29.

4. Mary Beth Norton, *Founding Mothers and Fathers: Gendered Power and the Forming of American Society* (New York: Vintage Books, 1996) esp. chap. 4. Else L. Hambleton also argues that a woman's sexual reputation was of primary importance in order for her to marry in her *Daughters of Eve: Pregnant Brides and Unwed Mothers in Seventeenth-Century Massachusetts* (New York: Routledge, 2004).

5. William Hand Browne, ed., *Archives of Maryland* (Baltimore: Maryland Historical Society, 1883–1972), 10:499, 500, 531–533, cited in Debra Meyers, *Common Whores, Vertuous Women, and Loveing Wives: Free Will Christian Women in Colonial Maryland* (Bloomington: Indiana University Press, 2003), 48–49.

6. Kathleen M. Brown suggests that some servants might have tried to arrange their sexual encounters during times when they expected they would not get

pregnant. Kathleen M. Brown, *Good Wives, Nasty Wenches, and Anxious Patriarchs: Gender, Race, and Power in Colonial Virginia* (Chapel Hill: University of North Carolina Press, 1996), 99.

7. William Bradford, *Bradford's History of Plymouth Plantation, 1606–1646*, ed. William T. Davis (New York: Charles Scribner's Sons, 1908). Available at: Early Americas Digital Archive, http://www.mith2.umd.edu/eada/html/display.php?docs=bradford_history.xml.

8. William Blackstone, *Commentaries on the Laws of England*, chap. 15, bk. 1. Available at: The Avalon Project at Yale Law School, http://www.yale.edu/lawweb/avalon/blackstone/blacksto.htm.

9. Benjamin Wadsworth, *The Well-Ordered Family, or Relative Duties* (Boston, 1712), 22–47, quoted in *America's Families: A Documentary History*, ed. Daniel M. Scott and Bernard Wishy (New York: Harper and Row, 1982), 89.

10. Laurel Thatcher Ulrich, "Vertuous Women Found: New England Ministerial Literature, 1668–1735," in Cott and Pleck, *A Heritage of Her Own*, 61.

11. Brown, *Good Wives, Nasty Wenches*, 84–85; *John Hammond, Leah and Rachel, or, The Two Fruitful Sisters Virginia and Mary-land: Their Present Condition, Impartially Stated and Related*, 1656. Available at: http://www.digitalhistory.uh.edu/learning_history/servitude_slavery/servitude_account2.cfm.

12. Cited in Brown, *Good Wives, Nasty Wenches*, 92.

13. Meyers, *Common Whores*, 50–51.

14. Christine Daniels, "'Liberty to Complaine': Servant Petitions in Maryland, 1652–1797," in *The Many Legalities of Early America*, ed. Christopher L. Tomlins and Bruce H. Mann (Chapel Hill: University of North Carolina Press, 2001), 239.

15. Verse quoted in Meyers, *Common Whores*, 50.

16. Meyers, *Common Whores*, 52–53.

17. George Fox, *A Collection of Many Select and Christian Epistles, Letters, and Testimonies* (Philadelphia, 1831), 2:180–81, quoted in Scott and Wishy, *America's Families*, 82.

18. W. W. Hening, ed., *The Statutes at Large, Being a Collection of all the Laws of Virginia, 1619–1792* (Richmond, 1809–1823), 2:86–87, quoted in Scott and Wishy, *America's Families*, 35.

19. J. William Frost, *The Quaker Family in Colonial America: A Portrait of the Society of Friends* (New York: St. Martin's Press, 1973), 156.

20. Ulrich, *Good Wives*, 122.

21. *Records and Files of the Quarterly Courts of Essex County, Massachusetts* (Salem: Essex Institute, 1916), 1:180; 2:242, quoted in Hambleton, *Daughters of Eve*, 114.

22. Hambleton, *Daughters of Eve*, 115–16.

23. William Whateley, *A Bride Bush: or, A Direction for Married Persons* (London: Robert Midgley, 1689), 93–94, quoted in Meyers, *Common Whores*, 55.

24. Maryland Archives, LIV, 109–10, cited in Norton, *Founding Mothers and Fathers*, 111.

25. Mehitable Parkman to Mr. Deliverance Parkman, Salem, 1683, Curwen Family Papers, Essex Institute, Salem, MA, quoted in Ulrich, *Good Wives*, 109.

26. Quoted in Frost, *The Quaker Family*, 162.

27. *The Complete Practice of Physick* (London, 1655), 503, quoted in Thomas A. Foster, "Deficient Husbands: Manhood, Sexual Incapacity, and Male Marital Sexuality in Seventeenth-Century New England," *William and Mary Quarterly* 56 (October 1999): 728.

28. William Gouge, *Of Domestical Duties* (1622); Foster, "Deficient Husbands," 728.

29. Ulrich, *Good Wives*, 130–31.

30. Jacques Guillemeau, *Child-Birth or, The Happy Deliverie of Women* (London, 1612), quoted in Marylynn Salmon, "The Cultural Significance of Breastfeeding and Infant Care in Early Modern England and America," *Journal of Social History* 28 (Winter 1994): 251.

31. Anne Bradstreet (ca. 1612–1672), "In Reference to Her Children, 23 June 1659." Original text: Anne Bradstreet, *Several Poems*, 2nd ed. (Boston: John Foster, 1678); cf. *The Complete Works of Anne Bradstreet*, ed. Joseph R. McElrath, Jr., and Allan P. Robb (Boston: Twayne, 1981): 184–86. Available at Representative Poetry Online, http://rpo.library.utoronto.ca/poem/215.html. Online text copyright © 2005, Ian Lancashire for the Department of English, University of Toronto.

32. William Brigham, ed., *The Compact with the Charter and Laws of the Colony of New Plymouth* (Boston: Button and Wentworth, 1836), 299, quoted in Norton, *Founding Mothers and Fathers*, 145.

33. Terri L. Snyder, *Brabbling Women: Disorderly Speech and the Law in Early Virginia* (Ithaca, NY: Cornell University Press, 2003), 122–23.

34. Ibid., 123–26.

35. Ibid., 127–39.

36. Daniel K. Richter, *The Ordeal of the Longhouse: The Peoples of the Iroquois League in the Era of European Colonization* (Chapel Hill: University of North Carolina Press, 1992), esp. 18–21.

37. Franklin Dexter, ed., *New Haven Town Records*, 2 vols. (New Haven, 1917–1919), 2:228–29, and Middlesex County Court Records, Massachusetts State Archives, Columbia Point, Boston: Order Book for 1681–1686: file 38 quoted in Richard Godbeer, *Sexual Revolution in Early America* (Baltimore: John Hopkins University Press, 2002), 29–30.

38. Hambleton, *Daughters of Eve*, 83–85.

39. George Percy, *Observations Gathered out of a Discourse of the Plantation of the Southerne Colonie in Virginia by the English, 1606. Written by that Honorable Gentleman, Master George Percy*. Available at: The Virtual Jamestown Project, http://etext.lib.virginia.edu/etcbin/jamestown-browse?id=J1002.

40. See Brown, *Good Wives, Nasty Wenches*.

SUGGESTED READING

Brown, Kathleen M. *Good Wives, Nasty Wenches, and Anxious Patriarchs: Gender, Race, and Power in Colonial Virginia*. Chapel Hill: University of North Carolina Press, 1996.

Carr, Lois Green, and Lorena S. Walsh. "The Planter's Wife: The Experience of White Women in Seventeenth-Century Maryland." In *A Heritage of Her Own: Toward a New Social History of American Women*, ed. Nancy F. Cott and Elizabeth H. Pleck, 25–57. New York: Simon and Schuster, 1979.

Hambleton, Else L. *Daughters of Eve: Pregnant Brides and Unwed Mothers in Seventeenth-Century Massachusetts*. New York: Routledge, 2004.

Norton, Mary Beth. *Founding Mothers and Fathers: Gendered Power and the Forming of American Society*. New York: Vintage Books, 1996.

Richter, Daniel K. *The Ordeal of the Longhouse: The Peoples of the Iroquois League in the Era of European Colonization*. Chapel Hill: University of North Carolina Press, 1992.

Salmon, Marylynn. "The Cultural Significance of Breastfeeding and Infant Care in Early Modern England and America." *Journal of Social History* 28 (Winter 1994): 247–69.

Ulrich, Laurel Thatcher. *Good Wives: Image and Reality in the Lives of Women in Northern New England, 1650–1750*. New York: Oxford University Press, 1982.

2

⎯⎯∞⎯⎯

Women and Law

In seventeenth-century America, as in most of the Western world, women had few legal rights. In many ways, however, the law was a very real part of their lives, as it defined who they were and how they lived within their society, whether single, married, widowed, servant, or slave. Single women were usually governed by their fathers or guardians, servants and slaves by their masters, and married women by their husbands under the legal construct of coverture (discussed in Chapter 1). Under coverture, married women or *femes covert* had no separate legal identity. They could not sue or be sued separately from their husbands, nor could they make contracts or pursue other legal transactions without their spouses. As *The Lawes Resolutions of Womens Rights* (1632) put it, "It is true, that man and wife are one person; but understand in what manner. When a small brooke or little river incorporateth with Rhodanus, Humber, or the Thames, the poor rivulet looseth her name; ... it beareth no sway; it possesseth nothing during coverture. A woman as soon as she is married, is called *covert* ... clouded and overshadowed; she hath lost her streame."[1]

This merging of identities did not necessarily apply to colonies not under British rule, who treated wives and widows differently. For example, under Dutch law in New Netherland, marriage was considered an equal partnership between men and women. Dutch women could continue to manage, buy, and sell businesses and property after they married. Upon widowhood, Dutch women in New Netherland received half of their husband's estate and the assurance that they could administer the other half for their children. After the British gained control of New Netherland and renamed it New York in 1664, Dutch women gradually lost the independence they had had to conduct business and legal affairs on their own.[2]

Although conditions in the early colonies meant there were some differences between common law and common practice, all of the British colonies in America enacted legislation maintaining English precedent regarding coverture. However, colonists did not always strictly follow the letter of the law. In Virginia, for instance, married women sometimes went to court by themselves in the early part of the century. Even though judges may have assumed that the women had the consent of their husbands, in effect, these married women were coming before the court as femes sole, or single women. By 1680, however, justices in Virginia were taking the law more literally. In one such ruling in 1683, justices in Norfolk declined to let Mrs. Wealthen Jones Lister proceed with her suit against her former master, Thomas Scott, for the corn and clothes she said he owed her, "she being under couvert and having noe power from her husband."[3]

For the most part, husbands accompanied their wives when they appeared in court, except for when the women were petitioning for divorce or fighting defamation of character suits, which were traditionally tried in ecclesiastical courts, and thus, not subject to the restraints of coverture.[4] Yet women found ways to bypass the law through informal means and arrangements. One method was by making verbal agreements with other women. For example, one Virginia matron offered to pay a midwife "12 hens" for her services when the woman went into labor. Husbands also sought to get around coverture by writing prenuptial agreements permitting their wives to accept gifts and allowing them to bestow their property to heirs in their own wills. Sometimes, too, wives acted for their husbands in business matters, such as buying and selling items or receiving the payment of debts. Because these transactions were not strictly legal, they were subject to invalidation by the courts if someone chose to challenge them. Husbands could legally give their wives power of attorney, but even then, they could renounce the actions their wives made.[5]

Powers of attorney could vary. They could provide wives with a one-time instruction, or give them almost total independence. Sometimes they even served as a type of separation agreement, as in the case of Jane (Ludwell) Parke. Jane's husband, Daniel Parke, granted her power of attorney two times. In the first in 1689, he gave her limited power, but in the second, he gave her great legal control over their property and business concerns. This power served her well, as she was able to resolve business issues and debts, make investments, and rent land. She did this because

Daniel left her in Virginia while he served as governor of the Leeward Islands. In the Leeward Islands, Governor Parke kept a mistress, a married woman. He acknowledged the mistress and their child in his will. Although Jane died before Daniel, she undoubtedly knew that he was not faithful to her, since this was not the first time he had been publicly involved with another woman. As one historian states, "In the context of this shadow life, the power of attorney that Daniel twice granted to Jane Parke takes on a distinctive meaning. In other families, powers of attorney indicated the ways that women played a part in trade networks. Jane Parke's powers of attorney, especially the second, seem to have served as an effective separation agreement.... In effect, this power of attorney allowed Jane Parke much of the power of a separation agreement but without the complications."[6]

Under coverture, however, a husband could both repudiate a contract made by his wife and challenge decisions made by the courts based on statements and actions presented by his wife, even when he had granted her power of attorney. This could work to a husband's advantage, if, for example, his wife had made ill-advised business decisions. On the other hand, since married women did not have separate legal identities, their husbands were liable for any debts they accrued. In addition, in criminal cases, a husband was responsible for court costs and expected to post bonds for his wife—even if she was charged with adultery or loose behavior.

As a result then of this legal device, which made husband and wife one person under the law, married women had few rights of their own. Moreover, as husbands were expected to have "dominion" over their households, they were permitted to physically correct their wives, children, and servants. Even though few condoned excessive wife beating, authorities and neighbors seldom interfered if a man chose to moderately correct his wife. Massachusetts Bay Colony and Plymouth Colony passed laws prohibiting spouse abuse but did not grant divorces solely on the grounds of cruelty. In fact, some men did not bother to hide the fact that they were abusing their wives, as they considered it to be acceptable behavior well within their role of husbands. Indeed, the early modern wifely ideal— whether Puritan or not—was of a woman unquestioningly obedient to her husband, and many women, raised to be submissive, may not have believed they should or could challenge an abusive spouse.

Nevertheless, most people considered excessive cruelty of a husband toward his wife to be wrong, and friends and neighbors did step in to aid a wife being battered, especially if they feared her life was in danger. Yet cruelty was not grounds for divorce, even in the colonies that granted divorces. Wives who had been forced to flee from their husbands because of abuse, however, often submitted testimonies of beatings and other cruelty inflicted upon them as part of their court depositions. Their accounts served to show judges that they had not been "bad" wives who chose to neglect their marital duties by deserting their spouses or by wanting to end their marriages.[7]

In one example from the 1670s, the well-to-do Boston matron Katherine Naylor asked for a divorce from her husband, Edward, only after the court found him guilty of repeated infidelity with two different women and "severe Cruelty in Abuseing his wife and Children." Mistress Naylor had endured years of physical and emotional abuse from her husband without asking for help from her wealthy extended family, friends, or authorities. However, the silence was broken when Mary Read, who was a maid in the Naylor household, became pregnant. Edward Naylor assisted her in running off to New Hampshire so that her baby could be born in secret. Unfortunately for Naylor, while in labor, Mary revealed to a midwife that he was the father of her child. In 1671–1672, Naylor was found guilty of fornication with Mary Read, "uncivil Cariage with mary Morse," and cruelty toward his wife. During the court proceedings, servants in the household, as well as tavern keepers and washerwomen, provided vivid testimony of the life Katherine Naylor described as "an intolerable bondage." A few months after that, she filed a petition for divorce.[8] It is possible that she had a chance to get even, however. Archeologists who have excavated the site of the Naylors' privy have found scraps of expensive clothing and a fashionable men's shoe. Perhaps she threw her former husband's things into the privy after he asked her to send clothing to him in Maine, noting "I have none to wear, especially linen and shoes."[9]

Divorce was possible in the seventeenth-century New England colonies, as marriage was a civil contract there rather than a sacrament, and thus it was a matter for secular courts. Massachusetts Bay began hearing divorce cases in 1639. In contrast, neither Virginia nor Maryland permitted divorce in the seventeenth century; however, both colonies granted legal separations and separate maintenances. William Penn's Great Law of 1682 permitted divorce in Pennsylvania to a man or woman whose spouse had been convicted of adultery, but it does not appear that any divorces were granted under this statute. In New Netherland, there were three divorces granted in 1655–1664, when the colony became the English colony of New York. The Duke's Laws of 1665 permitted a legal separation if a wife was found guilty of adultery, although it did not make provisions for divorce. However, some English governors in New York did grant divorces in 1664–1675 for adultery of the wife. Within the New England colonies, grounds for divorce varied somewhat from colony to colony and over time, but generally included adultery, bigamy, desertion, and impotence.[10] Although Puritans believed that marriage and family were central to the maintenance of society, they also recognized that occasionally a man or woman should be permitted to dissolve a marriage in which one spouse had violated the matrimonial contract by infidelity or desertion, or by the inability to consummate the marriage. Successful petitions brought by women usually indicated that the husband was unfit as a husband because he did not provide for the family.[11] Nevertheless, the dissolution of a marriage was not taken lightly. Women who had been deserted by their husbands were often left without financial support but still considered femes covert. Divorces for these women kept them from becoming a burden to the community and from entering into unsanctioned relationships with other men. Thus, in seventeenth-century New England, more women than men petitioned for divorce, usually on the grounds of desertion, and most of their petitions were granted.[12]

Nevertheless, judges granted divorces for other reasons, such as impotence of the husband. One historian noted that approximately one in six divorce petitions filed by seventeenth-century New England women "involved charges of male sexual incapacity."[13] The Massachusetts Court of Assistants granted Anna Lane a divorce in 1658. Anna stated that she "hath been deceived in contract of marriage with Mr. Edward Lane ... expecting the performance of an husband on his part, wherein he hath been from first to last altogether deficient." The couple remarried in 1659 after Anna became satisfied "in his sufficiency as a man."[14] Undoubtedly, the remarriage pleased Edward Lane for several reasons, not the least because a man divorced for impotence was not usually permitted to remarry. Consequently, he could not be the head of a household, as seventeenth-century men and women defined the term. Women who successfully sued for divorce because of the sexual incapacity of their husbands were allowed to marry again, as that would then put them under the governance of a husband and keep them from sexual temptation.

In seventeenth-century New Haven and Connecticut colonies, judges granted divorces as a means of keeping men and women from sinful behavior. Indeed, they were so concerned with preserving family life and households that they were willing to ignore both canon and common law. For example, they granted divorces to couples even when they knew that both spouses wanted a divorce. This practice went against the intention of divorce laws of this time, which were not meant to easily dissolve the bonds of matrimony for frivolous reasons, but rather to assist men and women whose marriages were already destroyed due to a spouse who had deserted them or who had been unfaithful. Between 1669 and 1702, Connecticut justices even granted divorces to three women and one man who had committed adultery. Elizabeth Reynolds, for example, was granted a divorce despite having been convicted and whipped in 1701 for bearing a child fathered by another man while her husband was away. Canon law did not permit adulterers to marry their lovers, but seventeenth-century Connecticut officials believed it was better to have couples marry than to risk having them continue their sinful behavior.[15]

In some cases, divorce might be used as a method to not only regulate marriage but also as a means to preserve English society. In 1668, Elizabeth Stevens petitioned the Massachusetts Bay court for a divorce from her husband, Henry. Noting that she had fled her home in Rhode Island and lived apart from her husband only after years of violence and physical abuse, Elizabeth then made the shocking assertion that her husband had committed "adultry wth severall Weomen & that nott wth those of our owne Nation onely but [with] the very heathen that Live among us." In 1670 Massachusetts authorities granted Elizabeth Stevens the right to remarry, thus ensuring that she would be able to live as a wife within a proper English Puritan household.[16]

Women living without a male head of household were considered at great risk of becoming involved in licentious behavior and of tempting men into sin. Early modern legal and religious authorities condemned anything that endangered marriage, as they considered it the cornerstone of society. All of the British American colonies enacted laws against extramarital sex, whether adultery, fornication, or sodomy, because such behavior undermined marriage. The regulation of marriage was of great importance to seventeenth-century Americans, as it was the basis of family formation, and nearly every colony enacted marital legislation within the first decades of establishment (discussed in more detail in Chapter 1). Anglo-Americans considered sexual relations between husband and wife to be an important part of marriage, but fornication, adultery, and sodomy, indeed, any nonprocreative or nonmarital sex acts, were deemed criminal. Adultery was particularly odious, since it threatened the husband's authority within the household and denied him exclusive rights to the body of his wife. In the seventeenth century, adultery occurred when a man had sexual relations with a married woman who was not his wife. The marital status of the man was irrelevant. Married men who had sexual relations with unmarried women were accused of fornication, not adultery. Thus, a double standard was built into the law, but it was in accordance with the views of many at this time.

Puritans considered adultery particularly evil, since it undermined the role of the husband and weakened the household. In the New England colonies adultery was a capital crime, although Massachusetts imposed the death penalty only one time for this crime, in the case of Mary Latham and John Britton, in March 1643–1644. Nevertheless, the Puritan authorities kept the statute on the books—indicating its importance— while finding ways to avoid executing those who were obviously guilty of the crime. In some cases, the courts declared individuals guilty of lesser crimes, such as "unchaste behavior" or "lascivious carriage," terms that were used for single men and women who engaged in nonmarital sexual relations. Moreover, as mentioned earlier, officials occasionally over-looked or discounted instances of adultery in granting divorces to individuals so that they could be joined in matrimony with their lovers and not live in sin. Although authorities in New England were reluctant to execute individuals for adultery, they did punish transgressions with whippings, banishment, and in at least one case, a symbolic hanging in which the couple had to sit at the gallows with ropes around their necks, after which the woman was banished.[17]

The double standard evidenced in laws on adultery can also be seen in the records of those prosecuted and convicted of fornication and bastardy. There were, however, differences in how the various colonies prosecuted such cases. In early modern England, cases of fornication and bastardy were usually tried in church courts, but these tribunals did not exist in the colonies. In early Virginia, justices presiding over such cases often imposed sentences requiring public penance, as well as secular punishments, such as fines, whippings, and increasing the terms of a servant's indenture, until after the Restoration, when legal reforms were put into place.[18]

Yet prosecutions of bastardy cases in the Chesapeake were due less to moral reasons than to economic ones—the loss of a pregnant or nursing servant's labor and the cost of raising her child. Unlike the young men and women of New England who lived within families, were supervised by household members and neighbors, and inculcated from birth with the beliefs and values of the Puritan theocracy in which they lived, the young people of the early Chesapeake generally lacked parents and strong church leadership to counsel and advise them. Consequently, they were less likely to abstain from premarital sexual encounters. At the same time, planters there sought to regulate the behavior of their servants. They had an economic motive for wanting to limit the number of illegitimate births—the region's economy was tied to the labor-intensive crop of tobacco, making it necessary for successful planters to have servants who could work unhampered by pregnancy and childbirth.[19]

Poor women, who faced an uncertain future in England, sailed for the American colonies, usually unaware of the dangers they faced there. They were lured by promoters, such as William Bullock, who wrote that female servants who "come of an honest stock and have a good repute ... may pick and chuse their Husbands." Since the number of men far outnumbered the number of women in the Chesapeake colonies, to some extent Bullock's statement about marriage was true—if the women did not become victims of the fever-producing environment of the region. Thus, the woman who emigrated with expectations of working as a house servant for a short time and then making a comfortable marriage may have been particularly tempted to believe the pledges of marriage uttered by men who only wanted to seduce them.[20]

Anne Orthwood was one such woman, a twenty-four-year-old indentured servant who sailed from her home in Bristol, England, to Virginia in 1663. Her first master, William Kendall, sold her after only a few months of service to separate her and his nephew, John. Despite these precautions, Anne became pregnant by John and died soon after giving birth to a son, Jasper. If John Kendall had married Anne, her status would have changed from indentured servant to wife of a well-connected and wealthy man. The birth of a child too soon after a wedding might have caused some embarrassment, but would not have been a big issue in the Chesapeake, as traditionally, betrothed couples often engaged in intimate relations before marriage. However, John did not marry Anne, and she died soon after childbirth. John later married an heiress. Anne's indentured status, her pregnancy, and the birth of her son, Jasper, led to four separate but related court cases, stretching over two decades and involving the issues of servitude, fornication, and bastardy.[21]

Most women who survived servitude in the Chesapeake did marry, but servants who gave birth to illegitimate children were treated more harshly by midcentury, as taxpayers grew resentful of having to support the children. It cost approximately 1,000 to 1,200 pounds of tobacco per year for a parish to support a bastard child. A man who was convicted of impregnating a servant had to pay her master for the time she could not work. The Virginia Assembly made the pregnant servants "lible to equall punishment" with their partners in 1660, but in 1662, the women alone were made responsible. Under law, they had to either pay their masters 2,000 pounds of tobacco or serve an additional two years of service. In addition, the woman had to pay a "fornication fine" to the parish. If her master paid for her, she had to compensate him by extending her indenture for an additional six months. If he did not pay her fine, she could be whipped. Had Anne Orthwood survived, she would have faced extended servitude.[22]

In the southern colonies, race added another dimension to fornication and bastardy cases. For example, in Virginia, a 1691 statute outlawed all interracial sex. White servant women and their children, however, were the ones most often punished. Between 1680 and 1710, at least 81 percent of all interracial prosecutions were white servant women.[23]

Female servants were at risk of sexual abuse from their masters in New England, as well. Most young women in New England, regardless of their class, spent some time living in other people's houses. As in England, parents sent their daughters to live in other households, often those of relatives, to learn the skills needed to become a housewife. Although parents expected their daughters to be well supervised, this was not always the case. In some situations, young women became the victims of sexual predators. That the culture encouraged girls and women to be submissive and to respect the male head of the household may have made some of these young women less able to protest or too scared to tell when attacks did occur. In other cases, they may have been seduced by promises of marriage. In Essex County, Massachusetts, 40 percent of the female defendants in seventeenth-century fornication and bastardy cases were servants.[24]

Even though some of these women were victims of rape or sexual coercion, Puritan laws and beliefs still held them responsible for having sinned. In fact, neighbors could quickly change their minds about a woman's character when faced with the undisputed proof that she had engaged in premarital sexual relations. In seventeenth-century Essex County, despite witnesses' testimony indicating that Samuel Appleton had forced sixteen-year-old Priscilla Willson to have sexual intercourse with him, Appleton was never prosecuted for rape, and he was acquitted of fornication charges. According to early modern beliefs, a woman could not become pregnant by rape. Therefore, since Priscilla did become pregnant, she must have consented to having sexual relations with someone. Even those closest to her believed that Priscilla had given in to sinful pleasures. However, in an unusual step, fourteen of her neighbors signed a statement that testified to her good character, noting that "from her childhood shee behaved herselfe soe modestly and Civilly all her time before this transgression as that none of us ever saw or heard of any Immodest or Uncivil behavior or wantonnesse and that wee beleeve she was overcome by some subtill slights and temptations of one that beguiled her to yeeld to his lust."[25]

Yielding to Appleton's position and honor as a gentleman, the judges took him at his word when he denied paternity. Nevertheless, they still required him to pay half the court costs, which included, among other things, the fee for the midwife, care for the baby, who only lived for a few weeks, and the costs to summon Priscilla's witnesses. Thus, Appleton's honor was saved, but the court still held him responsible for fathering Priscilla's bastard child. Nevertheless, Appleton went on to become a respected member of society who held a number of courtesy titles when he died in his seventies. On the other hand, Priscilla Willson is not mentioned again in any public records, and there is no indication that she ever married.[26]

In New England, unlike the Chesapeake, most women who became pregnant outside of wedlock faced a stigma. Few of them married, and sometimes the courts took their babies away from them, even using force in some cases. Susanna Durin, for example, was still breastfeeding her baby when it was taken from her. Her partner, William Reeves, begged the court to allow the distraught mother to visit her infant, but to no avail. Despite the belief that the primary role of a woman was to be a mother, Susanna was not permitted to keep her child. Undoubtedly, this was because marriage had not preceded the birth, and therefore, Susanna was not a fit mother. William Reeves, however, was still expected to pay support for the baby.[27]

Puritan New England prosecuted men and women for a variety of moral and sexual offenses, not just bastardy or fornication. Not only did Puritans regard extramarital acts as immoral, but they feared that if left unchecked, such behavior would destroy their whole society by not only damaging family life, but also by breaking their covenant with God. Thus, both men and women who committed fornication were punished, and men and women whose first child appeared too soon after the wedding were both prosecuted. Yet for single women who were involved with either single or married men, the consequences of engaging in extramarital sex (whether consensual or not) were worse for them than for their partners. In seventeenth-century Essex County, Massachusetts, women received harsher sentences in 75 percent of cases prosecuted. Moreover, the majority of these women did not marry, which kept them from engaging in the lifestyle of most women of that time and place. In contrast, most of the men who fathered bastard children were either already married, or they married soon afterward.[28]

Throughout the colonies, a double standard existed that put the onus on women to control sex and also held them responsible for sexual misconduct. This was particularly true in New England, although only a small number of individuals there actually engaged in extramarital relationships. By policing and regulating sexual behavior, it may be that New England Puritans were able to promote a new standard that conflated chastity and femininity while maintaining the common early modern belief in women as lust-filled temptresses.

These competing ideas about women made the prosecution of rape difficult. The combination of a submissive woman who might have been afraid to challenge a man, especially one who held a position of authority, and an assertive man, who viewed women as lustful daughters of Eve, made the determination of consent difficult. Women were questioned about why they did not cry out, or why they did not complain. Mary Rolfe of Newbury, Massachusetts, told her mother that Henry Greenland "is in Creditt in the Towne, some take him to be godly &say hee hath grace in his face, he have an honest loke, he have such a carriage that he deceive many: It is saide the Governor sent him a letter Counting it a mercy such an Instrument was in the Country, and what shall such a pore young women as I doe in such a case, my husband being not at home?"

Mary Rolfe might have been flattered initially by the imposing stranger's notice of her, but she did not know how to stop his actions, and she lacked the confidence to challenge him before others. It took her mother's prying into what was troubling Mary and then her persistence in pursuing the matter to bring Henry Greenland to court. Greenland was convicted of attempted adultery and fined thirty pounds. After Mary's fisherman husband, John, returned from sea, he sued Greenland for damages. The court granted John Rolfe's suit, since Greenland's attempted adultery conviction meant he had violated Rolf's "property," Mary.[29]

To secure a conviction of rape, a woman had to have witnesses who would testify that they saw the rape and that the woman called for help. Making it even more problematical to label a rape were early modern beliefs about conception. As in Priscilla Willson's case, when confronted with a pregnancy, the colonists of British American could not believe the woman had been raped. Michael Dalton's *The Countrey Justice*, a widely used judicial manual, stated this idea succinctly: "if a Woman at the time of the supposed Rape, do conceive with Child by the Ravisher, this is no Rape; for a Woman cannot conceive with Child except she doth consent."[30]

In the New England colonies, legislators wrote and rewrote laws concerning rape. In 1642, following the sexual abuse of two young girls, Dorcas and Sarah Humphrey, Massachusetts made the rape of a girl under ten years old a capital crime. There was no law on the books at this time addressing the rape of children. The rape of a married woman or of one who was engaged was made a capital crime, but whether the rape of a single woman should be a capital crime was left to the justices to determine in each case. In 1648, the law was revised to address only the rape of single women over ten; the rape of married women would be covered under the laws against adultery. After the rape of an eight-year-old girl in 1669, the law was again revised to make the rape of a female child a capital crime.[31]

Although Puritans and non-Puritans considered the rape of a child to be detestable, they did not consider the victimized young girls to be entirely blameless. John Winthrop, governor of the Massachusetts Bay colony, described Dorcas Humphrey as the instigator of her abuse, which began when she was seven years old. In one of the few Virginia cases in which a man was convicted for sexual assault, the court ordered the mother of the seven-year-old victim to correct her "for that her fault and for that there appeareth in her signe of more grace and greife for her offence."[32] The belief that all women, even female children, had difficulty controlling their sexual appetites made it difficult for authorities to convict men for rape.

By the end of the seventeenth century, race became more of a factor in rape prosecutions. Black men and Native American men were more likely to be charged and convicted of rape involving a white woman. As black and slavery became synonymous, black women seldom brought accusations of rape against their attackers—black or white. Since by definition a slave belonged to her master, he could use her body as he wished, and children born of their coupling became his property, as well.

Although Africans, African Americans, and Native Americans were perceived as being especially promiscuous, the notion that women could not control their sexuality meant any woman who did not live under male authority chanced being suspected of lewd or unseemly behavior and risked sexual coercion from men who viewed them as vulnerable. Nearly all white women in the seventeenth century did marry, but women who had been married but no longer had a husband because of desertion or death were also suspected of being sexually voracious. This was because people believed that having already experienced intimacy with a man, they would not be able to withstand temptation. In addition, because widows were no longer under coverture and had more legal rights and control over their estates, some viewed them as dangerous. Thus, often widows were encouraged to remarry.

Yet there were some women who chose not to marry at all. For example, Margaret Brent, who arrived in Maryland in 1638 with her sister, Mary, and her brothers, Fulke and Giles, remained single and conducted business for herself and the colony. Because her single state is so unusual in this time and place, some historians speculate that Margaret and Mary had taken vows of celibacy. Maryland was a Catholic colony, and the Brents were a Catholic aristocratic family. Whatever the reason for her single state, as an unmarried woman, Margaret Brent was permitted to own land and manage it on her own. She went to court regularly to take care of her affairs, such as collecting debts. That she was able and respected can be seen in that shortly before his death, Governor Leonard Calvert made her the executor of his estate. Then the Provincial Court appointed her "attorney-in-fact" for Lord Baltimore, as the colony was in the middle of a crisis as a result of an attack on it by forces under Richard Ingle (discussed in more detail in Chapter 6). Thus, Margaret appeared before the Maryland Assembly in 1648 asking for two votes—one for herself as a landowner plus one as a representative of Lord Baltimore. She was not granted the right to vote, although the Assembly openly noted her abilities.[33]

Unlike most women who came to the Chesapeake, Margaret Brent was wealthy and wellborn, and able to achieve some prominence both because of her abilities and because she remained single. Since most white women were married, however, they were not normally involved in either legal or political affairs of this nature. Nevertheless, married women did hold some power and were listened to in situations that concerned women and women's bodies. In cases of rape, fornication, and bastardy, and in other situations where authorities wanted a woman's body to be examined, they asked midwives or panels of matrons to perform the examination, to ask the woman questions, and to testify before the court. Since men were generally excluded, childbirth was under the control of midwives and other women who attended and helped with the birth. In effect, these women became expert witnesses. Throughout the colonies, midwives demanded to know the name of the baby's father from a woman in the midst of labor. (Midwives are discussed in more detail in Chapter 4.) It was widely believed that during those moments, a woman, in pain and facing possible death, would not lie. For example, Virginia midwife Alice Wilson noted that she demanded of "Ollive Eaton in the instant tyme of her payne in travail, to declare who was the true father of the child she was then to be delivered of, she answered William Fisher."[34] Sometimes a midwife even threatened to withhold her help until a laboring woman named the man who was responsible for her condition. In numerous cases throughout the colonies, as in the cases of Anne Orthwood, Priscilla Willson, and Mary Read, women in travail revealed their lover's name to a midwife who then testified in court.

However, a midwife's testimony could also help exonerate couples accused of fornication when a baby was born too soon after the wedding date. For example, in the case of Humphrey and Elizabeth Devereaux, the midwife Wiborough Gatchell testified that: "Elizabeth Devereaux, whom according to the best of my judgement, came before her time occasioned only by the stroke of a cow upon her body when she was milking, and my self and the women that were assistant there did judge that the child was born before its time."[35] As an expert on childbirth, Gatchell's statement that in her opinion Elizabeth Devereaux's child was born too early as a result of an accident was given due consideration by the court.

Midwives and married women also reported on other matters concerning women. For instance, the County Court of York County, Virginia, asked three married women in 1646 to examine a woman who they believed had been abused by her husband. The court also asked for testimony from a midwife. In 1633, the General Court of Virginia asked a Jury of Matrons to examine and decide whether a woman who had been sentenced to die for killing her child was now pregnant.[36]

In seventeenth-century British America, midwives and matrons provided a link between the formal legal system and traditional, informal systems of justice. Thus, Elizabeth Perkins, Sr., and Agnes Ewens told the Essex County Court in 1664 that:

what had brought them forth was the busy prattling of some other, probably the one whom they had taken along with them to advise a young woman, whose simple and foolish carriages and words, having heard of, they desired to advise better.... They desired to be excused from testifying because what was told them was a private confession which they had never to that day divulged, and the woman had never offended since that time but had lived gravely and soberly.[37]

As they stated, Elizabeth Perkins and Agnes Ewens investigated a situation known to them and known about by other women, but having talked to the young woman in question and given her the benefit of their wisdom, gleaned from experience, they now considered the matter over. It was clear to them that there was no need for the court to deal with the matter.

Sometimes women chose not to share gossip with men, particularly knowledge gained at childbirths. Women gathered together for childbirth in the seventeenth century, but men were excluded. During childbirth, the laboring woman might reveal who the father was, but sometimes the women discovered other secrets or observed something that men would not see. For example, a number of Boston women knew about the "monstrous birth" of Mary Dyer in 1637. Dyer was a follower of Anne Hutchinson, the religious dissenter who was tried and excommunicated for her beliefs. (Anne Hutchinson and Mary Dyer are discussed in Chapter 5.) Although Mary's deformed baby was born in October and was "whispered by s[ome] women in private to some others," Governor John Winthrop and the other magistrates did not hear about the story until Anne Hutchinson was excommunicated in March 1638, and then it was only by chance.[38]

Nevertheless, colonial courts investigated and admitted gossip as evidence. Women, especially married women, who could not easily take legal action against their neighbors could, however, talk about them. Thus, the "busy prattling" of women served as a type of social regulation and control in the colonies. Rumors about a woman's moral character, or lack thereof, spread quickly in the seventeenth century, and such rumors could injure her reputation severely, especially if the gossip was admitted as evidence.

Gossip was also one method women could use in attempts to regulate their households or to get revenge on neighbors or spouses. In one well-documented case from Virginia in 1694, Joanna Delony made several remarks about Jane Hide, after which Robert and Jane Hide sued Lewis and Joanna Delony for defamation. According to Joanna Delony, Jane Hide had had a sexual relationship with Lewis Delony. In addition, Joanna Delony accused Jane Hide of sleeping with her own father-in-law and drinking "a dose" that caused her to abort when they thought she was pregnant. Finally, Joanna Delony insisted that Jane Hide would even sleep with a black man—an enormous slur on Hide's reputation. Moreover, to thoroughly ensure that her words were heard by people throughout the area, and thus besmirch the reputations of both of the Delonys and of her own husband, Joanna Delony made her declarations on the way to church and around the tobacco fields. Thus, she made speeches in public space, and even in front of slaves.[39]

The Hides were of a much higher social status than the Delonys. Smearing Jane Hide's reputation was one of the few ways in which Joanna Delony could exact revenge. The Hides won the suit, but Joanna Delony refused to apologize as the court had ordered her to do. Lewis Delony did pay fines on behalf of his wife several months later. Yet, Joanna Delony may have achieved some revenge after all by causing a rupture in the Hide household. In 1697, Jane Hide petitioned the court for a separate maintenance from her husband.[40]

In some cases, however, gossip started and spread as a means to "get even," could lead to a woman being charged with and possibly executed for witchcraft. Most women in colonial America who were accused of being witches were married women. As married women, they could not own property or businesses, or hold office. Therefore, it was more difficult to take revenge against them. Gossip then was one way in which a person could successfully attack a married woman, as it was difficult to refute stories, once they started to spread.

Early modern Europeans and their colonial counterparts believed that through *maleficium*, the supernatural ability to cause harm, witches could make crops fail, make milk go sour, cause people to get sick or die, and prevent couples from consummating marriages. In a society that valued social order, witches turned things upside down, disrupting marriages, threatening the power of the head of the household, and engaging in or causing others to engage in sexual relationships with people other than their spouses, as well as animal familiars and the devil. Not all accused witches were women, but women were considered to be most vulnerable to the devil due to their weakness and inherently lustful natures.[41]

Although the Salem witchcraft crisis of 1692 is the most famous, there were many other examples of witchcraft scares in the British American colonies. (Witchcraft and Salem witchcraft crisis are discussed in more detail in Chapter 5.) In the early years of settlement, the heretical beliefs of Anne Hutchinson, Jane Hawkins, and Mary Dyer linked them to witchcraft, but none of the three was ever formally charged with witchcraft. However, between 1647 and 1663, seventy-nine people in New England were accused of being witches, and sixty-one of them were women. The first witch to be executed in Massachusetts Bay was Margaret Jones, a midwife, who was executed in 1648. The first witchcraft "outbreak" occurred in Hartford, in 1662–1663. Women were accused of being

Witch Riding Backward on a Goat, Accompanied by Four Putti, ca. 1505. Engraving by Albrecht Dürer. This engraving depicts the early modern belief in the sexual power of witches and their ability to cause chaos. Riding backward symbolized disorder, while goats were symbols of lust. Courtesy of Library of Congress.

witches throughout the colonies. For example, in 1626, the neighbors of Virginia midwife Goodwife Wright accused her of being a witch. Midwives, who seemed to have power over life and death and oversaw the mysteries of childbirth, were frequently accused of witchcraft. This intimate knowledge of birth and death led to witchcraft accusations by Goody Wright's neighbors in Virginia because she "became too good at predicting death in a society overwhelmed by mortality."[42]

Throughout much of the seventeenth century, as frontier colonial societies far away from the mother country, the British American settlements sought to enact laws and maintain order in the wilderness. In attempting to transfer their English traditions to a world that was new to them, colonists often changed or adapted laws and traditions. In the Chesapeake colonies, for instance, a young, mostly male servant population in the early years led to some tolerance of clandestine marriages, premarital sexual relations, and interracial sexuality. In New England, however, more stable families, and a faith-based, more homogenous population meant little toleration for extramarital relations.

In both areas, women, particularly married women, helped to maintain social order by investigating other women, examining their bodies, and passing along knowledge of what they had seen or heard to the courts. In doing so, they served as a link between the courts, local authorities, and female sexual offenders.[43]

By the late eighteenth century, the image of women as chaste beings became the province of white women, and the image of the sexually insatiable siren became associated with women of color. Nevertheless, white women who transgressed or violated the social codes—even if it was not their own fault—were often seen as having some sort of moral failure or of causing their own problem. Therefore, women had to be protected from potential seducers or anything that might enflame their passions.

NOTES

1. *The Lawes Resolution of Womens Rights; or, The Laws Provisions for Womens* ... (London, 1632), reprinted in *New World, New Rules: A Documentary History of Women in Pre-Industrial America*, ed. Sylvia R. Frey and Marian J. Morton (Westport, CT: Greenwood Press, 1986), 92–94, quoted in Linda L. Sturtz, "'As Though I My Self Was Pr[e]sent': Virginia Women with Power of Attorney," in *The Many Legalities of Early America*, ed. Christopher L. Tomlins and Bruce H. Mann (Chapel Hill: University of North Carolina Press, 2001), 252.

2. Carol Berkin, *First Generations: Women in Colonial America* (New York: Hill and Wang, 1996), 79–87.

3. Kathleen M. Brown, *Good Wives, Nasty Wenches, and Anxious Patriarchs: Gender, Race, and Power in Colonial Virginia* (Chapel Hill: University of North Carolina Press, 1996), 287–88.

4. Mary Beth Norton, *Founding Mothers and Fathers: Gendered Power and the Forming of American Society* (New York: Vintage Books, 1996), 82–83.

5. Ibid., 84.

6. Sturtz, "'As Though I My Self Was Pr[e]sent,'" 267. For Daniel Parke's exploits in the Leeward Islands, see Natalie A. Zacek, "Sex, Sexuality, and Social Control in the Eighteenth-Century Leeward Islands," in *Sex and Sexuality in Early America*, ed. Merril D. Smith (New York: New York University Press, 1998), 198–200.

7. This behavior continued in the eighteenth century. Connecticut included cruelty as grounds for divorce in 1786. Pennsylvania was the first state to include cruelty as grounds for divorce in its 1785 divorce law. Under this law, women could receive a divorce from bed and board with alimony. See Merril D. Smith, *Breaking the Bonds: Marital Discord in Pennsylvania, 1730–1830* (New York: New York University Press, 1991).

8. Laurel Thatcher Ulrich, "Big Dig, Little Dig, Hidden Worlds: Boston," *Common-Place* 3, no. 4 (July 2003). Available at: http://www.common-place.org.

9. Norma Jane Langford, "Colonial Boston Unearthed," *Archaeology* (September 26, 1997). Available at: http://www.archaeology.org/online/features/boston.

10. Brown, *Good Wives, Nasty Wenches*, 336–39; Norton, *Founding Mothers and Fathers*, 89–91; Smith, *Breaking the Bonds*, 16–17; Roderick Phillips, *Untying the Knot: A Short History of Divorce* (New York: Cambridge University Press, 1991), 39.

11. D. Kelly Weisberg, "'Under Greet Temptation': Women and Divorce in Puritan Massachusetts," *Feminist Studies* 2, no. 2/3 (1975): 187.

12. Cornelia Hughes Dayton, *Women before the Bar: Gender, Law, and Society in Connecticut, 1639–1789* (Chapel Hill: University of North Carolina Press, 1995), 110–11.

13. Thomas A. Foster, "Deficient Husbands: Manhood, Sexual Incapacity, and Male Marital Sexuality in Seventeenth-Century New England," *William and Mary Quarterly* 56 (October 1999): 727.

14. Quoted in Foster, "Deficient Husbands," 737.

15. Dayton, *Women before the Bar*, 115–19.

16. Massachusetts Archives Series, Massachusetts State Archives, Columbia Point, Boston, vol. 9, documents 52, 55, cited in Ann Marie Plane, *Colonial Intimacies: Indian Marriage in Early New England* (Ithaca, NY: Cornell University Press, 2000), 81.

17. Norton, *Founding Mothers and Fathers*, 341–43.

18. Brown, *Good Wives, Nasty Wenches*, 189.

19. Lois Green Carr and Lorena S. Walsh, "The Planter's Wife: The Experience of White Women in Seventeenth-Century Maryland," in *A Heritage of Her Own: Toward a New Social History of American Women*, ed. Nancy F. Cott and Elizabeth H. Pleck (New York: Simon and Schuster, 1979), 25–57.

20. William Bullock, *Virginia Impartially Examined, and Left to Public View, to be Considered by All Judicious and Honest Men* (London, 1649), 54, quoted in John Ruston Pagan, *Anne Orthwood's Bastard: Sex and Law in Early Virginia* (New York: Oxford University Press, 2003), 14.

21. See Pagan, *Anne Orthwood's Bastard*, for the entire story of Anne Orthwood and the trials.

22. Pagan, *Anne Orthwood's Bastard*, 84–85.

23. Brown, *Good Wives, Nasty Wenches*, 197–200.

24. Else L. Hambleton, *Daughters of Eve: Pregnant Brides and Unwed Mothers in Seventeenth-Century Massachusetts* (New York: Routledge, 2004), 24, 44.

25. M. G. Thresher, ed., *Records and Files of the Quarterly Court of Essex County, Massachusetts*, vol. 9 (Salem, MA: Essex Institute, 1975), 64, quoted in Else L. Hambleton, "The Regulation of Sex in Seventeenth-Century Massachusetts: The Quarterly Court of Essex County vs. Priscilla Willson and Mr. Samuel Appleton," in *Sex and Sexuality in Early America*, ed. Merril D. Smith (New York: New York University Press, 1998), 92.

26. Hambleton, "The Regulation of Sex," 95–96; 109–10.

27. Hambleton, *Daughters of Eve*, 49.

28. Ibid., 154–55.

29. This case is examined in Chapter 5 of Laurel Thatcher Ulrich, *Good Wives: Image and Reality in the Lives of Women in Northern New England, 1650–1750* (New York: Oxford University Press, 1982).

30. Michael Dalton, *The Country Justice* (1690), vol. 153, 392. Available at: Maryland State Archives, http://www.msa.md.gov/megafile/msa/speccol/sc2900/sc2908/000001/000153/html/am153–392.html.

31. Hambleton, *Daughters of Eve*, 136–39; Norton, *Founding Mothers and Fathers*, 347–49.

32. Hambleton, *Daughters of Eve*, 31; Brown, *Good Wives, Nasty Wenches*, 193–94.

33. Lois Green Carr, "Margaret Brent: A Brief History." Available at: Maryland State Archives, http://www.msa.md.gov/msa/speccol/sc3500/sc3520/002100/002177/html/mbrent2.html. Carr discusses the likelihood that Brent had taken a vow of celibacy.

34. *County Court Records of Accomack-Northampton, Virginia, 1640–1645*, ed. Susie M. Ames (Charlottesville, VA: University Press of Virginia, 1973), 129, cited in Pagan, *Anne Orthwood's Bastard*, 82.

35. Essex County, April 1684, 36-10-1, cited in Hambleton, *Daughters of Eve*, 110.

36. York, VA, Deeds, Orders, Wills, 2, September 24, 1646, cited in Brown, *Good Wives, Nasty Wenches*, 98.

37. *Records and Files of the Quarterly Courts of Essex County, Massachusetts* (Salem, MA: Essex Institute, 1911–1975), vol. 3, 194, quoted in Ulrich, *Good Wives*, 98.

38. Quoted in Norton, *Founding Mothers and Fathers*, 223.

39. Terri L. Snyder, *Brabbling Women: Disorderly Speech and the Law in Early Virginia* (Ithaca, NY: Cornell University Press, 2003), 82–86.

40. Ibid., 86.

41. Norton, *Founding Mothers and Fathers*, 248–52; Brown, *Good Wives, Nasty Wenches*, 30–33; Carol F. Karlsen, *The Devil in the Shape of a Woman: Witchcraft in Colonial New England* (New York: Vintage Books, 1987), esp. chap. 4.

42. Brown, *Good Wives, Nasty Wenches*, 103.

43. Ibid., 97.

SUGGESTED READING

Berkin, Carol. *First Generations: Women in Colonial America*. New York: Hill and Wang, 1996.

Block, Sharon. *Rape and Sexual Power in Early America*. Chapel Hill: University of North Carolina Press, 2006.

Brown, Kathleen M. *Good Wives, Nasty Wenches, and Anxious Patriarchs: Gender, Race, and Power in Colonial Virginia*. Chapel Hill: University of North Carolina Press, 1996.

Dayton, Cornelia Hughes. *Women before the Bar: Gender, Law, and Society in Connecticut, 1639–1789*. Chapel Hill: University of North Carolina Press, 1995.

Godbeer, Richard. *Sexual Revolution in Early America*. Baltimore: Johns Hopkins University Press, 2002.

Hambleton, Else. *Daughters of Eve: Pregnant Brides and Unwed Mothers in Seventeenth-Century Massachusetts*. New York: Routledge, 2004.

Karlsen, Carol F. *The Devil in the Shape of a Woman: Witchcraft in Colonial New England*. New York: Vintage Books, 1987.

Norton, Mary Beth. *Founding Mothers and Fathers: Gendered Power and the Forming of American Society*. New York: Vintage Books, 1996.

Pagan, John Ruston. *Anne Orthwood's Bastard: Sex and Law in Early Virginia*. New York: Oxford University Press, 2003.

Smith, Merril D., ed. *Sex and Sexuality in Early America*. New York: New York University Press, 1998.

Snyder, Terri L. *Brabbling Women: Disorderly Speech and the Law in Early Virginia*. Ithaca, NY: Cornell University Press, 2003.

Ulrich, Laurel Thatcher. *Good Wives: Image and Reality in the Lives of Women in Northern New England, 1650–1750*. New York: Oxford University Press, 1982.

3

———— ∞∞∞ ————

Women and Immigration

The seventeenth century was a time of large-scale immigration and migration. However, little is known about the individual lives of the vast numbers who immigrated. For women, this is particularly true. Unless their names appear in court or ships records, or in other legal documents, or unless they achieved some fame or notoriety, it is not even possible to discover who they were. Yet women moved from their birthplaces, just as men did, to find jobs or to remain with their spouses or other family members. This chapter focuses on the roles of white women who came from Europe, mostly voluntarily, to help settle the colonies, of African women who were brought to the colonies by force, and of Native American women who moved about because of social and work roles within their societies and as a response to contact with Europeans.

Within most countries of Europe, both men and women moved around to find work, to escape religious or political turmoil, and to satisfy a thirst for adventure. Even the sons and daughters of the gentry were sent to live in other households to prepare for their future roles. Thus, the migration of individuals, especially young men and women, was not an uncommon occurrence in early modern Europe, but it increased during times of economic or social disruption. England during the seventeenth century faced economic woes, crowds of homeless people, increased crime, bouts of plague, religious dissent, and civil war, which increased the movement of people both within its borders and away from them.

However, many of the problems actually began in the sixteenth century, when landowners began to enclose "common" land and evict tenants, exacerbating the crisis caused by rising food prices, population growth, and wages with decreased buying power. From the late sixteenth century into the seventeenth century, there were many years with particularly bad harvests; the 1590s and the 1620s were especially dire decades. Some of the poor died from malnutrition or related diseases such as scurvy as they were uprooted from homes and unable to find employment; others became more vulnerable to the outbreaks of plague and smallpox. The landed gentry, business owners, church officials, and other authorities feared that large numbers of unemployed men and women would cause severe social disruption. As a result, they encouraged the passage of legislation in the sixteenth century to regulate apprenticeships and wages and to punish vagrants. Those in authority believed that unemployed or idle women, as well as men, were also a threat to social order. One law passed during this time required unmarried English-women who were between twelve and forty years old to spend time in spinning. Given this social climate, many among the elite saw emigration to the new colonies as a welcome solution to England's problems—a method of ridding the country of its crowd of hungry, homeless, and trouble-making people, while at the same time providing revenue for England.[1]

In Elizabethan England, men such as Richard Hakluyt attempted to convince Queen Elizabeth and wealthy backers that establishing colonies was necessary to maintain England's economic and political power. Moreover, Hakluyt noted that establishing colonies would help England by providing employment to people who "work in and by working linen," mariners, soldiers, and the children "of the wandering beggars of England that grow up idly and hurtful and burdenous to this Realm."[2] In the seventeenth century, the Council for New England repeated the suggestion that the poor of England be sent to work in the colonies, using wording similar to Hakluyt's. In 1623, the council reported that colonization would "afford a world of employment to many thousands of our nation" and that it would "disburden the commonwealth of a multitude of poor that are likely daily to increase to the infinite trouble and prejudice of the public state."[3]

Nevertheless, by 1629, the Massachusetts Bay Company knew that it wanted a colony composed of hardworking, reliable, and moral settlers, not vagrants and criminals. The group of Separatists (now known as the Pilgrims) who established a colony in Plymouth, Massachusetts, in 1620 included some nonbelievers from the first.[4] In establishing their colony in Massachusetts, recruiters for the Massachusetts Bay Company implored skilled laborers and craftsmen to immigrate—they wanted men with skills that would help the colony to become successful. In learning from the mistakes made by earlier settlements, by 1630, the Massachusetts Bay

Company recruiters also sought respectable women and family groups. By including women, they hoped to ensure the continued growth of the colony through reproduction. As well, they hoped that the existence of families would ensure stable and moral households, thus keeping order with the colony. Consequently, a good many of the seventeenth-century immigrants to New England were not poor nor without property, and they arrived with or later brought over immediate family, distant kin, servants, and neighbors.

In particular, this profile fits the Puritan families that arrived in the 1630s. Many of the Puritans seeking refuge from persecution and wishing to build a new society away from the immorality of England's society were reasonably well to do. Both male and female Puritans felt a call or sense of mission to build and live in a new Zion. This urge escalated in the 1630s, after Parliament was dissolved and persecution of Puritans escalated.

Thus, Anne Marbury Hutchinson was not unusual in experiencing a powerful desire to immigrate to New England. Anne Marbury was born in 1591. Her father, the Reverend Francis Marbury, was an Anglican clergyman who for a time was removed from his pulpit because of controversial teachings; her mother, Bridget Dryden Marbury, was a midwife. By 1602, Francis Marbury was again preaching, and the family later moved to London, where the Reverend Marbury died in 1611. The next year, Anne Marbury married William Hutchinson, a merchant tailor, and they settled in Alford, Lincolnshire, England.

At about the same time the newlywed couple settled in Alford, the Reverend John Cotton began preaching in nearby Boston. Anne Hutchinson was drawn to Cotton's sermons and began to view him as a sort of religious advisor or teacher. When Cotton came under scrutiny by Anglican authorities, he fled England for Puritan Massachusetts. After his departure, Anne Hutchinson believed that God had given her a sign that she, too, should emigrate, and the following year, 1634, Anne and William Hutchinson, along with their eleven children and some relatives, arrived in the Massachusetts Bay Colony.[5]

In many ways, the Hutchinsons were like other Puritans who came to New England. They were motivated to emigrate by spiritual, rather than economic reasons. Unlike the majority of immigrants who traveled to other English colonies, a considerable number of Puritans actually gave up prosperous lives in England. They made the perilous journey across the Atlantic to become part of what they expected to be a model society.

However, not everyone who immigrated to New England did so for religious convictions. As one historian notes, "although the *purpose* of the colony was decidedly religious, its *people* were varied in their motives and characters." On every ship filled with devout Puritans, there were also those who came for adventure, economic gain, or to escape from troubles in England. Moreover, many Puritans who did feel a sense of mission were *also* motivated to venture to New England because they thought they had a better chance of prospering there than in England.[6]

Whatever their motivation for immigration, those who decided to go had to make extensive plans and preparations. Preparing to emigrate was quite a serious and expensive undertaking. The price of passage for one person was about £5. The cost of transporting a family to New England in the 1630s was £30–50 for the passage alone, plus approximately £50–100 to transport food and supplies.[7] Landowning emigrants had to sell or rent their land, business affairs had to be put in order, and plans had to be made for dependents left behind. Some immigrants had new wills drawn up in case they perished at sea or somewhere across the Atlantic. Some refused to follow their spouses. Despite societal beliefs that women should obey their husbands, more than one wife who feared the voyage announced that she would rather be "a living wife in England than a dead one in the sea."[8] Yet those leaving spouses or other loved ones in England had to find ways to cope with the sorrow of parting, even if was meant to be only a temporary separation. For example, before Governor John Winthrop left for Massachusetts in 1630, he and his wife, Margaret, decided to "meet in spirit" each Monday and Friday at five o'clock at night.[9]

Those who had made the voyage gave advice to those who were planning on immigrating. The Reverend Francis Higginson warned immigrants that "you shall meete neither taverns nor alehouse, nor butchers, nor grosers, nor apothecaries shops to helpp what things you need, in the midst of the great ocean, nor when you are come to land here are yet neither markets nor fayres to buy what you want."[10] Although by midcentury many items could be purchased in Boston and other port cities, this was not the case in the early years of settlement, when each arriving ship of immigrants strained the resources of the colony. Immigrants were told to take enough provisions for a year. Most of their provisions were stored in the hold and were not available until the passengers disembarked, but some items that would help to make their bland, boring diets more interesting were kept within reach.

Several lists were published in the 1630s listing items that immigrants should bring. Artisans, of course, had to bring their tools, but nearly all the things that most people counted on having on hand had to be brought over with them. As well as basic food items such as meal, oatmeal, oil, and vinegar, the lists included articles of clothing, tools for farming and building, household necessities, such as pots, kettles, and dishes, and additional things, including carts, wheels, and pitchforks. For those who could afford to do so, Reverend Higginson in one frequently reproduced publication advised bringing sugar, pepper, cloves, mace, cinnamon, nutmeg, and fruit, as well as cheese, bacon, and books.[11]

Families and individuals engaged in many of the same activities aboard ship as they had on land, but there were some differences that required adjustments. For example, even those accustomed to crowded living conditions on land probably were not used to the extremely close quarters they shared with other passengers below deck. In addition, sheets and mattresses were packed and stored in the hold, so passengers had to use rugs and blankets as bedding. Because ships to New England carried many family groups, there were women on board who could perform the particular tasks usually done by women and who could care for children, as they would have done at home on land. Women's roles aboard ship were generally the same as on land—only the conditions changed. For example, women cooked meals, but because the number of cooking fires was limited for safety, several families often shared a fire. Women also would have mended clothing and other items as necessary during the voyage.

Moreover, on these transatlantic journeys, women continued in their roles as mothers. For example, at least three women were pregnant on the *Rose*. One of them was Joan Leeds, who bore twin sons two months after the *Rose* arrived in Massachusetts in June 1637. This was not an isolated example. The Reverend Thomas Welde wrote to his former parishioners in England that one of the pregnant women aboard his ship "delivered of a lusty child within forty hours after she landed, she and child well." Accounts from passengers on other ships also reported pregnant women on board, and sometimes that a woman had given birth. Oceanus Hopkins was born on the *Mayflower* as it sailed across the Atlantic in 1620, and Peregrine White was born in November 1620, as the *Mayflower* sat in the harbor in Provincetown.[12]

To assist the laboring women, some women aboard ship acted as nurses and midwives—some with more skill than others. Although most married women were familiar with the mechanics and rituals of childbirth, no doubt all involved preferred to have an experienced midwife supervise when a woman actually gave birth. John Winthrop noted an occasion on his voyage to Massachusetts when a woman on his ship went into labor, and a midwife had to be brought from another ship. The *Jewel* had moved far ahead of Winthrop's ship, the *Arbella*. To get the attention of the *Jewel*, a cannon was fired on the *Arbella* and sailors lowered the topsails.[13]

Yet even a ship loaded with passengers possessing a variety of skills and enough provisions to last an extended voyage could encounter unforeseen perils. In addition to organizing their thoughts and belongings, immigrants needed to prepare both physically and spiritually for the

Cradle of Peregrine White. Courtesy of Pilgrim Society,
Pilgrim Hall Museum.

dangerous crossing. Ships normally left in March or April, with the voyage usually lasting eight to ten weeks. However, some journeys were
much longer. John Winthrop explained that one ship took 26 weeks to
make the trip to New England, due first to stormy weather and then to
fog once they reached New England.[14]

Occasionally, the voyage across the ocean resulted in more disastrous
and unforeseen consequences. During one voyage to Maryland in 1654,
four ships sailing from England encountered a storm that filled at least
one of the ships with water. As a passenger, Father Francis Fitzherbert,
related, the male passengers, as well as the crew, "sweated at the great
pump in ceaseless labor, day and night." The ship changed course,
attempting to get to Barbados, but the storm continued for two months,
preventing them from getting there. Finally, people began speculating that
a witch caused the tempest. They seized "a little old woman suspected of
sorcery," examined her, and executed her. Father Fitzherbert noted that
the storm did not cease with the woman's execution, but instead, people
began to get sick, and some died. (For more on witches and witchcraft,
see Chapter 5.)[15]

Although ships often encountered storms at sea, it was not often that
witches were accused of causing them. Frequently, however, the stories of
ships wrecked while sailing the Atlantic were attributed to God's judgment. In contrast, those who survived shipwrecks were described as being

favored or spared by God's mercy in the accounts that were circulated in both manuscript and published form. For example, Anthony Thacher wrote of the ordeal he and his wife faced when their ship was destroyed off the New England coast. Their children died and the couple were washed ashore nearly naked. Anthony Thacher found a knapsack with flint, steel, and powder to light a fire, and then the couple found clothing and provisions on the beach. Thacher believed God had sent these things to sustain them.[16]

On the journey, passengers were often seasick until they adjusted to the motion of the ship. Women and children were especially affected, as they were more likely to be closed-in below decks. On May 24, 1635, the first day of his voyage, the Puritan minister Richard Mather noted that the wind grew stronger in the morning, "and the ship daunced, and many of our women and some children were not well; but sea-sicke, and mazy or light in their heades, and could scarce stand or go without falling, unless they tooke hold of something to uphold them."[17]

Seasickness was unpleasant and uncomfortable, but it seldom caused anyone to die. However, sometimes more serious diseases such as small-pox did break out aboard ship. In general, there were fewer deaths on the ships carrying Puritans to New England than on other voyages of the time, but men and women faced potentially fatal risks and hazards during the journey across the ocean simply due to the nature of travel during this time period. Ships were often dangerous places. For example, both passengers and crewmembers had to be careful not be swept overboard during storms, and they had to watch where they stepped. In April 1630, John Winthrop noted that "a maid of Sir Richard Saltonstall fell down at the grating by the cook-room, but the carpenter's man, who occasioned her fall unwittingly, caught hold of her with incredible nimbleness, and saved her; otherwise she had fallen into the hold."[18]

In a voyage taken fifty-three years later, Francis Daniel Pastorius, who founded Germantown, Pennsylvania, also suffered accidents aboard ship. Pastorius reported back to friends about one time in which "two carved lugs over the ship's bell" fell on his back, and that in another instance during a storm, he "fell so severely upon my left side that for some days I had to keep to my bed." Pastorius also described the illnesses, births, and deaths that occurred, and complains about the awful rations on his ship. He advised those who planned on making the journey to bring additional provisions as he did, following the advice of his "good friends in England."[19]

Despite the dangers, or perhaps because of them, the actual voyage often produced a bond among the immigrants, born of the danger they faced crossing the ocean to a home in the wilderness, and in some cases their shared religious convictions.[20] Edward Johnson, who helped to found the town of Woburn, Massachusetts, provides one view of how a

Puritan man looked at the journey. Looking back at these events from 1653, Johnson describes the Puritans who first ventured to Massachusetts as weak beings—including pregnant women and mothers with young children—who were strengthened by God to be missionaries in the wilderness.

> the condition of those persons [that] passed the Seas, in this long and rest-lesse Voyage (if rightly considered) will more magnifie the grace of Christ in this great Worke. First, such were many of them that never before had made any path through the Waters, no not by boat, neither so much as seene a Ship, others so tenderly brought up that they had little hope of their Lives continuance under such hardships, as so long a Voyage must needs inforce them to indure, others there were, whose age did rather call for a quiet Couch to rest them on, than a pinching Cabbin in a Reeling Ship, others whose weake natures were so borne downe with Disease that they could hardly craule up the Ships-side, yet ventured their weake Vessells to this Westurne World. Here also might you see weakly Women, whose hearts have trembled to set foote in Boate, but now imboldened to venter through these tempestuous Seas with their young Babes, whom they nurture up with their Breasts, while their bodies are tossed on the tumbling Waves; also others whose Wombes could not containe their fruit, being ready for the Worlds-light, travailed and brought forth upon this depthlesse Ocean in this long Voyage, lively and strong Children yet living, and like to prove succeeding Instruments in the Hands of Christ, for furthering this worke; ... by all this and much more that might be said, for almost every one you discourse withall will tell you of some Remarkable Providence of God shewed toward them in this their Voyage, by which you may see the Worke of Christ, is not to bee laid aside because of difficulties.[21]

Upon reaching shore, these Puritans and others who traveled with them found a society that was as stratified as the one they had left behind in England. In part, this was because they were still very much English men and women and they wanted to replicate an English lifestyle in Massachusetts, but without what they believed to be immoral behavior and practices. Consequently, they built English-style houses and slept inside of them on beds with familiar bed coverings. They dressed as they would have in England. They brought familiar livestock, such as cows and goats for dairy production, and seeds for wheat, barley, and hops, so that they could bake wheat bread and brew beer. The English men and women who ventured to New England were very conscious of wanting to keep their English ways and fearful of becoming like the indigenous people they encountered. Thus, they expected women would work within the homes and gardens—preparing the food, brewing beer, and making clothing, but they would not be involved in agricultural labor, as Indian women were, or go about partially naked, as Indian women did.[22]

Puritans also believed that the stratification of society was divinely sanctioned in both old and New England. As Governor John Winthrop stated in his famous address "A Modell of Christian Charity," given aboard the *Arbella* in 1630, "GOD ALMIGHTY in his most holy and wise providence, hath soe disposed of the condition of mankind, as in all times some must be rich, some poore, some high and eminent in power and dignitie; others mean and in submission."[23] As members of the privileged group, the Hutchinsons, for example, were given a prime lot in Boston, Massachusetts; William Hutchinson was elected to the General Court, and Anne Hutchinson became part of the elite group of Boston matrons. It was within this circle of women that Mistress Hutchinson first started her religious discussions. Word of Mistress Hutchinson's discussions was slow to reach male authorities, but once the meetings began to include men along with women, the authorities perceived them—and her—as a threat to the community. (Anne Hutchinson's religious beliefs and trials are discussed in Chapter 5.)[24]

Women had to be careful about speaking out and expressing opinions, especially opinions that might disagree with those of the men around them. Anne Hutchinson was unusual in that she was the one who initiated the plan to emigrate, rather than her husband. Although some wives adamantly refused to immigrate when their husbands proposed the idea, others were more guarded in their refusal. For example, Governor John Winthrop's sister, Lucy Winthrop Downing, was not in favor of her family leaving their home and moving to Massachusetts. Yet she was cautious in voicing her dissent. As she told her brother, "I am but a wife, and therfore it is sufficient for me to follow my husban." Still she raised enough objections that it took several years before her husband, Emmanuel, finally succeeded in moving the family to New England.[25]

Anne and William Hutchinson, the Winthrops, and many others were participants in the Puritan Great Migration. Although the Pilgrims settled in Plymouth, Massachusetts, in 1620, it was and remained a small colony later to be swallowed by the larger Puritan colony surrounding it. The Great Migration truly began in 1630, when Governor John Winthrop and a group of Puritans set sail for Massachusetts, and continued for the next decade, as more than 20,000 Puritans emigrated from England. When civil war broke out in England, the migration of Puritans from England almost stopped, and in fact, a small reverse migration began, as a few people returned to England to offer their services to the new government.

Most of the immigrants to New England came in family groups. In general, these families consisted of husbands, wives with a few children (with more to be born in New England), and a servant or two. The families tended to be established and prosperous, but not extremely wealthy. Unlike the Chesapeake settlers, only about 17 percent of the Puritan migrants arrived as servants. Once in Massachusetts, the Puritan immigrants aspired to establish their city on a hill with a society based around well-ordered families. (The role of women within the family is discussed in more detail in Chapter 1.)

Yet not all Puritans were happy living in New England, especially in the early years of settlement. John Winthrop's brother-in-law Arthur Tyndal left Massachusetts in 1631, along with many others. Ten people left Massachusetts on the *Lion's Whelp* in 1632, and thirty more left on the *Elizabeth Bonadventure* in 1633. The colony expelled troublemakers such as Anne Hutchinson and sent others back to England, especially if they had no means of support. The widow Abigail Gifford was sent back to England in 1634 because she was found to be "sometimes distracted, and a very burdensome woman." Elizabeth Avis, "a poor lame maid," had become a burden to her master, and she also longed to return to England. The colony sent her back home in 1654.[26]

Once they reached New England, many Puritans continued to migrate until they found a permanent settlement that suited them. Most settlers arrived during the summer. As Boston and other port towns became more crowded commercial centers, most immigrants did not stay there long after their arrival; however, the establishment of commercial areas permitted them to purchase supplies and gain information about other locations in which they might settle. Most chose to migrate to new towns, either those just established or less than two years old, to be granted the best land and have a voice in town politics.[27]

The Puritan poet Anne Bradstreet moved several times with her husband, Simon, and her parents, Thomas and Dorothy Dudley. Although they were among the original settlers of Salem, Massachusetts, and shared the religious convictions of the founders, the Bradstreets and Dudleys did not enjoy the cramped, cold house they shared there, and they moved to Charlestown in 1630. The following year, they moved again, this time to Newtown (now Cambridge). In the next few years, the families moved to Ipswich and then to Andover. Each time, Simon Bradstreet and Thomas Dudley moved, they achieved more powerful political positions, rose in social status, and built larger estates. (Anne Bradstreet and her poetry are discussed in Chapter 7.)[28]

Yet most immigrants to England's colonies were not Puritans seeking a religious haven. Seventeenth-century emigration from England actually reached its high point in the late 1630s, as the Great Migration was ending. For the next twenty-five years, between 11,000 and 12,000 immigrants left England each year. Most of these English immigrants traveled to the West Indies and the Chesapeake colonies, while others went to Ireland, Germany, and the Netherlands. Most of them were single, young men. However, after the earliest all male settlements proved unsuccessful, the colonies actively recruited women, as well.

Most of the women who came to the Chesapeake were young, and like their male counterparts, they came as indentured servants. Anne Orthwood, discussed in Chapter 2, was just one of the many women who sought a better life in the colonies than they could expect to have had by staying in England. Female indentured servants might live in rugged conditions and die early from diseases complicated by childbirth, but they also had the potential to earn more money and become the wife of a landowner, choices that would not be available to them in England.

In a rebuttal to less favorable accounts about the conditions faced by indentured servants in the Chesapeake, George Alsop, an indentured servant himself, wrote his own description of indentured servitude there. He believed that the situation for women indentured servants was especially good.

> The Women that go over into this Province as Servants, have the best luck here as in any place of the world besides; for they are no sooner on shoar, but they are courted into a Copulative Matrimony, which some of them (for aught I know) had they not come to such a Market with their Virginity, might have kept it by them untill it had been mouldy, unless they had to let it out by a yearly rent to some of the Inhabitants of *Lewknors-lane* [a disreputable neighborhood in London].... Men have not altogether so good luck as Women in this kind, or natural preferment, without they be good Rhetoricians, and well vers'd in the Art of perswasion.[29]

Not all of the women who traveled to Virginia were indentured servants or of low birth. In 1621, fifty-seven women sailed to Virginia to become the brides of the male settlers there. These women came from respectable gentry or artisan families. Several of the women no longer had mothers or fathers who were living, and thus, had no means of support or protection. The women sailed with letters of recommendation stating their virtue, piety, and domestic skills. Although a good many of the women did marry, many of them died in the Indian attack in March 1622 or during the following bleak winter when many died of hunger and illness.[30]

Free or indentured, women and men arrived from many nations and settled in areas outside of New England and the Chesapeake. Many of them were seeking relief from religious persecution. For example, twenty-three Jewish men, women, and children arrived in New Amsterdam aboard the *St. Catherine* in September 1654. They came from Recife, a Dutch settlement in Brazil. When Recife was taken over by the Portuguese in 1654, the 600 Jews living there fled, as they feared they would be subjected to the Inquisition. Little is known about the daily lives of the Jewish immigrants who came to New Amsterdam. However, their journey to New Amsterdam was not easy or pleasant. After they finally left Brazil, they faced another danger immigrants and other travelers sometimes encountered—pirates. Pirates attacked the *St. Catherine* and stole the passengers' belongings. Upon reaching New Amsterdam, the captain of the *St. Catherine* sued the passengers for unpaid fares. The court in New Amsterdam ordered a sale of the passengers' luggage to pay the debts. One passenger, a widow named Rycke Nounces, became tangled in a legal battle. She believed that her luggage was sold for an amount "over and above her own debt," and that a man named Asser Leveen had profited. Asser Leveen sued the Widow Nounces for money owed him by her late husband. She countersued, and ultimately, the court agreed with her.[31]

Peter Stuyvesant, the governor of New Netherland, did not want the Jewish immigrants to settle in his colony. Since he had not objected to the Jewish male traders who had arrived the summer before, it seems likely that he objected to the group of immigrants because they included women. The presence of Jewish women meant there could be a real Jewish community in New Amsterdam, as opposed to just a few merchants or traders living in the town.[32]

French Protestants were also persecuted. Approximately 200,000 French Protestants, known as Huguenots, left France between 1680 and 1710. They were escaping religious persecution in France, which increased during the reign of Louis XIV, especially after he revoked the Edict of Nantes, which had accorded them some freedom of religion. In 1686, some of the Huguenots settled in the English colony of Carolina. In the next decade, more French citizens continued to arrive, many from urban areas. Often families traveled together in order to ease the burden of traveling to a new land.

Fugitives for Conscience Sake Leaving the Flemish Coast for America, by J. B. Hunt, ca. 1880. Courtesy of Library of Congress.

As with settlers arriving from England, the French Huguenots experienced unpleasant and difficult voyages across the Atlantic. Upon reaching Charleston, they found a small settlement with sparse resources. Judith Giton, who arrived in Carolina as a twenty-year-old woman, wrote, "I was in this country a full six months without tasting bread, and whilst I worked the ground, like a slave." Judith Giton had already endured the death of her mother during the voyage and the death of her eldest brother shortly after their arrival. She was penniless when she married a shoemaker, John Royer, but her second husband, Pierre Manigault, became a wealthy man.[33]

Although most of them did not sail across the ocean, many of the Native Americans with whom these various groups of European settlers came into contact did migrate. Sometimes they did so because of changes brought about by contact with Europeans. As European diseases decimated Indian villages, those few who survived probably traveled until they found homes in other villages.

Yet some tribes had a long-standing pattern of seasonal migration, traveling to different hunting and fishing grounds, or moving to plant crops in far away fields. Among the Algonquin, women were the ones

Virginia Discovered and Discribed by Captayn John Smith, 1606. Engraving by William Hole in 1624. Detail shows Chief Powhatan with his concubines. Courtesy of Library of Congress.

who decided when it was necessary to move to begin sowing crops in new fields. Men assisted in the process by clearing trees from the new areas to be planted. However, after the final corn harvest in the fall, entire villages moved to hunting grounds for the winter, where women helped to set up temporary villages.[34]

Some Native American chiefs used their children to establish alliances, just as European monarchs did. Thus, some Native American women were sent or taken to other villages in temporary or permanent moves as a result of diplomatic tactics. Before the establishment of Jamestown in 1607, Powhatan, the powerful chief of the Powhatan Indians in Virginia, consolidated his power by defeating and taking over other tribes, such as the Kecoughtan Indians, the Chesapeakes, and the Piankatanks. To further strengthen his power, Powhatan married close to one hundred women who came from villages throughout his domain. Powhatan sent many of these wives back to their home villages after he fathered a child with them. This practice helped to display his power to even remote villages.

Powhatan appointed his sons as *wereowances*, or chiefs, in many villages. He also attempted to marry his daughters to men who would help him achieve more power, although he did not gain much politically from the most well-known match, the marriage of his daughter, Pocahontas, with the Englishman John Rolfe. Pocahontas converted to Christianity, took the name Rebecca, and in 1616 sailed back to England with her husband and infant son in a type of reverse migration. As Rebecca, Pocahontas transformed her role of Indian chief's daughter to Christian, English wife; a transformation documented in a famous engraving probably completed while Pocahontas was in London. In this engraving, Pocahontas is dressed in the latest fashion, but her skin appears darker than that of Englishwomen in similar portraits produced in this era. She impressed the royal court with her ability to speak English and with her manners, and helped to increase interest in and encourage investment in the Virginia Company by demonstrating how a "savage" woman could be transformed into an English lady. This demonstration was the real reason for the trip to England. Unfortunately, Pocahontas died as she was set to return to Virginia with her husband and son. In March 1617, they boarded a ship, but Pocahontas/Rebecca became ill, most likely from pneumonia or tuberculosis, and was removed from the ship. She died in Gravesend, England, in March 1617.[35]

Englishmen wrote all the accounts of Pocahontas' life that are now in existence; therefore, it is impossible to know how Pocahontas truly felt about her roles as the daughter of a powerful Indian chief or as the wife of an English gentleman (and mother of their child). Nor do we know whether she felt that the English or her own people were using her as pawn. Her nickname, Pocahontas, meant "Little Wanton," and she seems to have been

Matoaks als Rebecka daughter to the mighty Prince Powhatan Emperour of Attanoughskomouck als virginia converted and baptized in the Christian faith, and wife to the worshipful Mr. Joh. Rolff.

Pocahontas after her marriage to John Rolfe. Engraving from the portrait painted in London, 1616. Courtesy of Library of Congress.

playful, adventurous, and poised. There is nothing to indicate that she was unwilling to marry John Rolfe or to travel with him to England.

In contrast to the white English women and Native American women who usually chose to move, African women were captured and brought to the Chesapeake by force. In the seventeenth century, however, once they arrived in the Chesapeake, they were often treated as indentured servants. Like most inhabitants of the seventeenth-century colonies of Maryland and Virginia, few details remain of individual lives, unless they appear in court records.

One African woman who does appear in Chesapeake records was known as Mary. In 1622, Mary arrived in Virginia on the ship the *Margarett and John*. Little is known about Mary's life prior to this—not even the name she was known by in Africa. Mary arrived in the spring, just after the Powhatan Indians attacked the colony. There were very few

Africans in Virginia at this time—only twenty-three are listed on the 1625 muster. Of those, only ten were women, including Mary.[36]

Most likely Mary's journey to Virginia began after she was either captured or traded and then marched to the coast of West Africa. There she probably boarded a Portuguese slave ship and endured a hellish transatlantic voyage, the infamous "middle passage," before arriving in the Caribbean, and then on to Virginia. The middle passage was a portion of the transatlantic slave trade in which European goods were brought to Africa and exchanged for African products and slaves. The slaves were then transported to the Americas, and articles grown or produced there, often with the help of slave labor, were brought back to Europe.[37]

Although white colonists feared the transatlantic journey, the mortality rates on ships carrying immigrants to the colonies were neither as high, nor the trip as terrible, as it was for Africans transported by force across the ocean.[38] In favorable sailing conditions, the voyage took about six to eight weeks. Slaves were packed in the ship's holds. Some captains

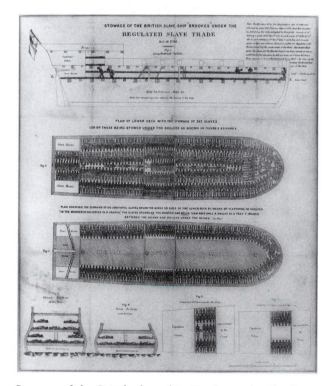

Stowage of the British slave ship *Brookes* under the Regulated Slave Trade Act of 1788. African men, women, and children were chained and packed tightly together in ships to be transported as slaves. Courtesy of Library of Congress.

Landing Negroes at Jamestown from Dutch Man-of-War,
1619. Courtesy of Library of Congress.

believed in "tight" packing, and squeezed in as many slaves as possible. They believed that if they carried greater numbers of slaves, then it would not matter if many died of disease. Other slave ship captains believed in "loose" packing to deter deaths brought about by the close and unhealthy situation aboard the ships. Diseases such as dysentery, smallpox, and typhus spread quickly on the slave ships. Male slaves were usually kept chained below deck. Slavers frequently kept women on deck, where they had fresh air, but were also subject to sexual abuse by the crew. Slaves were traumatized both physically and psychologically. Many slaves believed that the white slavers planned to kill them and eat them.[39]

The historical records do not show exactly where Mary came from or what she experienced before she arrived in the Chesapeake. Like other slaves and many indentured servants, she was probably sold a few times. Once in Virginia, she had to learn a new language, a new culture, and a new way of life. Because there were few Africans in Virginia at this time—and it is not known whether they spoke the same language or shared the same culture—Mary was probably forced to learn English quickly to communicate. She became a slave or servant of Robert Bennett. Bennett owned a large tobacco plantation on the James River. There she met the slave "Antonio," one of the five survivors of the Powhatan Indians' attack. At some point, Mary and Antonio were freed, although the details are unclear. They married, or at least lived as husband and wife, for forty years. They had four children, and all of them were baptized. Mary and Antonio became known as Mary and Anthony Johnson. The Johnsons then migrated to a new area on the Pungoteague River, where by about 1650, they owned more than 250 acres.

Similar opportunities were not easy to find for former slaves later in the century. Conditions for African men and women became more difficult toward the end of the seventeenth century, as slavery became more entrenched and codified. Generations of slave women discovered that there was always the threat of forced migration, as they or members of their families could be sold and taken far away from their homes at any time. For *all* women in seventeenth-century America, immigration was a key factor in the roles they played. Although women who immigrated to the colonies from England considered themselves Englishwomen, inevitably their lives were different from those of women who remained in England. The cultural constructions of their homeland were transformed in the colonies by the physical realities of their new homes, where they were introduced to new foods (and perhaps mourned the loss of familiar ones from home), to towns and plantations carved out of "the wilderness," to new institutions of government, and to new groups of people. Moreover, white women, Native American women, and African women were compared with one another, and increasingly, their roles and their work became segregated not only by gender and class, but also by race.

NOTES

1. Kathleen M. Brown, *Good Wives, Nasty Wenches, and Anxious Patriarchs: Gender, Race, and Power in Colonial Virginia* (Chapel Hill: University of North Carolina Press, 1996), 22–24; Gloria L. Main, *Peoples of a Spacious Nation: Families and Cultures in Colonial New England* (Cambridge, MA: Harvard University Press, 2001), 25–27. See the Statute of Artificers (1563). Available at: http://www.constitution.org/sech/sech_081.txt.

2. Richard Hakluyt, *Discourse of Western Planting* (1584). Available at national humanitiescenter.org/pds/amerbegin/exploration/text5/hakluyt.pdf.

3. H. M. C., *Report on the Records of the City of Exeter* (London, 1916), 166–69, quoted in David Cressy, *Coming Over: Migration and Communication between*

England and New England in the Seventeenth Century (New York: Cambridge University Press, 1987), 41–42.

4. Cressy, *Coming Over*, 39–40.

5. Mary Beth Norton, *Founding Mothers and Fathers: Gendered Power and the Forming of American Society* (New York: Vintage Books, 1996), 360–61.

6. Cressy, *Coming Over*, 85, 94.

7. Ibid., 119.

8. John Dunton, *The Life and Errors of John Dunton* (London: J. Nichols, Son, and Bentley, 1818), 91–92, quoted in Cressy, *Coming Over*, 147.

9. Richard Godbeer, *Sexual Revolution in Early America* (Baltimore: Johns Hopkins University Press, 2002), 57.

10. Virginia DeJohn Anderson, *New England's Generation: The Great Migration and the Formation of Society and Culture in the Seventeenth Century* (Cambridge: Cambridge University Press, 1993), 53.

11. Cressy, *Coming Over*, 112–18; Anderson, *New England's Generation*, 53–57; Maureen Richard, "Recreating the Material Culture of Mayflower II." Available at: http://www.plimoth.org/discover/behind/materialculture.php.

12. Anderson, *New England's Generation*, 72; *Letters from New England: The Massachusetts Bay Colony, 1629–1638* ed. Everett Emerson, The Commonwealth Series (Amherst: University of Massachusetts Press, 1976), 95, cited in Anderson, *New England's Generation*, 73. Information on Oceanus Hopkins and Peregrine White is available at http://www.pilgrimhall.org/F-cradles.htm.

13. John Winthrop, *Winthrop's Journal, History of New England, 1630–1649*, ed. James Kendall Hosmer (New York: Charles Scribner's Sons, 1908), 45.

14. Anderson, *New England's Generation*, 71.

15. "Execution of a Witch at Sea, 1654," in *Major Problems in American Women's History*, ed. Mary Beth Norton (Lexington, MA: D. C. Heath, 1989), 50–52.

16. Julie Sievers, "Drowned Pens and Shaking Hands: Sea Providence Narratives in Seventeenth-Century New England," *William and Mary Quarterly* 63 (October 2006): 743–44. Cotton Mather published Thacher's account almost fifty years later.

17. "Journal of Richard Mather," Dorchester Antiquarian and Historical Society, Collections, no. 3 (Boston, 1850), 6, 8–9, 11–12, 14, 17, quoted in Anderson, *New England's Generation*, 75.

18. Winthrop, *Winthrop's Journal*, April 5, 1630, 25.

19. Daniel Pastorius Francis, "Compare the Ship That Bore Them Hither with Noah's Ark: Francis Daniel Pastorius Describes His Impressions of Pennsylvania, 1683," *History Matters*. Available at: http://historymatters.gmu.edu/d/7439.

20. Anderson, *New England's Generation*, 89.

21. Edward Johnson, "Johnson's Wonder-Working Providence, 1628–1651," in Original Narratives of Early American History, ed. J. Franklin Jameson (New York: Charles Scribner's Sons, 1910), chap. 16. Available at: http://www.rootsweb.com/~usgenweb/special/history/providence.

22. Main, *Peoples*, 37.

23. John Winthrop, "A Modell of Christian Charity" (1630), in *Collections of the Massachusetts Historical Society*, 3rd ser., 7 (Boston, 1838), 31–48. Available at: Hanover Historical Texts Project, http://history.hanover.edu/texts/winthmod.html.

24. Norton, *Founding Mothers and Fathers*, 361.

25. *Winthrop Papers*, 1498–1649 (Boston: Massachusetts Historical Society, 1929–1947), vol. 3, 279–80, quoted in Norton, *Founding Mothers and Fathers*, 77. Norton

notes that the Winthrop Papers contain many examples of husbands and wives who did not agree about plans to emigrate.

26. Cressy, *Coming Over*, 195–97. Quotes from *Massachusetts Archives*, vol. 9:23, vol. 69:40, cited in Cressy, *Coming Over*, 197.

27. Anderson, *New England's Generation*, chap. 3.

28. Wendy Martin, *An American Triptych: Anne Bradstreet, Emily Dickinson, Adrienne Rich* (Chapel Hill: University of North Carolina Press, 1984), 24–246.

29. George Alsop, *A Character of the Province of Maryland (1666)*, ed. Newton D. Mereness (Cleveland: Burrows Brothers Company, 1902), 52–61, excerpt cited as "'They Live Well in the Time of Their Service': George Alsop Writes of Servants in Maryland, 1663."Available at: History Matters, http://www.historymatters.gmu.edu/d/5815.

30. David R. Ransome, "Wives for Virginia, 1621," *William and Mary Quarterly* 48 (January 1991): 34, 13, 14–15, 17–18.

31. Hasia R. Diner and Beryl Lieff Benderly, *Her Works Praise Her: A History of Jewish Women in America from Colonial Times to the Present* (New York: Basic Books, 2002), 3, 11; "Fact Sheet on 1654." Available at Jewish Women's Archive, http://jwa.org.

32. Diner and Benderly, *Her Works Praise Her*, 5.

33. Molly McClain and Alessa Ellefson, "A Letter from Carolina, 1688: French Huguenots in the New World," *William and Mary Quarterly*, 3rd series, 64, no. 2 (April 2007), esp. 377–82.

34. Brown, *Good Wives, Nasty Wenches*, 48–49.

35. Ibid., 42–45, 50–52.

36. Ibid., 107–9; Carol Berkin, *First Generations: Women in Colonial America* (New York: Hill and Wang, 1996), 103–7.

37. The Middle Passage, The Mariner's Museum. Available at: http://www.mariner.org/captivepassage/middlepassage/index.html.

38. For an analysis of mortality rates during the Middle Passage, see Herbert S. Klein, Stanley L. Engerman, Robin Haines, and Ralph Shlomoiwitz, "Transoceanic Mortality: The Slave Trade in Comparative Perspective," *William and Mary Quarterly* 58, no. 1 (January 2001): 93–117.

39. John Thornton, "Cannibals, Witches, and Slave Traders in the Atlantic World," *William and Mary Quarterly* 60, no. 2 (April 2003): 273–94.

SUGGESTED READING

Anderson, Virginia DeJohn. *New England's Generation: The Great Migration and the Formation of Society and Culture in the Seventeenth Century*. Cambridge: Cambridge University Press, 1993.

Diner, Hasia R., and Beryl Lieff Benderly, *Her Works Praise Her: A History of Jewish Women in America from Colonial Times to the Present* (New York: Basic Books, 2002.

Brown, Kathleen M. *Good Wives, Nasty Wenches, and Anxious Patriarchs: Gender, Race, and Power in Colonial Virginia*. Chapel Hill: University of North Carolina Press, 1996.

Cressy, David. *Coming Over: Migration and Communication between England and New England in the Seventeenth Century*. New York: Cambridge University Press, 1987.

Main, Gloria L. *Peoples of a Spacious Nation: Families and Cultures in Colonial New England*. Cambridge, MA: Harvard University Press, 2001.

Norton, Mary Beth. *Founding Mothers and Fathers: Gendered Power and the Forming of American Society*. New York: Vintage Books, 1996.

4

Women and Work

For seventeenth-century women, whether white, black, or Native American, work consisted mainly of preparing and cooking food, bearing and caring for children, and doing all the other tasks deemed necessary to maintain a household and its inhabitants. The work that any particular woman did, however, depended on her race, class, marital status, and where and when she was living. Moreover, each culture had its own ideas and beliefs about what constituted the proper work for women.

When English explorers and settlers first encountered the native inhabitants of the Chesapeake region, they were struck by differences between the work that Indian women did and that which women did back in England. The English observers believed that Indian women, who planted and harvested crops, among other chores, were mistreated, and that Indian men, who spent time hunting, were lazy. According to Captain John Smith, an early leader of the Jamestown colony, "the men bestowe their times in fishing, hunting, wars, and such manlike exercises scorning to be seene in any woman like exercises; which is the cause that the women be verie painefull and the men often idle. The women and children do the rest of the worke. They make mats, baskets, pots, morters; pound their corne, make their bread, prepare their victuals, plant their corne, gather their corne, beare al kind of burdens, and such like."[1]

In England, women worked in the fields only occasionally, for instance if extra help was required at harvest time, and hunting was generally considered to be a sport or something men did for fun. Among the Powhatan Indians, however, both the agricultural tasks of women and the hunting and fishing done by men were necessary requirements for subsistence. Women grew maize, beans, and squash, foraged for nuts and fruit, and were highly valued for their contributions to the household diet. Through hunting, men were able to supply their families with meat, usually wild turkey and deer, which was their major source of protein. In addition, deerskin provided them with clothing and blankets. According to English observers, Powhatan, the paramount chief of the Powhatan Indians, demanded tribute in deerskins; moreover, all deerskins had to be presented to him first so that he could choose which ones he wanted. Consequently, Powhatan men had to kill many deer to pay tribute and still provide food and clothing for their families. For these reasons, we can assume that the Powhatan took hunting very seriously. Both hunting and planting contributed to the maintenance of households. As a result, Powhatan men's work and women's work were separate, distinct, and based on gender, but both were necessary to maintain households within their tribe.[2]

Because of the great number of deer being hunted, families frequently moved to new hunting grounds. Women were in charge of moving both the houses and household goods when in late fall after the crops were harvested, families left the more permanent towns to travel to locations where deer were more prevalent. Women carried most of the household items so that the men could move quickly to hunt or to provide protection.[3]

Powhatan women also built the houses, called *yi-hakan* (yeee-ha-cahn), which were made of saplings placed in two parallel lines. The saplings were bent and lashed together at the top to form a roof, and then the whole structure was covered with bark or weeds. A smoke hole in the center of the roof permitted smoke to exit and light to enter the house. The doorway was covered with mats. Within the houses, women kept a cooking fire going all of the time.[4] The houses could be disassembled quickly when families moved. Most of the furnishings, such as ceramic pots, gourds, and other cooking utensils, baskets, and bedding, could also be easily moved. Bed frames were the only large pieces of furniture in the houses. They were built from short posts hammered into the ground at each side of the house. The posts were covered with smaller posts lashed together and placed over them. The frame was then covered with mats and skins for blankets.[5]

As well as building and moving their homes and furnishings, Powhatan women made the mats, pots, baskets, spoons, mortars, and other tools needed for everyday domestic life. They gathered wood for the fires, cooked and prepared meals, and gave birth to and reared children. In addition, they planted corn, prepared it by pounding or drying it, and made stews or bread from it. George Percy, who later became president of the Jamestown Colony council, observed Native American women baking bread: "The manner of baking bread is thus. After they pound their wheat into flowre, with hote water they make it into paste, and worke it into round balls and Cakes, then they put it into a pot of seething water: when it is sod throughly, the lay it on a smooth stone, there they harden it as well as in an Oven." Corn was very valuable, and thus, women held high status among the Powhatan, since they were the producers of corn.[6]

The English inhabitants of Jamestown did not understand the significance of growing corn and the status it gave Powhatan women. Corn was important because of its value as a food source, of course, but the Powhatan also considered it a form of wealth. Because women managed corn production every step of the way from planting and harvesting it to preparing and distributing it, they were therefore the controllers of great wealth. Those who still possessed a supply of corn late in the winter, when many people had depleted their stores, held even greater status.[7]

To the Jamestown settlers, however, agricultural work was the province of men. Moreover, in their worldview, fields were supposed to be cleared in an orderly fashion and planted to produce crops that would support a family through the year. To Englishmen such as John Smith, the seasonal migration of Powhatan villagers indicated that their harvests were inadequate, and this was because women planted the crops instead of men. In addition, their fields did not resemble the neat and orderly fields of England. To the English, the failure to fence and tame the wilderness and the practice of having women do the agricultural work clearly marked Native Americans as uncivilized and inferior.

In turn, the Powhatan viewed the Englishmen as weak and foolish because of their loud stomping in the woods and their need for food and assistance from the Indians. Furthermore, the English did not understand the concept of reciprocity in Powhatan society. When Powhatan offered Englishmen the company of Powhatan women he viewed it as a demonstration of his ability to share his wealth, as only a great chief would have so many women. Since there were no English women in the first group of Jamestown settlers, Powhatan may also have hoped to obtain an alliance with the English by using the bodies of Indian women. The English, however, not only interpreted the gift of women as a tribute to the power of white men, but the gift reinforced their belief that Indians were naturally licentious. Consequently, cultural discrepancies in gender roles played a large part in the mistrust and hostility evident in both the English and the Powhatan.[8]

Those who lived in the early Jamestown settlement keenly felt the lack of women and women's labor. The few English women who lived in the early colony had to work in adverse conditions without such basics as enough thread or soap. Nevertheless, the promotional literature for the colonies, which was intended to attract settlers, assured English women that they would only have to perform the chores that would have been expected of them if they had remained in England, that is, domestic work, not fieldwork. As John Hammond explained in his *Leah and Rachel, or, The Two Fruitful Sisters Virginia and Mary-land: Their Present Condition, Impartially Stated and Related* (1656): "The women are not (as is reported) put into the ground to work, but occupy such domestic employments and housewifery as in England, that is dressing victuals, right up the house, milking, employed about dairies, washing, sewing, &c." This was an idealized version of women's work in many places in the world, but especially in seventeenth-century Virginia. Because of the importance of tobacco in the economy and the lack of sufficient laborers needed to produce the crop, many women who came to Virginia did have to work in the tobacco fields. Few households in the early Chesapeake settlements had dairy cows or dairying equipment or furniture, and most had little in the way of kitchen tools or other items necessary for much in the way of "housewifery." In addition, there were no markets in which women could sell domestic products, such as butter or cheese, soap, or beer, even if they did produce them.[9]

No doubt some women felt a sense of betrayal once they reached Virginia and found conditions there far different from what they had imagined. One of several popular ballads of this time period, "The Trappan'd Maiden," expresses the sense of betrayal and unhappiness felt by some women who came to Virginia as indentured servants. "Five years served I, under Master Guy / In the land of Virginny-o," the narrator reports. She describes how her mistress "sits at her meat, then I have none to eat," and states that she "played my part, both at plow and cart." Each stanza ends with the sad refrain, "When that I was weary, weary, weary-o." Although this is a ballad, it captures the feelings that some female servants must have experienced.[10]

In reality, some female servants complained in court when they had to perform hard physical labor or agricultural chores. Anne Belson reported in 1640 that she was forced "to beat at the mortar" [pound corn in a mortar] despite her master's promise to "use her more like his child than his servant." Alice Rogers noted that her master forced her to "work in the ground and beate at the mortar though conditioned to the contrary."[11]

Recent archeological analyses demonstrate how architecture in the Chesapeake region developed and changed throughout the seventeenth century. The archeological evidence reveals not only changes in the types of building material used and the size and patterns of Chesapeake structures, but also the changing lifestyles and culture of its inhabitants.[12] From excavated structures and artifacts, scholars can also develop an understanding of how household members interacted. The first English settlers in Jamestown lived in barracks style housing in palisaded villages. As tobacco production developed and grew in importance, settlers began to live in scattered plantations and to build small two-room dwellings in which both family members and servants lived. Archeologists observe that:

> In the second and third quarters of the seventeenth century, Chesapeake colonists established many more aspects of the plantation landscape. The home lots of these farmsteads held the main dwelling house with a few detached service structures. Occasionally, planters built separate quarters for their indentured servants during this period, but servants continued to be an integral part of the household where they worked, ate, socialized, and slept. Houses more than fourteen or sixteen feet in width were large enough to offer headroom beneath the slope of the rafters. The loft reached by a ladder stair from the hall, supplied additional sleeping space and storage for produce. A few planters experimented with detached kitchens, but for the most the hall remained the principal room where meals were prepared.[13]

Toward the end of the seventeenth century, servants, slaves, and service spaces such as kitchen and food storage areas were commonly housed in outbuildings. Traveling in Virginia in 1687, a French observer commented that planters, "whatever their rank ... build only two rooms with some closets on the ground floor, & two rooms in the attic above; but they build several like this according to their means. They build also a separate kitchen, a separate house for the negro slaves, & several to dry the tobacco, so that when you come to the home of a person of some means, you think you are entering a fairly large village."[14]

Throughout much of the seventeenth century in parts of Virginia and Maryland, however, even the mistress of the house might work in the tobacco fields because tobacco was so profitable, and the additional labor of wives and children increased significantly the profits a planter made. Most likely, in these situations, women combined agricultural work with their household chores, including preparing meals, tending the livestock and garden, washing clothes, fetching the water for the household, and caring for children. Most Chesapeake households did not have spinning wheels or dairying equipment until after the mid-seventeenth century; however, by this time women who lived in larger and more prosperous households cooked more elaborate meals, especially for visitors. In addition, women who lived on plantations with orchards made apple cider. More wealth and perhaps additional servants may have freed some of these Chesapeake wives from the fields, but it did not reduce the amount of work they had to do, it only changed the nature of it.[15]

Because of the shortage of women in the early seventeenth-century Chesapeake region, men who did not have wives had to employ female servants, make arrangements with the wives of other men, do the work themselves, or have other men do "women's work." Most English men were not happy about having to perform chores normally done by women. Sometimes this could have disastrous effects. One fourteen-year-old Jamestown boy, who lived in a household with six other men, was forced to stay at the house and take care of all the domestic chores, while the others went out to take care of plowing and other agricultural duties. The young man killed himself.[16]

Although a wife might take over some of her husband's duties if he was away, for the most part, gender roles were strictly defined in the seventeenth-century Anglo-American world. Men and women wore distinctly different clothing and hairstyles; they also had different rights and did different types of work. King James denounced the female cross-dressing fad that became popular in London. In 1620, John Chamberlain wrote to his friend, Dudley Carleton, to tell him that the king had ordered the Bishop of London to inform the clergy that they had to condemn the fad, especially "against the insolency of our women, and their wearing of broad-brimmed hats, pointed doublets, their hair cut short or shorn, and some of them stilletos or poinards."[17] People in both England and its colonies were upset when these gender distinctions were blurred or made unclear in some fashion. One case that indicates the degree of uneasiness felt by seventeenth century colonists when faced with sexual ambiguity concerns Thomas or Thomasine Hall.[18]

Hall was born in England and christened Thomasine. Later, she cut her hair and dressed as a man to fight as a soldier. Perhaps while living in England she witnessed the fad for cross-dressing condemned by King James and the clergy. Following this stint in the army, she once again dressed as a woman and did fine needlework, a skill she would have been taught as a girl. Thomasine then once again became Thomas, who dressed in men's clothing and sailed across the ocean to Virginia as an indentured servant in 1627. In 1629, Thomas/Thomasine came to the attention of the court. Hall's familiarity with and demonstrated ability to do the tasks normally performed by women may have brought him to the court's attention. As well, Hall, who had entered the colony as Thomas, was known to dress in women's clothing. It is also possible that Hall may have chosen to repeatedly change his/her gender identity to earn money from another type of women's work—prostitution.[19]

At different periods, Hall deliberately chose a gender identity—sometimes male, sometimes female—by wearing the appropriate gender-specific apparel and usually performing the appropriate "men's work" or "women's work." (There appeared to be some crossover in that his male servant persona did the fine needlework that only women would be expected to know how to do, which led to gossip about him.) Yet his physical characteristics were more ambiguous. A group of women examined his body and declared him to be a man, but others were not so sure. When asked, Hall told his investigators that he was both, but that he could not use "the man's parte." Subsequent examinations did nothing to ease the confusion over Hall's genitalia or sex. Finally, the General Court ruled that Hall was to dress as both a man and a woman. He would wear men's breeches, but would be required to also wear the cap and apron of a woman. As a result, Hall was sentenced to life of marginality—neither man nor woman, although possessing characteristics of each. It is not known what happened to Hall after the sentence was determined; however, since it seems very clear that it was a combination of Hall's physical traits along with his/her changeable gender identity that confused and so upset his/her neighbors in Virginia, it does not seem likely that Hall would have had an easy life.[20]

The size of a man's penis and his ability to sustain an erection were important indicators of his ability to procreate. When wives accused their husbands of being impotent, their bodies were examined, just as Hall's was. Medical texts discussed men's genitalia and body hair, and associated particular characteristics with sexual drive and potency. Jane Sharp wrote in her book on midwifery that an average size "yard" was the most likely to "carry the Seed home to the place it should do." Philip Barrough in his *The Method of Physick* stated that men whose "yards" were too short to fertilize women were "half-geldings." Even marriage manuals discussed the male body. "Thou lovest thine husband because he is a proper man, and hath an active body," wrote the Puritan minister William Whately in *A Bride-Bush; or A Wedding Sermon* (1617).[21] Men who were sexually incapacitated could not marry and become heads of households. Consequently, the confusion about Hall's genitalia was of more significance than simply deciding what he/she should wear or what tasks he/she should do.

Clothing was also of great significance in seventeenth-century America. Several colonies passed sumptuary laws legislating what people could wear. Disturbed that common laborers and their wives were dressing above their station, Virginia laws decreed that only council members and "heads of hundreds" could wear gold in their clothing or silk. Distinctions in dress were even more important in early Virginia than in England, one historian notes, because many wealthy planters still lived in small cottages until near the end of the century.[22]

Massachusetts also had strict laws about clothing. A law passed in 1651 mandated that only the wealthy could wear such items as expensive lace, gold or silver buttons, silk hoods, and high leather boots. Plymouth colony did not enact this type of legislation, but popular beliefs and attitudes may have worked to keep people from dressing beyond their status. The clothing of both Puritans and Pilgrims came in a wide variety of colors, with black normally worn for formal or ceremonial occasions. Russet or orange-brown shades appear most often in inventories of clothing, but colonists also wore clothing dyed in shades of red, blue, green, yellow, and other combinations. Various types and combinations of wool, linen, and leather were used to make the clothing, but cotton was too expensive to be used very often. Both men and women generally avoided elaborate ruffs and other ostentatious displays. Most also avoided wearing jewelry, even wedding rings.[23]

Puritan and Pilgrim women wore gowns that unlike modern day dress consisted of separate pieces, the bodice, skirt, and sleeves. Women tied the sleeves to the armholes and covered them with shoulder pieces. Sometimes skirts were slit to reveal a special underskirt or elaborate petticoat. Since clothing was expensive, it was made to last, and often items such as petticoats were bequeathed to relatives. Closest to their bodies, women wore smocks, which were loose linen shifts, and over their gowns, they might wear an apron. On their legs and feet, women wore stockings, leather shoes, and perhaps clogs to avoid the mud. To complete the outfit, women wore kerchiefs around their necks, and a coif, or cap, made of linen on their heads. Women kept their heads covered as a sign of modesty.[24]

Men wore a close-fitting jacket called a doublet, full, knee-length breeches, and a cloak. These standard items were made of various fabrics, depending on the owner's class and status. Men might also wear a "jerkin" made from heavy material and a waistcoat. Under all of this, men wore linen shirts. Like women, men might wear all of these layers in cold weather, but they did not wear all of these items all of the time. On their legs, men wore wool or linen stockings, covered by canvas "boothose." For every day, men usually wore laced leather boots, but they wore black shoes when dressing more formally. Men were not required to wear head coverings, but most did wear some sort of cap. On formal occasions, men wore black felt hats.[25]

In the Boston privy belonging to Katherine Naylor and her family (discussed in Chapter 2) that was excavated during the Big Dig, archeologists found "158 fragments of silk and fine woolen textiles." These were high-quality, fashionable fabrics of the seventeenth century. Archeologists speculate that Katherine Naylor might have mended or trimmed her family's clothing, or perhaps servants threw away clothing to prevent being fined for violating the law.[26] Although it seems unlikely that servants would dispose of expensive clothing, perhaps it is more likely to have happened in Katherine's house, especially if her unfaithful husband gave some of his female conquests some cast-off clothing belonging to his wife.

Nobilis Matrona Pomeioocenſis.   VIII

A Noblewoman of Pomeiock. Engraving by Theodor de Bry, 1590, after a painting by John White. Courtesy of Library of Congress.

Distinctions in dress denoted both gender and class, and this was important in the world of seventeenth-century America. People expected to look at someone and instantly establish whether the person was a man or a woman, a master or a servant.[27] Colonists and other European observers were fascinated by the clothing and hair of Native Americans they encountered. George Percy, for example, described the difference in hair-styles for married and single Indian women.

> The Maids you shall always see the fore part of their head and sides shaven close, the hinder part very long, which they tie in a pleate hanging downe to their hips. The married women weares their haire all of a length, and is tied of the fashion that Maids are. The women kinde in the Countrey doth pounce and race their bodies, legges, thighes, armes and faces with a sharpe Iron, which makes a stampe in curious knots, and drawes the proportion of Fowles, Fish, or Beasts; then with painting of sundry lively colours, they rub it into the stampe which will never be taken away, because it is dried into the flesh where it is sered.[28]

Just as Anglo-American expected clothing to denote class and gender, they expected to see men doing "men's work" and women doing "women's work." Yet male/female divisions were not always so distinct. In addition to the fieldwork that some women did, there was the occa-sional woman who donned male clothing and like Thomas Hall became a soldier or sailor. Far more often, however, women went beyond their domestic world to aid their husbands and help them to run their busi-nesses. Wives routinely acted in their husbands' places when their hus-bands were away.

For example, Anne Devorix oversaw the spring planting, managed the family's finances, and protected their assets while her New England fisher-man husband was at sea. In 1674, Henry Dering of New Hampshire gave his wife, Anne, power of attorney to collect a debt owned him.[29] These are just two examples among hundreds. In most instances when a wife acted on her husband's behalf, it went unnoticed because it was so com-monplace. As one historian noted, "The fluidity of gender roles in the ru-ral economy had a one-way dimension: adult women were expected to act in their husbands' steads when the need arose, but men are rarely if even glimpsed in surviving records tackling cooking or housework."[30] Because spaces within and around houses were not yet highly specialized in most seventeenth-century New England homes, women were likely to overhear conversations taking place between the head of the household and other businessmen or creditors, as they conversed in the yard, hall, or parlor. In fact, men sometimes depended upon their wives, daughters, or sisters to remember details of business arrangements if they were required to testify in court. Although the ability of a wife to stand in for her husband could be challenged in court (see Chapter 2), the numerous examples from colonial courts indicate that many men trusted that their wives could do the job. In fact, communities throughout the British North American colonies expected wives to take over for their husbands when the men were away on business.[31]

For example, Puritan Samuel Sewall noted in his diary that his wife managed their family finances better than he did. After paying a Captain Belchar a sum of money, he gave the rest to his wife, and told her, "she shall now keep the Cash; if I want I will borrow of her. She has a better faculty than I at managing Affairs: I will assist her; and will endeavour to live upon my Salary; will see what it will doe. The Lord give his Blessing."[32]

Some women took over businesses from their husbands, or even ran them on their own. Seventeenth-century taverns, or ordinaries, were often licensed to or run by women. Diana White, for example, operated a tavern for about two decades toward the end of the seventeenth century in Albemarle, North Carolina. She first ran the tavern in the 1670s with her first husband. After his death, she continued to operate the tavern with and without the help of her next two husbands. During this time, she hosted court sessions on her own and hired employees and apprentices. By hosting court sessions, she became familiar with how the legal system worked. Despite coverture, she was involved in several debt suits—including a successful action against her third husband, Thomas White, in 1697. As a result of her petition, her debts were separated from his by court order, and Diana's house and belongings were restored to her. Other women in colonial North Carolina also hosted court sessions and ran taverns, as did women in Boston and other colonial cities.[33] Nevertheless, the good wife, whose work revolved around the domestic realm of home and family, remained both the ideal and the expectation for most seventeenth-century Anglo-American women.

Marital expectations were somewhat different for the Dutch women of New Netherland, as marriage there did not preclude women from engaging in business on their own. Under the English system of coverture, marriage subsumed women's right to own property, make contracts, and engage in commercial or legal undertakings separately from their husbands, even though some women did so in the seventeenth century. (See Chapter 2 for more on coverture.) Under the Dutch system, however, it was legal for married women to make contracts or go to court without their husbands.[34] Many Dutch women engaged in commercial activities separately from their husbands. This does not mean that marriage was unimportant or that they did not do household work; instead the Dutch believed that women's ability to undertake legal or business duties strengthened the family.

Margaret Hardenbroeck, for instance, arrived in New Amsterdam in 1659. She quickly established herself as an agent for a cousin who was a trader in the Netherlands, and then went on to prosper on her own as a merchant with connections to the fur trade. She continued to work throughout her marriage to merchant Pieter Rudophus DeVries. After his death, she inherited both his property and his prosperous business. With her second husband, Frederick Philipsen, Margaret acquired more property and built a transatlantic packet line. Under the Dutch government of the colony, many women participated in trade, and even though few were as involved in commercial trade as Margaret Hardenbroeck, and even fewer in transatlantic commerce, they were theoretically able to do so if they wanted to pursue such a course. Conditions for women changed after the colony became British. Although Margaret and Frederick continued to prosper after the British took over the colony in 1664, Margaret could no longer buy or hold property in her own name.[35]

Jewish women who arrived in New Amsterdam and in other colonial seaports also entered business, probably far more often than most other seventeenth-century women. Jewish wives worked with their husbands in stores and businesses. Unlike most settlers who arrived in the cities and then left to settle on farms, Jewish settlers tended to stay in the cities. In addition to seeking religious freedom, the twenty-three Jews who left Brazil and arrived in New Amsterdam in 1654 may also have been seeking business opportunities (see Chapter 3 on immigration).[36]

Even under English law, however, many women earned extra income through their domestic skills. Unless mentioned in a lawsuit, the money earned in this way usually went unrecorded. In the excavated privy of Katherine Naylor, for example, archeologists found an amazing number of seeds and pits from fruits and nuts. Along with this, they also discovered a large number of granary weevils and pollen from grains. Scholars speculate that Katherine Naylor may have earned some extra money from making preserves or baking cherry pies. If she did, no record exists of the transactions, as is true with most women's home-based businesses.[37]

School teaching was another option for some women, especially in New England, where officials believed everyone should know how to read. Teaching reading, which was done orally, permitted women to earn some extra income without having to leave their homes. (For more on education, see Chapter 7.) In these informal dame schools, or reading schools, women agreed to teach young boys and girls for a few hours a day in their homes. Most of these dame schools simply introduced reading to children of about three or four years old. Dame schools were not funded by the towns but did provide women with some money from parents who were willing to pay others to teach their children. In one situation, the Commissioners of the United Colonies of New England paid a female teacher to teach Indians to read. Impressed with her work, they increased her salary in 1653. As they wrote in a letter, "The wife of William Daniell of Dorchester hath for this three yeares last past bestowed much of her time in teaching severall Indians to Read and that shee hath onely

Receiued the summe of six pounds towards her paines; [we] thought fitt to allow her nine pounds more the time past."[38]

Even when they were involved with outside business dealings, most women would have been actively concerned with their households, as well.[39] The majority of women throughout the colonies were engaged in domestic work that included daily household chores, such as cooking; less often done chores, such as laundry; and seasonal tasks, such as preserving food or helping with planting or harvesting. The exact nature of a good wife's domestic chores depended on where and when she was living. In the mid-seventeenth century Chesapeake, most households still lacked much more than the very basics of subsistence.

In New England, however, the situation was different. Housewives there lived on family farms, in towns, and on the frontier. Early New England houses were small, clapboard houses of one or one and one half stories. The house usually had two rooms, with the inner room containing a furnished or curtained bed. The upstairs loft was used as sleeping quarters for the rest of the family and servants and also for storage.[40] Over time, homeowners might add a lean-to and additional rooms. Rooms were not used for specialized purposes for most of the seventeenth century. Most Puritan farmers invested their money in land, rather than in conspicuous displays of wealth.

In contrast, Boston merchants and their families, despite their Puritan convictions, tended to live in larger homes with fine furnishings. Governor John Winthrop lived in a two-story, nine-room house, while William Paddy, a wealthy merchant, but not the wealthiest, lived in an eight-room house that included a carpeted entrance hall containing eleven embroidered, leather chairs. Each of the seven beds in his house had a feather mattress, and there were mirrors on the walls.[41]

Women who lived in towns and cities had access to goods that might be produced by women living on a farm. A farm wife, for example, might begin her day with milking the cows. Breakfast would follow, consisting generally of easily prepared foods, such as toasted bread and cheese and items left over from the previous day, and beer or cider to drink with it, or perhaps milk in the summer. The main meal of the day came later, normally boiled meat with whatever vegetables were available at that time of year, and perhaps a pudding steamed on top in a cloth bag. Supper was a simple meal much like breakfast. Even a simple meal, however, required practice, skill, and timing, as cooking over an open fire—sometimes literally standing within the huge fireplace itself—was quite complex, since the cook might have several dishes cooking at different heights or distances from several small fires.[42]

It required even more skill to bake. Yeast breads began with a "sponge" made the night before. Women took yeast from the beer they brewed or from a piece of dough saved from a previous baking session. It was mixed with flour and water, and then set to rise overnight. Flour used for baking was often a mixture of wheat and other grains, such as rye. In the morning, along with her other tasks, the good wife added flour to the dough, kneaded, let it rise again, and eventually baked it in the oven built into the back of the fireplace. Learning how to regulate the temperature so that the bread baked without burning took time and practice.[43]

Although most seventeenth-century New England households had one or more cows, only some women engaged in serious dairying. Cows were raised for both meat and milk. They could graze in most areas, but only if they had sufficient meadowlands could they produce the milk needed to make butter and cheeses. Dairying was not a significant part of seventeenth-century Chesapeake life. For one thing, dairying was considered to be a female activity, and there were relatively few women there. In addition, cows in the Chesapeake were usually permitted to roam freely to forage instead of being situated in the high quality grazing areas that are necessary to produce abundant milk. The milk they did produce— on average only one to two quarts per day—was usually low in butterfat. A well-tended cow in seventeenth-century England might produce milk for about eight months. Colonial cows, which were not so well cared for, probably averaged only about four or five months of milk production.[44] Moreover, dairy products were likely to spoil easily because of the hot summers and the lack of cool streams that in other areas were used to keep dairy products cold.[45]

For those good wives who were engaged in dairying, the cycle began in the early spring when calves were born. Later in the summer, women preserved the fruits and vegetables grown in the garden or gathered from nearby areas. Autumn was the season for slaughtering animals and preserving the meat in various forms, including bacon and sausages. Good wives also made apple cider during the autumn months. Good wives made beer, too, either large quantities of strong beer, or weekly portions of "small beer."[46]

Spinning was another activity that good wives did, whether they owned sheep or not. Spinning was easily performed while taking care of small children, as it was a repetitious activity that could be easily started and stopped. Mothers taught their daughters how to spin, and even young girls could spin coarse thread.[47] Women could not stop working when they were pregnant, breastfeeding, or had small children. The care of babies and young children was simply part of the rhythms of their daily lives. Babies were carried around and cradles were kept close to the mother; toddlers might be put into "go-carts" later in the century to keep them amused and safe.[48]

"To the right hon'able the Earl of Moira, this plate, taken on the spot in the County of Downe, representing spinning, reeling with the clock reel, and boiling the yarn; is most respectfully dedicated by . . . Wm. Hincks / Wm. Hincks, del. et sculp., 1791." Spinning was an activity that could be done while looking after children. This portrayal of spinning also reflects the numerous household activities of many seventeenth-century women. Courtesy of Library of Congress.

Babies and young children's clothing had to be made, mended, and altered as they grew. Babies and toddlers of both sexes wore gowns, which were easier to handle than breeches when an infant needed to be changed or held over a chamber pot, and could be handed down from sibling to sibling. Infant clothing also needed to be washed and mended, as did the clothing of other family members. Washing and ironing were not jobs that were done daily or even weekly by many people, as it took time and a great deal of effort to heat the water and irons, strength to wring out the clothes, and space in which to dry them. Although woolen outerwear and petticoats were seldom washed, linen shifts, handkerchiefs, and shirts did need to be washed. Women with babies must have done laundry on a regular basis to take care of the infant's soiled diapers and bedding.[49]

Although each farm and household was different, the probate records from the Cole Plantation in St. Mary's County, Maryland, provide some

Woman Sewing, 1655. Courtesy of The Granger Collection, New York.

insight into the labor performed on one seventeenth-century tobacco plantation. Robert Cole settled the three-hundred-acre estate in 1652. He was a Catholic farmer from England with a wife and children. In 1662, he died while visiting England, leaving his neighbor, Luke Gardiner, to care for the plantation and his five children and one stepchild for the next eleven years until the oldest one, Robert, turned twenty-one. In 1673, Luke Gardiner submitted his records to the probate judge.[50]

Tobacco was the cash crop, but the male servants and Cole's sons also cultivated about eleven acres of corn to feed the family and servants and pay rent on the farm. Tobacco is a very labor-intensive crop, and it can only be grown in one spot for four years. Corn can be grown on the land for one to two years after that, but then the land has to lie fallow for twenty years before tobacco can be grown there again. Consequently, the male workers needed to clear an acre or two of land each year in addition to planting, cutting, stripping, and curing tobacco, planting, gathering, and storing corn, and slaughtering the hogs and cattle. All land cultivation was done with hoes, as Cole did not own a plow. Tobacco seeds were planted in mid-February, corn was planted in April or May, and tobacco was cut in late August or early September and then cured before the first frost. In the late fall, hogs and cattle were slaughtered, and the meat was salted for storage.[51]

Since Cole's children were motherless, as well as fatherless, Gardiner hired a housekeeper and a female servant to take care of the children, do the cooking, and do the laundry. On plantations without the means to hire enough male servants to work in the fields, the women had to take time from household chores to also do field work, but this was not the case on Cole's plantation. Yet Gardiner only kept the female help until Betty, the youngest Cole child, was seven years old. At that time, she was sent to live and to be schooled elsewhere. As scholars have noted, after this the men and boys probably "lived far less comfortably than before— that less washing was done, for example, and more vermin abounded." Most likely, the men and boys also had fewer vegetables to eat, since women tended vegetable gardens, and unless the younger boys did the milking, then they also did not have milk. Even if the boys did do the milking, it is unlikely that they produced butter or cheese.[52]

From the probate records, scholars can also observe what tasks were not done on the plantation. For example, even when women were living there, they did not make clothing. Instead, a tailor came each year to make and mend clothing for the family and servants. The women on Cole's plantation also did not spin or weave, as there is no record of spinning wheels or looms. On this plantation, as on most plantations in the area, all effort was put into producing food to eat and tobacco to sell. Money was not spent on other tools or equipment, or on extra building, and so servants and family members lived, worked, ate, and slept together.[53]

Except for those women isolated on tobacco plantations or in similar frontier settings, most seventeenth-century women frequently worked in communal settings. This social world of labor enabled women and girls to learn how to do particular jobs by watching other women do them.[54] In addition, these communal work situations gave women the opportunity to gossip and exert their moral authority. The separate strands that made up this social world of labor—women working together, women learning from one another, and women exerting their moral authority— were woven together most notably in the experience and rituals of childbirth.

Each birth was an event in the community of women. When a woman went into labor, female neighbors and family members gathered at her house. Although women encountered other women while performing daily chores, such as bringing water from the community well, only during births were they in an environment that excluded men entirely.

Giving birth is work—a statement with which any woman who has done so will agree. For colonists of seventeenth-century America, it was the most important work a woman could do, but only after she was married. The experience of childbirth separated women from men, but it also formed a bond between women. Many women gave thanks to God after coming safely through "travail" with a living child, yet the experience linked them to other women, even as it tested and proved their strength.

As women gathered at the laboring woman's house, the atmosphere might suggest a social event. The mother-to-be was expected to provide refreshments for her attendants, who might be there for quite a long time. Groaning cakes and groaning beer were a frequent offering during labor. At this early stage of labor, the laboring woman was encouraged to walk around, and she probably talked to the other women. Later, she might turn to one of them for physical, as well as emotional support, as she squatted on the midwife's stool.[55]

When a single woman gave birth, however, or the situation seemed unusual or irregular, the midwife became an inquisitor, empowered by the law to question the woman while she labored. When twenty-one-year-old Elizabeth Emerson of Haverhill, Massachusetts, went into labor in 1686, she was attended by her mother, her sister, Hannah Duston, who would later be captured by Indians and become famous for her escape, at least three neighbors, and the midwife, Johanah Corliss. The women began to quarrel after Johanah Corliss adopted her legal role and began to question the laboring woman. Elizabeth had claimed earlier that Timothy Swann had raped her after they had gone to see her parents' new bedchamber. At the birth, the women surrounding Elizabeth Emerson wondered why she had not fought Timothy Swann and cried out that she was being raped. They also asserted that conception could not occur from rape, which was believed by many physicians during the seventeenth century, as well. When the still unwed Elizabeth Emerson became pregnant a second time six years later, she killed the twin girls she delivered in secret, and she was executed for infanticide in 1693.[56]

In a case in Virginia when the indentured servant Anne Orthwood went into labor on July 29, 1664, the midwife, Eleanor Gething, questioned her and warned her that "she should answer at that dreadfull Day of Judgment where all harts shall be opened and all secrets made knowne, To Speake who was the father of the Child she went with." When Anne named John Kendall as the father and told the midwife when they had been intimate, Gething did not believe the story. To the midwife, the timing of Anne and John's trysts would have occurred too early to match what she believed was a full-term birth, and she continued to question Anne, noting that "[a]ccording to Computation of the tyme of your Reckninge, if you goe your full tyme wronge the young Man." Anne gave birth to twins after a difficult labor throughout which she insisted John Kendall was the father.[57]

One of the twins was stillborn or died shortly after birth, while the other, a son named Jasper, survived. The unfortunate Anne died shortly after delivery, and local gossip blamed Gething. The court reported that "Sum Reports hath past that Ellinor Gething appointed Midwife at the Labour of Ann Orthwood late Servant to Lieutenant Colonel William Waters used harsh Useage to her the said Ann by neglecting her in the tyme of her Labour." The court vindicated her and noted that the two women who had assisted at the birth reported that she had acted properly.[58]

Eleanor Gething held an important position both within the community of women and within the larger community, as was true of most colonial midwives.[59] A midwife's work was done in addition to her work as a wife and mother, although it was in some ways an extension of those roles.[60] She was often a leader or spokesperson for the community of women, but she held a position of authority in the male world, as well. Midwives were authorized by the courts to question single women when they gave birth or married women whose babies appeared too close to their wedding date. They also examined the bodies of women suspected of infanticide or witchcraft, as well as those under suspicion for other reasons, such as in the case of Thomas/Thomasine Hall.

Skilled midwives were in great demand and valued for their abilities to bring mothers and babies through the dangers of childbirth. Yet because they dealt with such intimate aspects of women's lives, they were also able to learn secrets that some women wished to hide, such as when a full-term baby was born too soon after the wedding date. Even so, what was revealed at a birth often remained a secret known only within the community of women. One extreme example of the community of women keeping a secret from men concerns the birth of the stillborn, deformed infant to Mary Dyer, a follower of Anne Hutchinson (discussed in Chapter 2). The birth was known among the women of the community, but word of it only reached the men—by chance—after several months.[61]

Although the midwife was the woman in charge at a birth, she was rarely the only woman in attendance. Similarly, when women went about their domestic duties, they often had daughters, servants, or slaves who assisted them or took over the routine or most onerous chores. Indeed, the ability of a married woman to engage in work outside of the usual domestic chores often depended upon having her daughters or servants who could complete the necessary tasks. Toward the end of the century in some parts of New England, it became much more difficult to find servants and to replace those who left. At the same time, newer themes of gentility and polite society began to merge with the older ideal of the good housewife. During this time, such items as extra chairs, looking glasses, table linens, and forks appeared much more often in inventories in northern New England. Although women aimed to appear refined and polished, they still had to do routine domestic chores, or they had to oversee servants who could do the chores.[62]

To give one example, in 1684, Elizabeth Saltonsall of Haverhill, Massachusetts, sent her sixteen-year-old daughter, Elizabeth, to Boston with the girl's father. Nathaniel Saltonsall was a magistrate in this frontier town, as well as a militia commander. Thus, the Saltonsalls were well respected and important, but Haverhill could not provide Elizabeth's daughter with the opportunities available in Boston to make her into a genteel woman. Even though there were chores to be done at home, and dairy season was about to begin, Elizabeth permitted her daughter to go. She thought she would have help from her servant, Betsey Warner, but Betsey's own mother called her home to help there. Elizabeth wrote to her daughter and told her, "Were it not that I aime at your good I should not be willing to deny myself as I do." Then she told her daughter, "It would be a very great trouble to me you should misuse your precious time or any way mispend it." Elizabeth believed that her own suffering was worth it, if it would improve her daughter.[63]

Five years later, daughter Elizabeth was married, but Elizabeth Saltonsall still suffered with having to do her ordinary work, plus having the extra responsibilities that went along with having a husband who was the militia commander. She had to cook and provide for soldiers who were billeted in their large house during a siege in 1694, and she had to be hospitable to strangers who appeared and needed a place to stay. She had to do so without the help of servants, since the young women who might have helped her were probably at home helping their own mothers.[64]

Aspirations of gentility were also apparent, if not more so, in Virginia by the end of the seventeenth century and continued into the eighteenth century. As the native-born population grew, the sex ratio became more equal, and the number of slaves in the colony increased, the number of white immigrants decreased. Society in Virginia became more stratified, and an elite planter class developed. Houses began to reflect a division of labor, with workspaces and living spaces carefully separated. The mistress of the house might oversee the labor performed in the work areas, but servants and slaves did the labor itself.[65]

Although there were few black women in Virginia in the early days of the colony, they had a great impact on the colony. The English perceived African women as different from white women and believed it was acceptable to put them to work in the fields. They may have been partially influenced by accounts of West African women performing heavy agricultural labor there. As the need for laborers increased, it became accepted that African women worked in the fields—along with doing domestic chores that white women did. The distinction between African women and white women became codified in 1643 when the Virginia Assembly decided that African women, but not white women, were "tithable" (taxable). The new law included "youths sixteen years of age [and] upwards, as also negro women at the age of sixteen years." Although free African families had to pay a tithe for husband, wife, and children of sixteen or above, white landowners did not have to pay a tax on their wives, children, or white female servants. They were categorized as dependents. As a consequence, even though some white women did work in the tobacco fields, lawmakers created a legal distinction that assumed white women worked at domestic pursuits, while African women worked as field laborers, despite the reality.[66]

Yet toward the last quarter of the seventeenth century, some women deliberately chose to breach the boundaries of gender, race, and class by picking up hoes in the Tobacco Cutting Riots in Virginia. In 1682, large and small tobacco planters were affected by the low prices of a glutted tobacco market. Rioters began to travel from farm to farm cutting down the tobacco plants until the militia and threats of harsh punishment forced them to stop. The insurrection did not end there, however. As Secretary Nicholas Spencer informed readers in his account of the Tobacco Cutting Riots, "the women had so cast off their modesty as to take up hoes that the rabble were forced to lay down."[67] Hoes were agricultural tools used by white male farm workers, male indentured servants, and male and female slaves. By the 1680s, free white women seldom worked in the tobacco fields. By picking up the hoes that male protesters had been forced to put down, these white women continued the political protest and linked themselves to servants and slaves. It is possible that slaves joined the protest, too, although it did not change their situation.

Although most Anglo-Americans considered it to be part of a wife's duty to have children who would help their parents in taking care of home, farm, and family, it was different for African women. Part of an African woman's work became to reproduce—sometimes as a result of coerced sex—to increase profits for the people who owned her. This became true after legislation passed in 1662 declaring that the offspring of a slave mother was a slave, even if the father was a white man. Consequently, any child born to a slave became the property of her master.

The work of all women, whether white, black, or Native American, played an important role in seventeenth-century American life. Their contributions as good wives, mothers, producers of domestic goods, and field laborers made it possible for the colonies to become established and to grow. Although women's work was not generally discussed or written about, except for when there was a problem, seventeenth-century colonists valued it and realized how necessary it was.

NOTES

1. John Smith, *A Map of Virginia, with a Description of the Countrey, the Commodities, People, Government and Religion* (1612). Available at: Virtual Jamestown, Virginia Center for Digital History, University of Virginia, http://etext.lib.virginia.edu/etcbin/jamestown-browse?id=J1008.

2. Kathleen M. Brown, *Good Wives, Nasty Wenches, and Anxious Patriarchs: Gender, Race, and Power in Colonial Virginia* (Chapel Hill: University of North Carolina Press, 1996), 57–58, 83–84; Helen C. Rountree, *The Powhatan Indians of Virginia: Their Traditional Culture* (Norman: University of Oklahoma Press, 1989), 38–39. Also see Karen Ordahl Kupperman, *Indians and English* (Ithaca, NY: Cornell University Press, 2000), 148–50. Kupperman notes that the English settlers in New England also believed that Indian women were hardworking and almost slaves to the lazy Indian men.

3. Rountree, *Powhatan Indians*, 41.

4. Ibid., 61.

5. Ibid., 62–63.

6. Ibid., 51–52, 89; Brown, *Good Wives, Nasty Wenches*, 66, 73; "Observations by Master George Percy, 1607," American Journeys Collection, Wisconsin Historical Society Digital Library and Archives, Document No. AJ-073, 18. Available at: http://www.americanjourneys.org.

7. Rountree, *Powhatan Indians*, 51, 89.

8. Brown, *Good Wives, Nasty Wenches*, 57–61, 65–67.

9. John Hammond, *Leah and Rachel, or, The Two Fruitful Sisters Virginia and Mary-land: Their Present Condition, Impartially Stated and Related* (1656). Available at: http://www.digitalhistory.uh.edu/learning_history/servitude_slavery/servitude_account2.cfm; Brown, *Good Wives, Nasty Wenches*, 84–85.

10. "The Trappan'd Maiden." Available at: http://www.contemplator.com/america/trappan.html.

11. Quoted in Brown, *Good Wives, Nasty Wenches*, 87.

12. For a detailed overview with illustrations of Chesapeake architecture, see Willie Graham, Carter L. Hudgins, Carl R. Lounsbury, Fraser D. Neiman, and James P. Whittenburg, "Adaptation and Innovation: Archaeological and Architectural Perspectives on the Seventeenth-Century Chesapeake," *William and Mary Quarterly* 64 (July 2007): 451–522.

13. Graham et al., "Adaptation and Innovation," 503.

14. [Durand de Dauphiné], *A Huguenot Exile in Virginia: Or, Voyages of a Frenchman Exiled for His Religion with a Description of Virginia and Maryland*, trans. and ed. Gilbert Chinard (New York, 1934), 119–20, quoted in Graham et al. "Adaptation and Innovation," 507.

15. Brown, *Good Wives, Nasty Wenches*, 84–86.

16. Ibid., 85. This is not to say that the young man committed suicide solely because he had to do women's work, but clearly he was unhappy. He may have been or felt that he was stigmatized because of the work he was doing. It is also possible that he was teased or abused.

17. The Norton Anthology of English Literature, Norton Topics Online, "Contesting Cultural Norms: Cross-Dressing." Available at: http://www.wwnorton.com/college/english/nael/17century/topic_1/mulier.htm.

18. I have used him when referring to Thomas Hall and her when referring to Thomasine Hall. When it is unclear, I have used his/her.

19. Elizabeth Reis, "Impossible Hermaphrodites: Intersex in America, 1620–1960," *Journal of American History* 92 (September 2005): 418; Mary Beth Norton, *Founding Mothers and Fathers: Gendered Power and the Forming of American Society* (New York: Vintage Books, 1996), 193.

20. Brown, *Good Wives, Nasty Wenches*, 75–80; Norton, *Founding Mothers and Fathers*, 183–97.

21. All quoted in Thomas A. Foster, "Deficient Husbands: Manhood, Sexual Incapacity, and Male Marital Sexuality in Seventeenth-Century New England," *William and Mary Quarterly* 56 (October 1999): 730–31.

22. Brown, *Good Wives, Nasty Wenches*, 89–90.

23. John Putnam Demos, *A Little Commonwealth: Family Life in Plymouth Colony* (New York: Oxford University Press, 1970), 53–54.

24. Ibid., 54–56.

25. Ibid., 56–57.

26. Norma Jane Langford, "Colonial Boston Unearthed," *Archaeology* (September 26, 1997). Available at: http://www.archaeology.org/online/features/boston.

27. The English were also fascinated by and discussed in great detail the clothing and hairstyles of the Indian men and women they encountered. Kupperman, *Indians and English*, 54–55.

28. Percy, "Observations," 19.

29. Laurel Thatcher Ulrich, *Good Wives: Image and Reality in the Lives of Women in Northern New England, 1650–1750* (New York: Oxford University Press, 1982), 40–41.

30. Cornelia Hughes Dayton, *Women before the Bar: Gender, Law, and Society in Connecticut, 1639–1789* (Chapel Hill: University of North Carolina Press, 1995), 75.

31. Ibid., 73–75.

32. Samuel Sewall, "Diary," Massachusetts Historical Society, vol. 2, 93, quoted in Edmund S. Morgan, *The Puritan Family*, rev. ed. (New York: Harper and Row, 1966), 43.

33. Kristi Rutz-Robbins, "'Divers Debts': Women's Participation in the Local Economy, Albemarle, North Carolina, 1663–1729," *Early American Studies* 4 (Fall 2006): 425–26, 428, 429–30.

34. Michael E. Gherke, "Dutch Women in New Netherland and New York in the Seventeenth Century," (PhD dissertation, West Virginia University, 2001), 130–31.

35. Carol Berkin, *First Generations: Women in Colonial America* (New York: Hill and Wang, 1996), 79–81; Gherke, "Dutch Women," 119–21.

36. Hasia R. Diner and Beryl Lieff Benderly, *Her Works Praise Her: A History of Jewish Women in America from Colonial Times to the Present* (New York: Basic Books, 2002), 44, 47, 49.

37. Langford, "Colonial Boston Unearthed."

38. David Pulsifer, ed., *Records of the Colony of New Plymouth, in New England, Acts of the Commissioners of the United Colonies of New England, 1653–1679* (Boston, 1859), 2:106, quoted in E. Jennifer Monaghan, "Literacy Instruction and Gender in

Colonial New England," in *Reading in America: Literature and Social History*, ed. Cathy N. Davidson (Baltimore: Johns Hopkins University Press, 1989), 59.

39. Gherke, "Dutch Women," 42.

40. Demos, *A Little Commonwealth*, chap. 1.

41. Virginia DeJohn Anderson, *New England's Generation: The Great Migration and the Formation of Society and Culture in the Seventeenth Century* (Cambridge: Cambridge University Press, 1993), 161–71.

42. Ulrich, *Good Wives*, 17–19.

43. Ibid., 20–21.

44. Joan M. Jensen, *Loosening the Bonds: Mid-Atlantic Farm Women, 1750–1850* (New Haven, CT: Yale University Press, 1986), 96.

45. Virginia DeJohn Anderson, "Animals into the Wilderness: The Development of Livestock Husbandry in the Seventeenth-Century Chesapeake," *William and Mary Quarterly* 59 (April 2002): 385.

46. Ulrich, *Good Wives*, 21–23.

47. Ibid., 29–30.

48. Ibid., 26.

49. Ibid., 28–29.

50. Lois Green Carr and Lorena S. Walsh, "Economic Diversification and Labor Organization in the Chesapeake, 1650–1820," in *Work and Labor in Early America*, ed. Stephen Innes (Chapel Hill: University of North Carolina Press, 1988), 149.

51. Ibid., 150–51.

52. Ibid., 151–52.

53. Ibid., 153.

54. Else L. Hambleton emphasized the point that New England women worked communally and used the phrase "social world of labor" in a private communication with me.

55. Ulrich, *Good Wives*, 126–29.

56. Else L. Hambleton, *Daughters of Eve: Pregnant Brides and Unwed Mothers in Seventeenth-Century Massachusetts* (New York: Routledge, 2004), 135–36.

57. John Ruston Pagan, *Anne Orthwood's Bastard: Sex and Law in Early Virginia* (New York: Oxford University Press, 2003), 87–88.

58. Ibid., 89.

59. Ibid., 81; Norton, *Founding Mothers and Fathers*, 225.

60. Laurel Thatcher Ulrich notes how the practice of the eighteenth-century mid-wife Martha Ballard advanced once her daughters were old enough to do the household chores, as well as spin and weave. When her daughters married and left home, Martha had to hire servants to help, or do the work herself—as well as deliver babies. *A Midwife's Tale: The Life of Martha Ballard Based on Her Diary, 1725–1812* (New York: Knopf, 1990), esp. 219–23.

61. This case is analyzed in Norton, *Founding Mothers and Fathers*, 223–24, 394–95.

62. Ulrich, *Good Wives*, 71–72.

63. Ibid., 72–73.

64. Ibid., 74–75.

65. Brown, *Good Wives, Nasty Wenches*, 250–51.

66. Ibid., 108–13.

67. Quoted in Terri L. Snyder, *Brabbling Women: Disorderly Speech and the Law in Early Virginia* (Ithaca, NY: Cornell University Press, 2003), 39.

SUGGESTED READING

Berkin, Carol. *First Generations: Women in Colonial America*. New York: Hill and Wang, 1996.

Brown, Kathleen M. *Good Wives, Nasty Wenches, and Anxious Patriarchs: Gender, Race, and Power in Colonial Virginia*. Chapel Hill: University of North Carolina Press, 1996.

Demos, John Putnam. *A Little Commonwealth: Family Life in Plymouth Colony*. New York: Oxford University Press, 1970.

Kupperman, Karen Ordahl. *Indians and English*. Ithaca, NY: Cornell University Press, 2000.

Norton, Mary Beth. *Founding Mothers and Fathers: Gendered Power and the Forming of American Society*. New York: Vintage Books, 1996.

Pagan, John Ruston. *Anne Orthwood's Bastard: Sex and Law in Early Virginia*. New York: Oxford University Press, 2003.

Rountree, Helen C. *The Powhatan Indians of Virginia: Their Traditional Culture* Norman: University of Oklahoma Press, 1989.

Ulrich, Laurel Thatcher. *Good Wives: Image and Reality in the Lives of Women in Northern New England, 1650–1750*. New York: Oxford University Press, 1982.

5

———— ∞∞∞ ————

Women and Religion

Religion was central to the lives of most seventeenth-century colonists who came to America. Many fled persecution in Europe because they would not renounce their passionately held convictions. Praying for a chance at a better existence elsewhere, they looked at the colonies being established across the sea and imagined new homes and opportunities there. In the New World, groups such as the Puritans and Quakers created societies based around their religious beliefs; however, the model societies they envisioned could not survive the divisiveness caused by the expansion of the settlements, nor the loss of mission felt by succeeding generations. Nevertheless, in these early American colonies, religion was such an integral part of life for most people that it cannot be separated from other aspects of people's existence.

This was particularly true in the Puritan colonies of New England. The Church of England was created in 1531 when Henry VIII broke from the Church of Rome and made himself head of the Church of England to divorce his wife, Catherine of Aragon, and marry Anne Boleyn. During the reign of his daughter, Queen Elizabeth (1558–1603), the Church of England (the Anglican Church) became firmly established. Yet Puritans believed that the Protestant Anglican Church continued the practices and symbols of Roman Catholicism in its rituals, in the vestments worn by its clergymen, and in the training and character of its clergy. They sought to purify the church in a number of ways, such as by eliminating all of the sacraments, except for baptism and communion. Under Elizabeth's successor, James I, Anglican bishops began to attack Puritans, while they strengthened their own position. Religion and politics merged as the merchants and less powerful gentry, many of whom were Puritans, began to oppose the king and nobles and struggled to gain power in Parliament. A Puritan/Parliamentary party emerged, and by the time James' son Charles I came to power, conditions were ripe for Civil War.[1]

Under Charles, the Anglican Church became more formal and closer in form to the Roman Catholic Church. It also became even less tolerant of Puritans. William Laud, who became Archbishop of Canterbury in 1633, took firm action against Puritan ministers; many were removed from their pulpits, and some were imprisoned. As early as 1626, some Puritans began to make arrangements to leave England to escape persecution there. In 1630, hundreds of settlers left England to establish a new colony across the sea, beginning the Great Migration. (See Chapter 3 on immigration.)[2]

Puritanism encompassed more than simply a way of looking at doctrine or church practices. It was an all-encompassing way of life. For Puritans, the secular and spiritual were completely interwoven. In the desire to create their "city on a hill," Puritans believed that what they did and how they behaved served both as a model for the world and as a testament to their covenant with God. Puritans did not just want to change the practices of the English church, they wanted to reform society.

The meetinghouses built by Puritans in New England reflected their belief that church and state should not be separated. Many were similar in design to English town halls, and in fact, the meetinghouses were used for town meetings. In keeping with their desire to simplify the church, the meetinghouses were austere, with walls painted white and without ornamentation. The seats faced the centrally located pulpit. Seating was assigned by churchwardens on the basis of wealth, age, and status in the community, and disagreements often arose over where a person was seated.[3]

Each congregation was composed of members who had demonstrated and testified about their personal relationship with God, but church attendance was required for both members and nonmembers. Churchwardens inspected houses to make sure that all townsfolk attended services. They were particularly interested in making sure that young maidservants who were left home to watch young children were not entertaining young men. Each congregation was independent and led by a minister and lay leaders. Although both men and women became church members, only men could become ministers, vote on church matters, or lead public prayers. Moreover, men generally testified publicly before the congregation, while women usually related their testimony in private, and had a male member read it to the congregation. Women were church members, but they were not supposed to speak in church.[4]

Churches were generally located in the center of town, and they were supported by taxes—paid by men—but women often influenced their husbands and fathers in private. Actually being able to get to a church in early New England was one issue of great concern to female church members. As towns grew, residents of farms far away from the town center sometimes found it difficult to make it to church. It was particularly inconvenient for women who were pregnant or nursing infants. As Hannah Gallop noted in a letter to her uncle, John Winthrop, Jr., when mothers had to spend all day in town without eating, those "that have young children sucking, manie times are brought exeding faint, & mutch weakened, & divers are not able to goe al winter."[5]

Faced with the difficulty of getting to church, some women took action to participate in services. For example, in 1677, the men of Chebacco, Massachusetts, petitioned the town of Ipswich to permit them to call a minister and form a church of their own because it was difficult for people to get to church. The town replied that there was not enough money and implied that the residents of Chebacco had brought about their problem by moving outside of the town. Yet, it was the women of Chebacco who were most inconvenienced. Several of the women decided "without the knowledge of theire husbands and with the advice of some few men went to other towns and got help and raised the house that we intended for a meeting house if we could git liberty." The women were fined for contempt of authority. Nevertheless, a few months later, Chebacco did receive permission to bring in a minister, and they had a meetinghouse for services.[6]

The role of women within the Puritan church was ambiguous. Theologically, all souls were equal and capable of achieving grace, but only men could become ministers or publicly espouse doctrine. Furthermore, although women could (and should) be pious and virtuous, they needed to be restrained, led, and guided by their husbands or fathers. According to popular belief, women were weak, dangerous, and lustful "daughters of Eve" who were easily tempted and who could easily lead men astray. By making the carefully ordered family the center of society, Puritans believed they could also keep society in order. Families were "the little commonwealth," and mirrored the hierarchical society of the seventeenth century. Even though women held an important place within the family as wives and mothers, it was the father who was the undisputable head of the family. (See Chapter 1.)[7]

Still, it was possible for any soul—male or female—to achieve salvation. As a consequence, Puritan clergymen and leaders might admit, albeit reluctantly, that God *could* speak through a woman; however, they were not likely to believe that anyone who threatened the patriarchal order or challenged the authority of ministers or magistrates was divinely inspired. Since many among the clergy believed women were weak, easily misled, and potentially evil, they were more likely to think that any woman who dared to speak in public and defy church leaders had been led astray by wickedness.[8] Many Puritan women internalized these negative views about female depravity. In conversion testimony, they frequently noted that they were wicked sinners and full of sin. In contrast, men more commonly confessed to particular sins without claiming to be inherently evil.[9]

In one example from the confessions recorded by Thomas Shepard, minister of the First Church of Cambridge Massachusetts, Mistress Mary Gookin stated, "I thought my sins were so great that I knew not what to say in presence of God, but to lie at his feet. . . . I saw I could do nothing but sin in all I did, sin in praying and hearing, and my sins appeared great in God's sight."[10]

Yet some women felt compelled to speak out, trusting that they were performing God's will. Anne Hutchinson, who with her husband and children immigrated to Massachusetts in 1634, believed she had a right to hold religious meetings in her home. (For more information about immigration, see Chapter 3.) She declared, "It is said, I will poure my Spirit upon your Daughters, and they shall prophesie, &c. If God give mee a gift of Prophecy, I may use it."[11]

Anne Hutchinson was a devoutly religious woman. When the Reverend John Cotton had to flee England because of religious persecution, she convinced her husband that they should also emigrate. Shortly after their arrival in Boston, she passed her membership examination, and both she and her husband, William, became members of the church. Yet within a few months, Anne Hutchinson was expressing religious views that questioned the teaching and thus, the authority of the religious leaders of the colony. Initially, she voiced her opinions only to women who gathered at the homes of women in childbirth. Although Anne Hutchinson was not the official midwife in Boston, she attended many births, and she was knowledgeable about childbirth and midwifery. She gave birth to fifteen children, thirteen of whom survived.[12] John Cotton later wrote, "she did much good in our Town, in womans meeting at Childbirth-Travells, wherein shee was not only skillful and helpfull, but readily fell into good discourse with the women about their spiritual estates."[13] Because these discussions took place when men were not present, it took some time for male authorities to learn of Mistress Hutchinson's opinions.

After a time, however, gossip about Anne Hutchinson spread, and it would have been difficult not to know that she was holding religious meetings. As her neighbor John Winthrop reported, she began holding meetings in her own home twice a week with sixty to eighty women attending each meeting. Eventually, some of the women began bringing their husbands to the meetings. Moreover, instead of simply explaining John Cotton's sermons, she began "to set forth her own stuffe." [14]

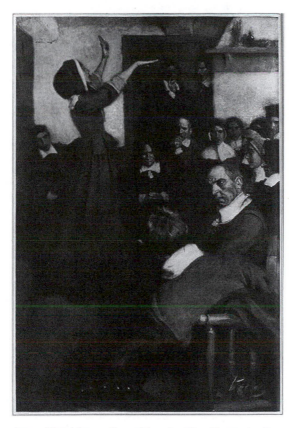

Anne Hutchinson Preaching in Her House in Boston, 1901. Courtesy of Library of Congress.

Anne Hutchinson's religious meetings came at a time when the colony was facing threats from outside in the Pequot War, as well as threats from within, as her followers questioned the authority of the colony's ministers. The colony's leaders also considered Anne Hutchinson's "own stuffe" threatening because she insisted that salvation came from God and that it could not be achieved through doing good works, reading the Bible, or behaving in a pious manner. Although this belief was consistent with Puritan thought, Anne Hutchinson and her supporters took it to an extreme so that people began to doubt the ministers.[15]

Edward Johnson, who moved to Boston in 1636 with his family, wrote about a conversation he had with one of Anne Hutchinson's followers. The man allegedly said to Johnson:

> Come along with me, says one of them, i'le bringe you to a Woman that
> Preaches better Gospell then any of your black-coates that have been at the

Ninneversity, a Woman of another kinde of spirit, who hath had many Revelations of things to come, and for my part, saith hee, I had rather hear
such a one that speaks from the meere motion of the spirit, without any
study at all, then any of your learned Scrollers.[16]

By the start of 1637, Anne Hutchinson's supporters, including Reverend John Cotton and Reverend John Wheelwright, her brother-in-law,
began to openly oppose the colony's ministers. Reverend Wheelwright
accused them of supporting the Covenant of Works over the Covenant of
Grace. Reverend Wheelwright was tried and banished from the colony,
and then Anne Hutchinson was put on trial on November 7, 1637, for
"traduceing the mi[niste]rs & their ministry in this country." This civil
trial was the first of her two trials. As a result of that trial, she was banished from the colony, and in the following church trial, she was
excommunicated.

Anne Hutchinson threatened the Massachusetts Bay Colony in a number of ways. In Anglo-American society, it was men who spoke publicly,
elucidated religious doctrine, made the rules, and held the political power.
In Puritan New England, where the well-ordered family was considered
the foundation of society, men were expected to control their wives, children, servants, and other female dependents. Anne Hutchinson threatened society both by going outside her female role—suggesting that she
was not under control of a man—and for her religious beliefs, which
emphasized an individual's direct relationship with God through revelations, thus making the spiritual guidance of ministers unnecessary.

Anne Hutchinson and her family moved to Rhode Island, a colony
populated by other Massachusetts Bay exiles and religious dissidents,
including Anabaptists and Quakers. Later, she moved to New Netherland.
After her exile, John Winthrop and others continued to record stories
about her in their journals and letters. They commented on the birth of
the "monster" to her follower Mary Dyer (discussed in Chapters 2 and 4),
which John Winthrop learned about as the two women left the church
following Anne Hutchinson's excommunication, and the subsequent birth
of a "monster" to Anne Hutchinson herself. Many viewed the births of
the deformed infants as a judgment of God on the women and their heretical beliefs. Similarly, when Indians killed Anne Hutchinson and fifteen
other people in New Netherland in 1643, they believed it was an act of
divine retribution.[17]

Historians have viewed Anne Hutchinson and the conflict that arose
over her meetings in various ways. Some have emphasized the theological
aspects of the episode; others have commented primarily on the political
ramifications, or on the gender issues that arose from it. The events of
the 1630s stifled both religious and political dissent, as a seditious libel

law was passed immediately after John Wheelwright's trial, and numerous troublemakers were banished from the colony. Moreover, after this time, authorities were more inclined to perceive any woman who questioned religious doctrine or practices as a major threat to the established hierarchical society.[18]

Most Puritan women did not challenge the church or its ministers; they were content with preparing for sanctification and becoming full members of the church. Indeed, by the eighteenth century, New England women were more likely to become church members than their husbands, and as their numbers grew, they exerted an informal influence over the church and its ministers. Yet even before that time, a minister who alienated his female parishioners did so at his own risk.[19]

The Reverend Jeremiah Shepard discovered this unfortunate fact in the town of Rowley, where he was invited to preach in 1672. The town's previous minister, Ezekiel Rogers, had died, but the town had another candidate for the position, Samuel Phillips, a minister older than Jeremiah Shepard, who was serving as a teacher in the town. The Reverend Shepard made it through his first year, and his invitation to preach was renewed. Yet a few months later his membership in the church was denied, and in fact, the church members voted to have him leave before his time was up. According to Samuel Phillips, the church thought he had disregarded his studies and his family, but apparently he had also upset Samuel Phillips and his wife. As he recalled:

> In the time of my wife's long and dangerous sickness he came below to look upon her and there took offense that she did not show him respect though my wife affirms that she bowed her head as well as she could being then entering into her ague fit, but he never would come to see her though I wished him to do it.[20]

In addition to upsetting Samuel Phillip's wife, it appears that Jeremiah Shepard also had difficulty with other women in the town. For example, he blamed Goody Elithorp for the church's opposition to his ministry. He exclaimed that "if she had an opportunity he doubted not but she would cut his throat, yea, so far as a man can know a woman's heart by her words she would actually do it."[21] Although Reverend Shepard may not have lived up to the expectations of the men of Rowley in some ways, it appears that his conflicts with the women of the town played a major role in the decision to let him go. The women of Rowley did not mount a public campaign against him, nor did they speak out in public forums; however, they influenced their husbands and other men who made the decision not to extend the minister's tenure in Rowley.

Some women challenged the religious orthodoxy of the Puritans in more overt ways. For instance, Anne Eaton, the wife of the governor of

New Haven, was excommunicated for her adherence to Anabaptist beliefs, specifically her opposition to infant baptism. She walked out of or did not attend church services, which made her actions "a public offence." Her crime was considered even worse because, she did not seek advice or counsel from her husband or pastor. To seventeenth-century Puritans, her marital problems and her disinclination to submit to her husband were a clear result of her heresy, and therefore, a threat to the social and political order of the colony. In addition, like Anne Hutchinson, she was a woman of high social status who could easily convince others, especially other women, to follow her heretical ways.[22]

Although Puritan authorities considered women such as Anne Hutchinson and Anne Eaton to be threats to society, they initially welcomed the women. The Massachusetts Bay Colony feared Quakers from the very beginning, however, and imprisoned, maimed, banished, and even executed them. Quakers attracted many women because they believed that all people should be open to the Holy Spirit (the Inner Light). Quakers permitted—even encouraged—women to speak in public and to become preachers. Several women connected with Anne Hutchinson subsequently became Quakers; for example, her sister, Katherine Marbury, and her supporter, Mary Dyer.[23]

At least to some extent, Quakers did pose a threat to the political and religious authorities of Massachusetts. Quakers believed that all people carried the inner light and could experience divine revelation. Therefore, there was no need for ordained clergy; women and men, educated, and uneducated, all could speak and preach the word of God. The religious beliefs of Quakers carried over to the social and political realms, and they rejected a social hierarchy based on class or wealth, since all people were equal before God. At the most basic level, their refusal to swear oaths in court or to doff their caps to their superiors, enraged their neighbors. As well, they believed that governments had no right to interfere with religious beliefs.

Whether Quakers posed an actual threat to order or not, Massachusetts Bay enacted severe laws against them in 1656 following the appearance in Boston of Quakers Anne Austin and Mary Fisher. The women were not the first Quakers to arrive in the colony, but they were the first in Boston. Both women were accused of witchcraft, and they were strip searched aboard their ship and their bodies examined for devil's marks before they disembarked. After that, they were imprisoned, and the books found with them were burned. The authorities in Massachusetts considered the women to be so dangerous that their cell windows were boarded up, and no one was permitted to speak to them. They were banished from the colony after being imprisoned for five weeks. After they were exiled,

Quaker Preaching, 1657. Quaker women traveled and preached throughout the colonies. This nineteenth-century engraving depicts Quaker women preaching in the streets of New Amsterdam. Courtesy of The Granger Collection, New York.

the General Court passed laws specifically against Quakers, which may have eliminated the need to charge Quakers with witchcraft in order to have them removed from the colony.[24] The laws against Quakers included fines for ship captains who knowingly brought Quakers to the colonies, fines for possessing Quaker books, and whipping and imprisonment for Quakers who came to the colony. In 1657, the laws were made harsher: male Quakers who returned to Massachusetts Bay after being banished would have an ear cut off. If the person returned again, his other ear would be cut off. Quaker women who returned to the colony after being banished would be whipped. A third return could bring branding of the tongue with a hot iron, while a fourth return meant execution for men or women.[25]

Mary Dyer was one of the Quakers who returned several times to test the law and challenge the authority of Puritan leaders. She was twice sentenced to death and eventually executed in 1660. Like Anne Hutchinson, she posed a threat to the male hierarchy of Puritan New England by speaking out and proclaiming her message in public. During Anne Hutchinson's church trial, the minister Hugh Peter declared, "You have stept out of your place, you have rather bine a Husband than a Wife and a preacher than Hearer; and a Magistrate than a Subject."[26] Anne Hutchinson was one woman who threatened the very structure of Puritan society, but Mary Dyer, as a Quaker, was even more dangerous. Because Quakers permitted and even encouraged women to preach in public, Puritans considered the whole sect an enormous menace to the social order. After Anne Hutchinson was banished from Massachusetts, she never returned. Mary Dyer, however, returned to Boston, even after she was sentenced to death the first time and forced to leave. At that time, she had been given a last-second reprieve and removed from the scaffold after the rope was already around her neck. Her two companions and fellow Quakers, William Robinson and Marmaduke Stephenson, had already been executed. Mary Dyer refused to be silent; she insisted that she was speaking the word of God when she spoke out against unjust and cruel laws. During her first trial, she urged the magistrates to search for the inner light within them and told them that they "will not repent that you were kept from Shedding blood though it were by a woman."[27] As she stood on the scaffold the second time, she refused to repent, and proclaimed again that she was called by God to testify against evil and unjust laws.[28]

By going beyond their role as wives and mothers, in fact, sometimes leaving their husbands and children to speak in public, it was obvious to the Puritan ministers and magistrates that Quaker women were hazardous to and perhaps even intent upon destroying the well-ordered family, and by extension, society. Puritan authorities believed that by subverting the hierarchy of the family, Quakers loosened other restraints, as well. They assumed, for instance, that Quaker women were sexually promiscuous because Quaker men did not restrain them, giving their innate lascivious natures free rein. Similarly, because they were not under the control of their husbands, rumors of infidelity had surfaced about Anne Hutchinson and Anne Eaton during their trials. Nevertheless, the fact that Quaker men condoned the independent behavior of Quaker women disturbed the sensibilities of Puritan and made Quakers appear to be a great menace to society.[29]

Religious crises often appear when there are other stresses or changes occurring in a society. This was true in New England. For example, during the Anne Hutchinson controversy, New England colonists were engaged in the Pequot War; furthermore, some of her supporters refused to fight because they felt the militia officers were wicked.[30] Another Indian War, King Philip's War, provoked additional stresses and changes in the 1670s. (For more on women and war, see Chapter 6.) Yet the Puritan colonies were never the totally homogenous, stable communities that the original colonists had envisioned. There were a few nonbelievers right from the beginning, but as the colonies grew and expanded, the population became much more diverse. Massachusetts had approximately 24,000 colonists in 1665; by 1690, its population had more than doubled. The city of Boston had over 5,000 inhabitants in 1690. As more settlers arrived, the colonies expanded farther west into the interior and north to Maine into Indian territory. Serious conflicts took place between English settlers and Native Americans, sometimes aided by the French. In addition, the increased commercial activity, as well as the expansion of Boston and port cities, brought people with different religions and cultural backgrounds to Boston and other seaports, creating more divisions in Puritan society.[31]

The tensions and disruptions caused by the New England colonies' expansion helped create a large witchcraft scare that began in 1692 in Salem, Massachusetts. This witchcraft outbreak was not the only one to take place in New England, nor were accusations of witchcraft limited to British North America. During the Middle Ages, some women and men had been accused and tried as witches, but larger and more prolonged witchcraft scares took place throughout Europe between 1550 and 1650. There were witch hunts in nearly every European county, and England and Scotland each had at least one massive witch panic in the seventeenth century.[32] The trials and executions of witches were particularly numerous and brutal in parts of Switzerland and Germany affected by the Reformation and the Thirty Years War. Historians suggest that ideas about women's innate evil and licentiousness combined with social and political tension helped to fuel these witch hunts.[33]

In both Europe and the American colonies, most accused witches were women. Men who were accused of being witches were often related to women who had been accused of witchcraft. Of the 344 people accused of being witches in New England in 1620–1725, 267 (78 percent) were women. The number is even higher for those tried: 103 people were tried as witches, and 89 (86 percent) were women.[34]

In both Europe and the British North American colonies, witches were accused of using *maleficium*, or using supernatural powers to harm others. Most commonly, witches were said to have hurt their neighbors by causing someone to become ill, or even to die. Often this was a baby or young child who had appeared healthy prior to the witch's spell. Witches were also accused of preventing women from reproducing by causing miscarriages, stillbirths, and horribly deformed infants. They were blamed for preventing men from fathering children with their wives by making them unable to maintain an erection, and they were also accused of seducing men and taking them away from their wives or betrothed. Problems with livestock, crops, and even domestic disturbances, such as spoiled beer, were all blamed on witches. Even foul weather, especially storms at sea, might be blamed on a witch. (For an example, see Chapter 3.)[35]

As in the witch hunts of Europe, some historians suggest that social and political unrest helped to fuel the largest witchcraft crisis in British North America—that of Salem—although witches were tried and a few were executed during other times and in other colonies. For example, in 1626 the neighbors of Goodwife Wright, a middle-aged Virginia midwife, accused her of being a witch. As they were associated with life and death, knowledgeable about healing and medicinal plants, and often knew the most intimate secrets of their neighbors, midwives were frequently accused of being witches. Witches were blamed for situations that perverted the role of women. Instead of giving life, they took it away; instead of breastfeeding infants, they nursed demons. When a mother or infant seemed to suffer or die under suspicious circumstances, the midwife was often accused of practicing witchcraft. Goodwife Wright seemed to have the ability to predict the deaths of her neighbors. Since life spans were short in the disease-filled Chesapeake area, it is not odd that her predictions came true, but they probably caused great anxiety in people who most likely were already fearful of dying. Since pregnancy and childbirth increased a woman's chance of dying, Goodwife Wright was probably not welcomed as a midwife. Although midwives were often well respected, her predictions and quarrels with other women made Goodwife Wright the target of neighborhood gossip, as were many accused witches.[36] Because so many women's "reputacons have been so much impaired and their lives brought in question," Norfolk, Virginia, passed a law in 1655 stating that people who spread rumors about women being witches would be fined one thousand pounds of tobacco if they could not prove the accusation.[37]

Throughout much of the seventeenth century, women who were seen as argumentative, disruptive, or not under the control of a man might be called witches. For example, John Winthrop suspected Anne Hutchinson was a witch because she was able to seduce upstanding citizens into supporting her heretical beliefs.[38] Most suspected women, however, were not formally tried as witches.

The crisis that began in Salem Village in 1692 differs from earlier witchcraft incidents in a number of ways. For one thing, the number of people accused during this crisis is a great deal larger than in any other witchcraft panic in the British North American colonies. Furthermore, those accused included some of the types of people normally accused of witchcraft—poor, widowed, disgruntled, middle-aged or elderly women—but also included those who would not normally be accused. The possessed accusers were mainly young, single women, many of them servants, a group who rarely spoke in public and whose opinions normally held no weight. In addition, although this event is usually referred to as the Salem witchcraft crisis, a majority of the accused came from nearby towns in Essex County, Massachusetts, and people from as far away as Boston and Ipswich were accused of being witches.

As a result of the Indian wars that had been taking place on the Maine frontier for two decades, many settlers fled the area. Many of them saw their family members and friends killed and their homes destroyed during raids by the Indians. A number of the refugees settled in Essex County, including some young women who lived as servants in other people's homes. Later, several of them became involved in the witchcraft crisis. Others involved in the crisis were not refugees, but they had a connection to Maine or to Indians because they were involved in trading, had fought there, or had relatives involved. Uncertainty was endemic to the frontier. The two decades of fighting produced enormous fear and anxiety in the population. (For more on the connection between the outbreak of witchcraft in Salem and the Indian Wars, see Chapter 6.)

These anxieties were coupled with other existing tensions within Salem Village. Salem Town was founded in 1626. The seaport grew and prospered, but new settlers seeking land settled outside of the town in what became Salem Village (not becoming the independent town of Danvers until 1752). Residents of Salem Village wanted their own church and minister, as it was difficult for them to get to the town center for services. The Massachusetts General Court finally gave them permission to have their own meetinghouse in 1672; however, Salem Village was still not totally independent of Salem Town. In fact, the residents of Salem Village were forced to ask for help from Salem Town, the General Court, or other governing bodies when disputes arose, and disputes did arise over each of the first four ministers in Salem Village.[39]

The Reverend Samuel Parris, the fourth minister, was hired in 1689, and dissent and division grew in Salem Village during his tenure there. Before Samuel Parris became the minister, there was no formal church in Salem Village—that is, no congregation composed of covenanted saints. With the hiring of Reverend Parris, a church was formed, initially consisting of twenty-six members plus the Reverend Parris, who was then ordained by nearby clergy. Only members of the church could take communion, and only an ordained minister could administer communion or baptize babies. Since the church also rejected the Halfway Covenant, which permitted baptism for the children of any baptized person, only infants who had at least one parent who was a church member could be baptized. Consequently, there was a sharp division between members and non-members, leading to many in Salem Village who were dissatisfied with the Reverend Parris's ministry. Some of the dissatisfied Salem Villagers refused to pay his salary or to make sure that he had firewood. In response, Parris's sermons contained sharp rebukes of his critics.[40]

In January 1691–1692, Parris's nine-year-old daughter, Betty, and his twelve-year-old niece, Abigail Williams, became afflicted with fits as if they were being bitten, pinched, and choked. After several weeks of these fits and consultations with a local doctor, it was decided that the girls were bewitched. Samuel Parris ordered fasting and prayers in his house and in the community, but a neighbor, who was a church member, asked the Reverend Parris's Indian slave, Tituba, to make a witch-cake, composed from the urine of the girls mixed with rye meal and baked in ashes. It was given to the family dog to eat. This ritual was supposed to reveal the identity of a witch, and is an example of the folk magic rituals still practiced in Salem Village, even by devout church members.[41]

Reverend Parris was outraged that the ritual was performed and spoke out in church against the neighbor, Mary Sibley. Meanwhile, the two afflicted girls accused Tituba of being a witch, and other girls began to be afflicted. Tituba confessed that she had signed a compact with the Devil, and named Sarah Good, a homeless beggar, and Sarah Osborn, a woman who had been involved in disputes in the village, as witches. Both ministers and magistrates were convinced that these women and perhaps many others in their community had conspired with the Devil.

In April, the number of accusations suddenly increased after Abigail Hobbs confessed on April 19 that she was a witch, named other witches, and connected the events in Salem, witchcraft, and attacks made by the Wabanaki Indians on New England settlements.[42] A spectral encounter by Ann Putnam, Jr. with Salem's former minister, George Burroughs, made the connections even stronger. As Ann, Jr. testified in a deposition to the Grand Jury, she had seen the "Apperishtion of a Minister" who tormented her and demanded that she sign his book. He then told her that:

> his name was George Burroughs and that he had had three wives: and that he had bewitched the Two first of them of death: that he kiled Mist. Lawson because she was so unwilling to goe from the village and also killed Mr. Lawsons child because he went to the eastward with Sir Edmon and preached soe: to the souldiers and that he had bewicthed a grate many souldiers to death at the eastward, when Sir Edmon was their, and that he had made Abigail Hobbs a wicth and severall wicthes more ... and he also tould me that he was above wicth for he was a conjurer.[43]

George Burroughs was an earlier minister whose time in Salem Village had been contentious. In fact, he and his parishioners clashed over the payment of his salary. Reverend Burroughs left Salem in 1683 and then moved to the frontier. He and his first wife lived with the Putnam family for the first few months of his time in Salem, and when Burroughs was later brought back to Salem in 1692 and tried and executed for being a wizard, the Putnams testified about his abusive behavior towards this wife. There were also rumors about Burroughs' mistreatment of his second wife. Women from his congregation in Maine reported that she had appealed to her neighbors for help and that Burroughs was extremely anxious to keep her from talking to other women. In fact, the female communities in both Salem and in Maine knew Burroughs' secrets—that he abused his wives. In all likelihood, Ann, Jr. and the other "afflicted" girls had heard the whispers about Burroughs in both Salem and in Maine, where Abigail Hobbs and some of the other girls had known each other.

The accusations against Burroughs and the connection to the frontier changed the course of the Salem crisis and turned it into an episode that differed substantially from previous witchcraft crises. Reverend Burroughs was named countless times as the leader of the witches and the man who united the invisible world with the visible devils, the Wabanakis. Since many of the residents of Essex County had had direct experience with the brutal Indian attacks, they had a great fear of Indians. As their stories circulated, they induced more fear among people living in the region. Burroughs had escaped Indian attacks in Maine, while others perished, and he had become involved in controversies in his frontier parishes, as well as in Salem. As a result of these April events, the afflicted girls continued to accuse more people, some of them well-respected church members.[44]

In May 1692, Sir William Phips, the newly appointed royal governor, arrived in the colony with a new royal charter. He created a special Oyer and Terminer Court to hear the witchcraft cases, which were overburdening the local courts, as the jails filled with accused witches. The accusations spread to towns outside of Salem, even as far as Boston. The court, headed by Lieutenant Governor William Stoughton, upheld the use of spectral evidence. This meant that the court accepted as evidence the testimony of a witchcraft victim who declared that the specter of a person was his or her tormentor, even though others could not see the specter. The admission of spectral evidence led to more arrests, and those arrested were presumed guilty. Moreover, since the beginning of the crisis, the accused witches had been examined in front of those they had supposedly afflicted, other afflicted girls, and the public. Forty-seven people eventually confessed to being witches and making pacts with the Devil. Many of them confessed after it became clear that those who did so would not be

Regni *ANNÆ* Reginæ Decimo.

Province of the Massachusetts-Bay.

AN ACT,

Made and Passed by the Great and General Court or Assembly of Her Majesty's Province of the Massachusetts-Bay in New-England, Held at Boston the 17th Day of October, 1711.   *Nat Lambert Salem*

Jan 28ª 1808

An Act to Reverse the Attainders of *George Burroughs* and others for Witchcraft.

FORASMUCH *as in the Year of our Lord One Thousand Six Hundred Ninety Two, Several Towns within this Province were Infested with a horrible Witchcraft or Possession of Devils ; And at a Special Court of Oyer and Terminer holden at* Salem, *in the County of* Essex *in the same Year One Thousand Six Hundred Ninety Two,* George Burroughs *of Wells,* John Procter, George Jacob, John Willard, Giles Core, *and his Wife,* Rebecca Nurse, *and* Sarah Good, *all of* Salem *aforesaid* : Elizabeth How, *of Ipswich,* Mary Eastey, Sarah Wild *and* Abigail Hobbs *all of Topsfield* : Samuel Wardell, Mary Parker, Martha Carrier, Abigail Falkner, Anne Foster, Rebecca Eames, Mary Post, *and* Mary Lacey, *all of Andover* : Mary Bradbury *of Salisbury* : *and* Dorcas Hoar *of Beverly* ; *Were severally Indicted, Convicted and Attained of Witchcraft, and some of them put to Death, Others lying still under the like Sentence of the said Court, and liable to have the same Executed upon them.*

A   The

Act to pardon those accused of witchcraft in Massachusetts, October 17, 1711. Courtesy of Library of Congress.

executed; however, some of them later recanted their confessions, raising doubt about the validity of all the confessions.

As respected and high-status people began to be accused, public opinion turned against the trials. The Reverend Increase Mather and other ministers asked Governor Phips to stop the trials, which he did in 1693. Mather's essay, *Cases of Conscience*, which was first given as a sermon, argued that the words of those who were possessed by the Devil could not be believed because the Devil lies. Confessing witches also were "not such credible Witnesses" because they lied or were deluded by the Devil. Accepting Mather's arguments meant witchcraft and the belief in witches was ending. Even cases of *maleficium* could no longer be brought before the courts because it could be the Devil causing harm by using the form of a particular woman when she was not responsible for the harmful acts. Criticism of the whole Salem episode began to grow, and there was public acknowledgment that some of the executed had been innocent.[45] As a result, Samuel Parris was ousted from his Salem pulpit in 1696. In 1697, Boston declared a Day of Repentance. Judges and jurors apologized for their part in the crisis, and Anne Putnam, Jr., one of the original afflicted girls and one of the most vocal of the accusers, confessed her crimes before the church congregation of Salem Village in 1706. In 1701, the colony of Massachusetts overturned all of the convictions in the Salem witchcraft trials. The belief in witches and spirits did not totally disappear, but it made way for the rational, scientific beliefs of the Enlightenment.

The Salem witchcraft crisis stands out for the sheer number of people involved. At least twenty-five people died—nineteen were executed by hanging, one was tortured to death, and five died while in jail. More than 160 people were accused of being witches, and nearly fifty of them confessed.[46] The Salem witchcraft crisis is also significant for other reasons—the admission of spectral evidence, the references to witches signing covenants with the devil instead of simply performing acts of *maleficium*, and the indulgence of authorities towards the girls and young women victims, who under normal circumstances would never have been permitted to speak in church, freely interrupting ministers and services. Although historians argue over the cause of their afflictions, it appears that the suffering of the girls was real—at least at first. After they began to receive so much attention, it must have been exhilarating to suddenly have the power and ability to make people listen to them. It seems likely that there was some collusion between the young victims, as they described similar specters and events, especially since they were examined together.

Nevertheless, the many connections to Indians and to the Maine frontier also set this crisis apart from others. Before the name of George Burroughs had even been mentioned, there was the involvement and the confession of Tituba, the Parrises' slave. She was known to be an Indian, although Reverend Parris probably purchased her in Barbados. Still as a woman and as an Indian, she was doubly suspected of being a creature of darkness, easily seduced by the Devil. As she was a slave, it was assumed that she was discontented—the type of person usually lured by the Devil.

Native Americans living in New England were often feared and demonized by Puritans. Frequently Puritan theologians described them as aiding the Devil, or being used by God to punish the Puritans. In fact, the association of Indians with the Devil goes back to earlier encounters the English had with Indians. George Percy, John Rolfe, and John Smith all described the American Indians they observed in Virginia as devil worshipers. Many also believed that witches incited them to partake in savage rituals.[47] Nevertheless, Puritans did make some attempts to convert Native Americans to Christianity. The most successful of their missionary attempts was on Martha's Vineyard, where many of the Wampanoags became Christians, filtering and interpreting Christianity through their own religious beliefs.[48]

Puritans were especially interested in changing Indian marital customs and household arrangements; however, these transformations were not always accomplished easily. Even Native American men and women who sincerely desired to become Christians sometimes posed questions that missionaries found difficult to answer. For example, they wondered what would happen if a man who had more than one wife became a Christian? Was the man supposed to cast off all but the first wife? What would happen to the other spouses and their children?[49]

Native American women had other questions. One woman wondered about a verse from Revelations 12:1–2: "there appeared a great wonder in heaven; a woman clothed with the sun, and the moon under her feet, and upon her head a crown of twelve stars: And she being with child, travailing in birth, and pained to be delivered." As the Indians believed women should not cry out in pain during childbirth, how could such descriptions be reconciled with their ways?[50]

Native American women who converted to Christianity found their lives changed in many ways. For example, women normally lived apart from their families while they were menstruating. For Puritans, however, women going out and living alone did not fit their model of the household in which a family, including all the single young women and men, lived together under one roof with the father in charge. Accordingly, they passed a law in "praying towns" assessing a twenty-shilling fine on menstruating women who performed the "old Ceremony of the Maide walking alone and living apart so many days."[51]

Nevertheless, missionaries who sought to mold Indian life to fit Puritan ideals sometimes had to adjust their methods and principles. Because Native American women were often more visible in the community than men, missionaries urged them to reform their husbands and to bring them to Christianity. In this context, they advised Indian women to speak out, even if it meant opposing or contradicting their husbands.[52]

Catholics in New France were also interested in converting the native population to Christianity. (French Catholics and English Protestants brought their political/religious rivalries to the American colonies, and placed the Native Americans in the middle.) The Catholic missions of New France included women, both laywomen and nuns. Jeanne Mance was not a nun, but she went to Montréal in 1642 and later took charge of the city's first hospital. Ursuline nun Marie Guyart, "Marie of the Incarnation," became the first woman missionary in New France when she arrived in 1639. She served there for forty years, founding a school for Native American children and publishing a French-Algonquian dictionary.[53]

The extreme importance of religion in the founding of the New England colonies, in the conflicts they had with Indians (and the French), and in events such as the Salem witchcraft crises sometimes overshadows the importance of religion in the other British colonies in North America. The English Civil War and the Restoration had an enormous effect on all of the colonies. Although some Puritans were involved in founding Virginia, the established churches in the colony were Anglican. The few ordained ministers there and the spread-out settlements, however, meant that there were few churches and little official religious presence in Virginia in the early years of settlement. Virginia was the last of the British North American colonies to submit to Oliver Cromwell's rule, and the first to welcome back the new monarch, Charles II, in 1660.

During the Civil War, religious dissenters fled to Virginia, just as they had to Massachusetts and other colonies. As in Massachusetts, they were suspected of trying to overturn the government, and after the Restoration, these dissenters, especially Quakers, were suspected of conspiring against the king. Norfolk County was an area of particular concern for Anglican justices and those concerned with the moral and religious wellbeing of the colony. In part, the problem was due to the lack of ministers. In some cases, ministers who were there refused to perform their duties, as in the case of Reverend Thomas Harrison, who "desented his Ministeriall Office" and would not administer the sacraments.[54]

The county was also a hotbed of dissent. Several times, for example, the whole county was presented by the Grand Jury for failure to observe the Sabbath. In the 1640s, officials tried to repress Puritan thought and keep the sect from meeting. After the Restoration, however, it was Quakers who were seen as a particular menace. Governor Berkley sent directives to local officials demanding that they keep Quakerism from spreading. As in England and New England, authorities were especially concerned with the threat to order brought about by the existence of Quaker women and the inability or disinclination of their husbands to keep them subdued. In Virginia, however, the concerns about Quaker women also included an additional threat: several Quaker women met in private with their slaves. Clearly, if Quaker women believed that not only they, but their slaves, as well, possessed the inner light, and that they were all equal before God, then they presented a very real danger to the social order.

In 1661, Governor Berkeley directed:

All women who should after publicacon of the said proclamation and explanacon continue their said unlawful meeting and breach their schismaticall and heretical doctrines and opinions should by their adjoying magestrate be tendred the oaths of Supremacy and allegeance and the refusees to be Imprisoned according to the Law.[55]

Directives such as these did not prove to be very effective in abolishing dissension in the colony. Moreover, as it began to codify a system of race-based permanent slavery, the colony passed a law in 1667 stating that baptism had no effect on a person's freedom or bondage. Consequently, African slaves who had counted on being freed because they were Christians could no longer count on their petitions for freedom being granted by legislators.[56]

The other Chesapeake colony, Maryland, was founded as a haven for Roman Catholics when Charles I granted a charter to Cecilius Calvert, 2nd Lord Baltimore. Catholics even built a large brick chapel in St. Mary's City in the 1660s. Yet, Puritans and Catholics fought bitterly during the English Civil War during an event known as Ingle's Rebellion or "the Plundering Time." (For more on war, see Chapter 6.) Although there were probably more Protestants in the colony than Catholics even in its earliest years, Anglicans (unlike Puritans) and Catholics usually tolerated one another and even intermarried. In 1692, with a new royal governor, and a Protestant Assembly, the Church of England was established in Maryland.[57]

Both Anglican and Catholic women in Maryland undertook the religious education of their children, especially since priests and ministers were in limited supply in the colony. In fact, many husbands even asked in their wills that their wives provide religion instruction for their children. For example, Catholic John Parsons requested that his wife Mary, "maintain and Educate my said Children bringing them up in the fear of God and the Holy Catholick Religion not at all doubting of her love to and tender care over them." In a similar vein, the Anglican Thomas Stockett wrote that he trusted his wife "will not neglect any Endeavor that shall be tending to [the children's] good both in Religious Education and for the advancement of their temporall ffortunes which I beseech the Lord of Heaven to give his assistance unto."[58]

In addition to providing their children with religious instruction, some Catholic and Protestant Maryland women had religious structures built on their land. The wealthy Catholic landowner Henrietta Maria Neale had a Roman Catholic chapel built on her property. Quaker Anne Ayres Chew donated the land her father left to her in 1658 to the Herring Creek Meeting, so that a meetinghouse could be constructed. There was enough land for a cemetery, as well. In contrast, Elizabeth Baker donated one hundred acres near her home for a church, school, and burial ground. The desire to sponsor and aid their faith was not limited to the richest and most powerful women. Some women who were not wealthy enough to build churches donated smaller sums of money to protect or purchase religious vestments and equipment.[59]

Some Maryland women, however, had the wealth and status to make men listen to their opinions. Mary Taney, who was married to the Calvert County sheriff, was upset about the lack of religious guidance in her community. In 1685, she wrote to the Archbishop of Canterbury and the king asking them to send the funds to build a church and support an Anglican priest, as well as asking them to supply her community with Bibles and religious books. The king sent the requested money, along with Bibles and other texts.[60]

Although Protestants of various sects and Catholics lived together in Maryland, the Middle Colonies of New York, New Jersey, and Pennsylvania had the most diverse populations with a variety of ethnicities and religions. New York had been the colony of New Netherland, founded by the Dutch West Indies Company in 1624, but in addition to the Dutch, there were immigrants from England and New England, French Huguenots, a community of ex-slaves, and a community of Jews from Recife, Brazil. (See Chapter 3.) The colony was taken over by the British in 1664, and East and West Jersey were separated from New York.[61]

During Dutch rule, the Dutch Reformed church had been the official church of the colony, but other religious groups were tolerated. Between 1666 and 1695, New York City had congregations of Jews, Quakers, and Dutch Lutherans, as well as Dutch Reformed and Anglican. Within the Dutch Reformed church, women outnumbered men, with many more women than men joining the congregation, especially between 1696 and 1730. Even Dutch women who were married to English men remained in or joined the Dutch Reformed church. This is not totally surprising, since Dutch religion centered on the home, where women held a great deal of influence.[62]

Though women were not permitted to take an active role in church government, the church did provide them with a sense of community with other women. As the women sat together, they were able to discuss matters of concern or get advice from their friends. Through membership in the Dutch Reformed church, Dutch women were able to continue the customs and traditions of their homeland. As English traditions and law began to supplant Dutch ways, removing the legal rights that Dutch women had had, membership in the church gave them a sense of power and belonging.[63]

Many Africans in New Amsterdam chose to have their children baptized in the city's Dutch church as means of securing their freedom. A

1644 law gave qualified freedom to some of the Dutch West India Company's long time slaves. The freed slaves were give plots of farmland at the outskirts of the city, but they were also warned that their children and future children would be "bound and obligated to serve the Honorable West India Company." Yet critics complained to the Company that it was "contrary to the laws of every people" that children born to free Christian mothers should be slaves, and Africans believed that ties to the Christian community would aid them in securing freedom for their children. To some extent baptism and other Christian rites did aid Africans, however, they did not guarantee freedom. For example, Judith Stuyvesant, the wife of Director-General Petrus Stuyvesant had the African children in her household baptized, but later an official from Curacao wrote Stuyvesant to apologize for the sale of the slave children, "since with great forethought on the part of Madam Stuyvesant . . . they were presented at the baptismal Font."[64]

In contrast to the ease with which the Dutch of New Amsterdam continued the practices of the Dutch Reformed Church, the Jews of New Amsterdam and later New York City and other seaports probably found it difficult to practice Jewish rituals as they had in Europe. Because the populations were not large enough at first, most Jews in the British North American colonies would not have been able to acquire kosher foods, obtain decisions on Jewish matters from rabbis, or even pray in a synagogue. Without a Jewish community that practiced their customs and patronized their businesses, Jewish merchants might have had a problem closing late on Friday afternoons to prepare for the Sabbath. Similarly, since women cooked and prepared food in the home and kept many of the rituals and traditions, it must have been a hardship for them. If a woman gave birth to a baby boy, would the couple be able to find a *mohel* to perform the ritual circumcision of the infant, as Jewish law required? As well, it is impossible to know exactly what married couples did about marital purity in the seventeenth century colonies. Observant Jewish women traditionally slept apart from their husbands during their menstrual periods. Seven days after the menstrual flow has finished, women are supposed to attend a ritual bath called a *mikvah* before they have sexual relations with their husbands. (This practice is still followed by many Jewish couples throughout the world.) In areas without *mikvahs*, it is not known what Jewish women did. Sources indicate that the synagogue in Newport, Rhode Island had a *mikvah* by 1731. By the eighteenth century, several cities in North America had synagogues and large Jewish populations, making it easier for Jewish families to practice their faith.[65]

Pennsylvania also had a diverse population. Although Pennsylvania was founded as a haven for Quakers, the colony followed a policy of religious toleration from the beginning. Charles II granted a charter for

Pennsylvania to William Penn in 1681. Penn was a landed gentleman who had become a member of the Society of Friends (Quakers). It may be that Charles II decided that granting a charter to William Penn was one way of getting rid of the pesky Quakers. Although Charles was not an admirer of the Quakers, who were frequently arrested and imprisoned in England, he demanded that Massachusetts stop maiming and executing them in 1662. It is also possible that Charles granted Penn the land to pay a debt he owed his father, Admiral Sir William Penn.[66]

People of many nationalities and religions flocked to the city of Philadelphia or settled on the rich, fertile farmland surrounding it. Even in 1683, the colony welcomed people from all nations. Francis Daniel Pastorius noted that on his voyage to Pennsylvania, there were men and women from France and the Netherlands, as well as England and Germany. There were also people of many faiths: Catholic, Lutheran, Calvinist, Anabaptist, Anglican, and one Quaker.[67] English Quakers controlled the politics of Pennsylvania until the mid-eighteenth century, but after a few decades they were a minority in the colony. In addition to the English Quakers, the colony boasted a sizeable population of Welsh Quakers, Anglicans, and German Mennonites, as well as people of other religions.[68]

As mentioned previously, Quaker women were considered a serious threat to the social order in both England and the colonies because they preached in public and did not appear to be under the control of their husbands or other male authority figures. George Fox, the founder of the sect, involved women in spreading his message from the start. Many of the earliest traveling ministers, or "public Friends," were women who traveled to the eastern Mediterranean and to Venice, as well as to England's colonies.[69]

Although Quakers had no ordained ministers and little organizational structure at first, George Fox created a structure of monthly, quarterly, and yearly meetings, which was in place by the 1660s. This organizational structure is still used today. Quakers in New Jersey and Pennsylvania were using this system by the 1680s. (Quakers from New England had set up meetings for worship in Shrewsbury and Woodbridge—then part of East Jersey—in the 1660s.) There were separate men's and women's monthly, quarterly, and yearly meetings, each with its own officers who were well-respected Quakers. Although the men's and women's meetings were separate, it was not set up that way because women were considered unworthy or below men, but rather so that sensitive issues could be discussed between groups of men or women. Moreover, this system permitted male and female Friends to share the workload equally.

In 1675, the women's meeting in Lancashire, England, sent out an epistle to other women's meetings, including some in the American colonies.

In the epistle, they noted that wherever there were men's monthly meetings, there should also be women's monthly meetings. The epistle described the types of transgressions the women's meetings should examine, as well as stating that it was "duely Incumbent upon us to look into our families, and to prevent out Children of running into the world for husbands, or for wives." In addition, before marrying both women and men were supposed to be examined first by the women's meeting and then by the men's meeting. Besides taking care of their own families and examining those Friends who wanted to marry, the epistle further observed that the women's meeting was responsible for caring for the poor and sick, and that a responsible woman should keep notes of their transactions.[70]

Well-respected men and women led each meeting and watched over the Quaker community, just as husbands and wives watched over their families.[71] George Fox wrote in 1672:

> For man and woman were helps-meet in the image of God, and in righteousness and holiness, in the dominion, before they fell; but after the fall in the transgression, the man was to rule over his wife; but in the restoration by Christ, into the image of God, and his righteousness and holiness again, in that they are helps-meet, man and woman, as they were before the fall.[72]

Thus, men and women worked together to monitor the behavior of Friends and to keep the community running smoothly.

Consequently, the role of women extended beyond women's meetings. At meetings for worship—attended by both men and women—women and men preached. Women traveled to other meetings—sometimes traveling quite a distance—and also preached there. In addition, there were both male and female elders who met with and commented on the behavior of those who seemed lacking in religious fervor or who disrupted services.[73]

The main duty of the women's meetings was to discipline women who had misbehaved, for example through immodest behavior, fornication, bastardy, or even to investigate why a woman had not been attending meetings. They also helped poor Friends, prepared certificates for women who were going to move, examined those who planned to marry, and investigated cases in which Friends married non-Friends. The men's meetings accepted the decisions made by the women's meetings, and it is doubtful that the men ever overturned any of the women's decisions.[74]

Female elders worked hard and took their roles seriously, even while caring for their own homes and families. For example, Martha Awbrey Thomas completed marriage inspections right up to the year of her death in 1727. Between 1695 and 1727, she examined 33 women. She and an assistant were given one month for each inspection. During these examinations, the elders determined whether the bride and groom were too closely related to marry, whether the woman had prior betrothals that might interfere with a marriage, and whether her behavior was appropriate for marriage within the Quaker community.[75]

Despite the importance of women's meetings, the first ones in the colonies were usually set up after the men's. This is not because they were not considered important, but rather because many of the first female Quaker settlers were in their twenties and thirties when they immigrated. Many of them had young children and were trying to set up households in a new environment. Women generally became most active in the meetings in their mid-thirties and forties, after they were married and their children were older. Most of them had husbands who were also active in the meetings.[76] The role of the women's meetings and of Quaker women continued to grow in the eighteenth century.

Religion was of vast importance to most seventeenth-century American women. Whether they were escaping religious persecution, persuaded by a sense of mission or by the inner spirit to testify their faith, or simply content to worship in church, many female colonists sought or belonged to a religious community. For most of them, religious belief and activities infused their everyday life in hundreds of ways, from determining where they lived, to how they dressed, when and how they worshipped, and how they educated their children.

Moreover, religious beliefs played a part in the struggle to conquer North America. French Catholics and English Protestants fought over both land and souls. (See Chapter 6.) Often women were the victims, as they were displaced, captured, or believed to be witches. Meanwhile, Native American women and African American women who became Christians discovered that conversion and baptism did not necessarily make them equal to their white neighbors, or bring them freedom.

NOTES

1. Marilyn J. Westerkamp, *Women and Religion in Early America, 1600–1850: The Puritan and Evangelical Traditions* (New York: Routledge, 1999), 12–13.

2. Ibid., 14.

3. Debra Meyers, *Common Whores, Vertuous Women, and Loveing Wives: Free Will Christian Women in Colonial Maryland* (Bloomington: Indiana University Press, 2003), 72–73; Francis J. Bremer, *The Puritan Experiment: New England Society from Bradford to Edwards* (New York: St. Martin's Press, 1976), 193.

4. Westerkamp, *Women and Religion*, 17, 21.

5. *The Winthrop Papers*, Part III, MHS Collections, 5th ser., 1 (Boston, 1871), 104–5, quoted in Laurel Thatcher Ulrich, *Good Wives: Image and Reality in the Lives of Women in Northern New England, 1650–1750* (New York: Oxford University Press, 1982), 218.

6. Records of Chebacco Parish, 1676–1726, 18, in Ulrich, *Good Wives*, 219.

7. Carol Berkin, *First Generations: Women in Colonial America* (New York: Hill and Wang, 1996), 42; Westerkamp, *Women and Religion*, 24–25.

8. Westerkamp, *Women and Religion*, 36.

9. Elizabeth Reis, *Damned Women: Sinners and Witches in Puritan New England*, (Ithaca, NY: Cornell University Press, 1997), 42–45.

10. Quoted in Reis, *Damned Women*, 44.

11. John Winthrop, "A Short Story of the Rise, Reign, and Ruine of the Antinomians, Familists, and Libertines," in David D. Hall, ed., *The Antinomian Controversy, 1636-1638: A Documentary History* (Middletown, CT: Wesleyan University Press, 1968), 268, quoted in Westerkamp, *Women and Religion*, 35.

12. Mary Beth Norton, *Founding Mothers and Fathers: Gendered Power and the Forming of American Society* (New York: Vintage Books, 1996), 360–64; Berkin, *First Generations*, 27–28.

13. John Cotton, "The Way of Congregational Churches Cleared," in *The Antinomian Controversy, 1636–1638*, ed. David D. Hall, 2nd ed. (Durham, NC: Duke University Press, 1990), 411–12, quoted in Norton, *Founding Mothers and Fathers*, 362.

14. Norton, *Founding Mother and Fathers*, 365.

15. Mary Beth Norton has written a very detailed account of Anne Hutchinson and focuses on "the controversy as a grave crisis in the system of gendered power." See *Founding Mothers and Fathers*, chap. 8.

16. Franklin Jameson, ed. *Johnson's Wonder-Working Providence 1628–1651* (New York: Charles Scribner's Sons, 1910), 127, quoted in Norton, *Founding Mothers and Fathers*, 368.

17. Norton, *Founding Mothers and Fathers*, 394–97.

18. Norton, *Founding Mothers and Fathers*, 374; Berkin, *First Generations*, 40–41.

19. Berkin, *First Generation*, 41–42.

20. Patricia Trainor O'Malley, "Rowley, Massachusetts, 1639–1730: Dissent, Division and Delimitation in a Colonial Town" (PhD dissertation, Boston College, 1975), 67–68, from the church book kept by Samuel Phillips, quoted in Ulrich, *Good Wives*, 220–21.

21. O'Malley, "Rowley," 69, quoted in Ulrich, *Good Wives*, 221.

22. See a detailed account of the controversy surrounding Anne Eaton in Norton, *Founding Mothers and Fathers*, 165–80.

23. Westerkamp, *Women and Religion*, 45–46.

24. Carol F. Karlsen, *The Devil in the Shape of a Woman: Witchcraft in Colonial New England* (New York: Vintage Books, 1987), 122.

25. Westerkamp, *Women and Religion*, 47.

26. Quoted in Norton, *Founding Mothers and Fathers*, 359.

27. Mary Dyer, Petition to General Court, 1659, Massachusetts State Archives, quoted in Westerkamp, *Women and Religion*, 49.

28. Westerkamp, *Women and Religion*, 47–49.

29. Ibid., 48–51.

30. Norton, *Founding Mothers and Fathers*, 360.

31. Berkin, *First Generations*, 45–46.

32. There was a massive witch panic in East Anglia, England, in 1645–1647; see James Sharpe, *Instruments of Darkness: Witchcraft in Early Modern England* (Philadelphia: University of Pennsylvania Press, 1997).

33. Meg Lota Brown and Kari Boyd McBride, *Women's Roles in the Renaissance* (Westport, CT: Greenwood Press, 2005), 79–81.

34. Westerkamp, *Women and Religion*, 62.

35. Karlsen, *The Devil*, 6–7.

36. Ibid., 144; Kathleen M. Brown, *Good Wives, Nasty Wenches, and Anxious Patriarchs: Gender, Race, and Power in Colonial Virginia* (Chapel Hill: University of North Carolina Press, 1996), 102–3.

37. Norfolk Wills and Deeds D, May 15, 1655, 150; Brown, *Good Wives, Nasty Wenches*, 146.

38. Karlsen, *The Devil*, 144; Norton, *Founding Mothers and Fathers*, 395.

39. Mary Beth Norton, *In the Devil's Snare: The Salem Witchcraft Crisis of 1692* (New York: Knopf, 2002), 16–17. Norton explores this crisis in depth and provides a new analysis by revealing its connection to the Indian wars. For court records, maps, and other material on the Salem crisis, see Salem Witch Trials: Documentary Archive and Transcription Project, University of Virginia, http://jefferson.village.virginia.edu/salem/home.html.

40. Norton, *In the Devil's Snare*, 17–18.

41. Ibid., 19–20.

42. Ibid., 78–81.

43. Paul Boyer and Stephen Nissenbaum, eds., *The Salem Witchcraft Papers: Verbatim Transcripts of the Legal Documents of the Salem Witchcraft Outbreak of 1692*, 3 vols. (New York: Da Capo Press, 1977), 164, quoted in Norton, *In the Devil's Snare*, 120.

44. Ulrich, *Good Wives*, 221–22; Norton, *In the Devil's Snare*, chap. 4.

45. Karlsen, *The Devil*, 41–42.

46. See the Overview of the Salem Witch Trials Documentary and Archive Transcription Project. Available at: http://jefferson.village.edu/salem/home.html.

47. Brown, *Good Wives, Nasty Wenches*, 61.

48. David J. Silverman, "Indians, Missionaries, and Religious Translation: Creating Wampanoag Christianity in Seventeenth-Century Martha's Vineyard," *William and Mary Quarterly* 62 (April 2005): 144.

49. Ibid., 160; Ann Marie Plane, *Colonial Intimacies: Indian Marriage in Early New England* (Ithaca, NY: Cornell University Press, 2000), 42–43.

50. Silverman, "Indians, Missionaries," 161.

51. Thomas Shepard, *The Day-Breaking If Not The Sun-Rising of the Gospel with the Indians in New-England* (London: Richard Cotes for Fulk Clifton, 1647), 22, quoted in Plane, *Colonial Intimacies*, 98.

52. Plane, *Colonial Intimacies*, 99.

53. Nancy F. Cott, *No Small Courage: A History of Women in the United States* (New York: Oxford University Press, 2004), 85.

54. Brown, *Good Wives, Nasty Wenches*, 142.

55. Quoted in Brown, *Good Wives, Nasty Wenches*, 144.

56. Brown, *Good Wives, Nasty Wenches*, 135–36, 223.

57. Willie Graham, Carter L. Hudgins, Carl R. Lounsbury, Fraser D. Neiman, and James P. Whittenburg, "Adaptation and Innovation: Archeological and Architectural Perspective on the Seventeenth-Century Chesapeake," *William and Mary Quarterly* 64 (July 2007): 482; Meyers, *Common Whores*, 24–30; Lois Green Carr, "Maryland's Seventeenth Century," Interpretive essay. Available at: Maryland's Humanities

Council, http://www.mdhc.org/resources/search_essays.htm?essay1=29&essay2=hist& essay3=1&search1.x=16&search1.y=10.

58. Wills, 4:317 (1688); Wills, 1:432 (1713), quoted in Meyers, *Common Whores*, 106.

59. Meyers, *Common Whores*, 104, 107–8.

60. Ibid., 108–9.

61. Westerkamp, *Women and Religion*, 77.

62. Joyce D. Goodfriend, "The Social Dimensions of Congregational Life in Colonial New York City," *William and Mary Quarterly* 46 (April 1989): 253, 257–58, 274–75.

63. Ibid., 276–77.

64. Joyce D. Goodfriend, "The Souls of African American Children: New Amsterdam," *Common-Place* 3, no. 4 (July 2003). Available at: http://www.common-place.org.

65. Hasia R. Diner and Beryl Lieff Benderly, *Her Works Praise Her: A History of Jewish Women in America from Colonial Times to the Present* (New York: Basic Books, 2002), 18, 34, 37.

66. Westerkamp, *Women and Religion*, 49; The Charter to William Penn, March 4, 1681. Available at: Pennsylvania State Archives, http://www.docheritage.state.pa.us/documents/charter.asp.

67. Francis Daniel Pastorius, "Compare the Ship That Bore Them Hither with Noah's Ark: Francis Daniel Pastorius Describes His Impressions of Pennsylvania, 1683." Available at: History Matters, http://historymatters.gmu.edu/d/7439.

68. Westerkamp, *Women and Religion*, 78.

69. Jean R. Soderlund, "Women's Authority in Pennsylvania and New Jersey Quaker Meetings, 1680–1760," *William and Mary Quarterly* 44 (October 1987): 724.

70. "An Epistle to Quaker Women," Lancashire Women's Meeting, 1675, in *Early American Women: A Documentary History 1600–1900*, Nancy Woloch, ed. (Belmont, CA: Wadsworth Publishing Co., 1992), 152–54.

71. Soderlund, "Women's Authority," 726–27.

72. George Fox, *A Collection of Many Select and Christian Epistles, Letters, and Testimonies, Written on Sundry Occasions, by That Ancient, Eminent, Faithful Friend, and Minister of Christ Jesus, George Fox* (Philadelphia, 1853), 2:39. Quoted in Soderlund, "Women's Authority," 726.

73. Soderlund, "Women's Authority," 726.

74. Ibid., 736, 744, 745.

75. Barry Levy, *Quakers and the American Family: British Settlement in the Delaware Valley* (New York: Oxford University Press, 1988), 209.

76. Soderlund, "Women's Authority," 729–30.

SUGGESTED READING

Berkin, Carol. *First Generations: Women in Colonial America*. New York: Hill and Wang, 1996.

Diner, Hasia R., and Beryl Lieff Benderly. *Her Works Praise Her: A History of Jewish Women in America from Colonial Times to the Present*. New York: Basic Books, 2002.

Karlsen, Carol F. *The Devil in the Shape of a Woman: Witchcraft in Colonial New England*. New York: Vintage Books, 1987.

Levy, Barry. *Quakers and the American Family: British Settlement in the Delaware Valley*. New York: Oxford University Press, 1988.

Norton, Mary Beth. *Founding Mothers and Fathers: Gendered Power and the Forming of American Society*. New York: Vintage Books, 1996.

———. *In the Devil's Snare: The Salem Witchcraft Crisis of 1692*. New York: Knopf, 2002.

Plane, Ann Marie. *Colonial Intimacies: Indian Marriage in Early New England*. Ithaca, NY: Cornell University Press, 2000.

Reis, Elizabeth. *Damned Women: Sinners and Witches in Puritan New England*. Ithaca, NY: Cornell University Press, 1997.

Soderlund, Jean R. "Women's Authority in Pennsylvania and New Jersey Quaker Meetings, 1680–1760," *William and Mary Quarterly* 44 (October 1987).

Ulrich, Laurel Thatcher. *Good Wives: Image and Reality in the Lives of Women in Northern New England, 1650–1750*. New York: Oxford University Press, 1982.

Westerkamp, Marilyn J. *Women and Religion in Early America, 1600–1850: The Puritan and Evangelical Traditions*. New York: Routledge, 1999.

6

⁓

Women and War

Seventeenth-century women were intimately connected with war. Wars in Europe, such as the Thirty Years War (1618–1648) and the English Civil War (1642–1649), displaced people and disrupted life for many throughout Europe. Young and old women, single women, married women, and widows all had to adjust to living in a new place and new situations. For some elderly women, it must have been especially difficult to leave a place that might have been home for a long time—especially if forced to flee because of war. For pregnant women and women with young children, traveling a distance carried additional worries. Single, young women, however, sometimes encountered options that did not exist in their homelands. Although war brought a real threat of being injured, killed, raped, or captured, for some it also brought an opportunity to begin a new life. For a single woman, even one who had to first work as a servant for several years, life in British North America brought the possibility of marriage to a man of property.

Yet life in the colonies was not without conflict. Political and religious disagreements in Europe followed settlers to the colonies. During the English Civil War, for example, New Englanders showed their support of the Parliamentary side with days of prayer and fasting. They believed that God was on their side and that England was following the Puritan vision of a godly society. Many of New England's intellectuals and their families even returned to England to participate in the new government there. In return, and to show his appreciation of New England's support, Oliver Cromwell, the Lord Protector, assisted New England in several ways, such as by sending captured Scots to the colonies as indentured servants to help ease the labor shortage there and by supplying military assistance to fight against the Dutch in New Netherland.[1]

In contrast, the English Civil War brought a different response in the Catholic colony of Maryland. Between 1645 and 1647, Maryland experienced a period known as "the plundering time." In February 1645, Richard Ingle, the Protestant captain of the ship *Reformation* sailed to St. Mary's City, Maryland, to attack "the Papists." With the help of Protestant settlers, Ingle attempted to take over the settlement. He and his soldiers then looted and destroyed the estates of the Catholic leaders of the colony. Governor Leonard Calvert escaped to Virginia, but the rebellion continued for two years, until he could bring troops from Virginia to retake the colony. Governor Calvert died a few months later, leaving Mistress Margaret Brent as his executrix to oversee a perilous situation. (For more on Margaret Brent, see Chapter 2.) The troops from Virginia demanded their payment, but the Maryland landowners whose properties had been plundered did not have any money. To solve the situation, the Provincial Court made Mistress Brent the attorney for the Proprietor, Cecilius Calvert, older brother of Leonard. As "his Lordship's Attorney," Margaret Brent was able to use revenue from his personal estate to pay the soldiers.[2]

Although Margaret Brent's use of his private resources to pay the troops angered Lord Baltimore, the Assembly answered his letter of complaint by stating, "we do Verily Believe and in Conscience report, that it was better for the collonys safety at that time in her hands then in any mans else in the whole Province after your Brothers death[;] for the Soldiers would never have treated any other with that Civility and respect and though they were even ready at several times to run into mutiny yet she still pacified them till at last things were brought to that strait that she must be admitted and declared your Lordships Attorney by an order of Court." The Assembly further noted that Lord Baltimore should thank Margaret Brent for her effort to maintain the "publick safety."[3]

As a single, propertied gentlewoman, Margaret Brent was not a typical seventeenth-century Maryland woman. Because of her status and her successes in the courtroom, where she won most of the suits she brought for repayment of debts owed her or her siblings, Governor Calvert appointed her his executrix. Nevertheless, if the colony had not been facing such a dangerous situation, she probably would not have been appointed to the role of Lord Baltimore's attorney. Yet it should be noted that her place in the colony was unique. As one historian notes, no other woman or man ever took on the sort of role she assumed in colonial Maryland.[4]

As the English Civil War carried over to the colonies, sparking conflicts there, so too did conflicts in other parts of the world. When Portugal took control of the Dutch colony of Recife, Brazil, in 1654, many of its Jewish residents fled. Under the Dutch, the Jewish population of Recife had been permitted to practice Judaism openly and without persecution, but under Portuguese rule, they would be subject to the Inquisition. Twenty-three Jewish individuals, men and women, chose to make a new start in New Amsterdam. Among them was the widow Rycke Nounces, who became embroiled in legal disputes shortly after surviving the hazardous voyage to New Amsterdam. (See Chapter 3 on immigration for more on Jewish emigration.)

Other refugees also sought a home in New Netherland. Sizeable numbers of German Protestants escaping the Thirty Years War, and French Protestants, known as Huguenots, who were fleeing persecution in Catholic France, found new lives there. The Calvinist Jacob Leisler (1640–1691), leader of a rebellion in New York against the supporters of the Catholic James II, donated one-third of his own land to Huguenots to establish New Rochelle in 1689.[5] Other Huguenots settled in New England and South Carolina. For example, after fleeing France to escape religious persecution, Judith Giton became one of the first French Huguenots to settle in South Carolina on land granted to them from Charles II. Despite the early years of hardship there, she and her second husband, Pierre Manigault, became wealthy and successful.

New Netherland was not the only colony the English took over from the Dutch. The English also conquered New Sweden in 1664. The colony had been founded by Sweden in 1638, but the Dutch took control of it in 1655. In 1669, a little-known conspiracy, or possible conspiracy, occurred involving a man known as Long Swede or Long Finn. Armegot Printz, a daughter of the former governor of New Sweden, was also implicated in the plot.[6]

Armegot Printz was born in Sweden around 1627, but she traveled to New Sweden with her father, Johan Printz, in 1643. Her father's assistant, Count Johan Papagoja, also made the journey to New Sweden. Both men wanted Armegot to marry Papagoja, but the sixteen-year-old woman refused. In fact, she kept on refusing for two years, despite pressure from her father, her suitor, the Church, and the Crown. Finally, she gave in and agreed to marry Johan Papagoja, after receiving a letter from the Queen of Sweden. Armegot and Johan had five children, but the marriage was not a happy one.

Both her father and her husband returned to Sweden in 1654, but Armegot remained in New Sweden, where she managed to bargain with the Dutch for her father's plantation on Tinicum Island, after they took over the colony. There she grew grain, raised hogs and cattle, and distilled liquor. She bought another house in Upland (now Chester, Pennsylvania). She also dropped her married name and went back to using her maiden name.[7] In 1669, when the alleged plot took place, she was "the colonist of highest status in the Delaware Valley," and she was one of the few who could read and write.

The Long Swede claimed to be a part of a noble Swedish family called Kônigsmark, and he was trying to gain supporters to reclaim the colony for New Sweden. In September 1669, the Long Swede was arrested, but English officials found three papers, "Copyes Two of them subscribed Coningsmark ye other Armgart Prins." It is unknown what exactly Armegot Printz did, or why, as some of the papers have been lost, and much of the information about the insurrection was not recorded in official documents. The governor of New York, Francis Lovelace, wrote "though what she hath Comitted was not of any dangerous Consequence, yet it was a demonstration of their Inclynation & temper to advance a strange power & a manifestation of her Ingratitude fro all those Indulgences & fauours she hath received from those in Authority over her." Despite these words and the evidence of the paper, Armegot was not punished, perhaps because of her high position and connections. In 1676, she returned to Sweden, probably due to age and ill health. The Long Swede, however, was "publickly & severly whipt & stigmatiz'd or Branded in the fface with the Letter (R) with an Inscription written in great Letters & putt upon his Breast." He was then sold as a servant and sent to the Caribbean in 1670. No record remains of him after that.[8] Even though much is not known about this insurrection, it gives some indication of the turmoil within colonies repeatedly overtaken and ruled by various European powers.

The conflicts between European nations also affected another group of people—the Africans brought as slaves to the Americas. As the nations of Europe juggled for dominance on the Continent, they carried their rivalries to Africa, Asia, and the Americas, fighting over the slave trade, trade routes, and colonies. For example, the Portuguese and Dutch fought over territory in Brazil. The Portuguese controlled the West African slave trade from the late fifteenth century until the mid-seventeenth century, while at the beginning of the seventeenth century, the Dutch were only involved in a limited way, buying or confiscating slaves from the Portuguese and Spanish and then selling them. After the 1630s, however, the Dutch dominated the slave trade and brought cloth and alcohol, as well as slaves to the ports of Virginia. By the 1640s, English merchants had begun to encroach on the Dutch monopoly, and by the mid-eighteenth century, England controlled the slave trade. Thus, it is likely that Mary Johnson, discussed in Chapter 3, was taken from Africa on a Portuguese ship, then sold to a Dutch merchant and brought to Virginia from the Caribbean, where she worked for an English master before achieving freedom.[9]

Although the policies and conflicts between rival nations affected the black, white, and Native American inhabitants in North America, it is probably the wars with Native Americans that most directly affected many of the white settlers in seventeenth-century America. In some areas, Indian wars went on for years, and settlers had to cope daily with fears of being attacked. Some of these conflicts developed or expanded because of European rivalries, with Native American tribes forming alliances at various times with the French, English, or Dutch. At other times, wars erupted when one side or the other felt the need for revenge. As white settlements grew, newcomers demanded access to lands occupied by Indians. Additional conflicts developed because of cultural misunderstandings about many things, including but not limited to gender roles, religion, warfare, and family.

These cultural misunderstandings are evident from first contact between Europeans and Native Americans. Many English people justified the conquering of the New World because they believed the native inhabitants there had failed to tame the wilderness, since they did not establish English-style farms and permanent settlements. In the view of the English, Indian men were lazy because they hunted, while their women did the agricultural chores. Furthermore, they did not use the land the way the English believed it should be used, that is, by clearing and dividing the land into tidy farms. Because many Indian tribes did not settle in permanent towns, promoters assured potential colonists and financers that the land was barely populated by the Indians and that there was more than enough available land for everyone. Moreover, because the Indians were not Christians, and indeed, according to the English, were probably devil worshipers, the English felt vindicated in occupying the land to bring civilization to its inhabitants.[10]

In accounts of warfare, the English tended to stress the superiority of their own weapons and the savagery of the Indians. Yet not all Englishmen viewed the Indians as animal-like savages. Although they viewed them through a lens of their own biases, the bodies of Indian women captivated many English observers. The strength of the women and their ability to bear children without pain, however, led some Englishmen to conclude that Indian women were either savage drones who were forced by their men to work at agricultural labor, or unspoiled creatures of nature who did not suffer from Eve's curse. In either case, they saw the women as different from and unlike European women.

Furthermore, in their early encounters with Native Americans, the Protestant English wanted to emphasize that they were morally superior to the Catholic Spanish, their enemies. English accounts of the Spanish conquest of the Americas in the fifteenth and sixteenth centuries stressed the Spanish conquerors' brutality toward and the ravishment of the indigenous population. English writers wanted to underscore the point that England's soldiers and settlers acted chastely and appropriately towards the native women they encountered. Nevertheless, despite the cultural differences, some Englishmen found Indian women attractive and wanted to marry them. Most Indian women probably did not believe these men would be good marriage partners, since by Indian standards they could not provide for them as well as the men in their tribes. Still, until about 1618, the Powhatan Indians may have encouraged their women to form sexual liaisons with the English, in the hopes that marriage, or even less permanent sexual relationships, would improve diplomatic relations. Peace between nations did not arise from the union of individuals, but English men and Indian women did form intimate relationships. In the early years of the Jamestown settlement when food shortages and harsh discipline made conditions there unpleasant, some of the male laborers deserted the compound to take their chances with the Indians in spite of the punishment they faced if caught.[11]

By the time Jamestown was settled by the English in 1607, the Powhatans they encountered were members of a large empire. Powhatan, the paramount chief of the Powhatans, was the ruler of over thirty chiefdoms. He had gone to war several times to take over other tribes and build his empire, but he and other Powhatans also went to war to obtain women or children to have as wives and future warriors, or to seek revenge. The Powhatans placed great value on a warrior's abilities and exploits, as did many other Indian tribes. Warriors were supposed to be stoic and able to withstand great pain, even when being tortured. Englishmen who were captured and tortured in the early years of settlement, however, died begging for their lives, while the Indians mocked them. In contrast, both Indian men and women praised warriors who were brave and skilled, and gave them public accolades and rewards. One famous warrior, Nemattanew, or "Jack of the Feather," was thought to be invincible. His tribesmen believed that the bullets of the English could not kill him. When he was mortally wounded in 1621, he asked his captors not to let his people know that English bullets had killed him.[12]

English observers believed that the death of Nemattanew sparked a revenge massacre by the Powhatans in 1622.[13] Although according to Virginia planter Robert Beverley, the attack came as a surprise. In an account he wrote several years later, he stated, "all men were lulled into a fatal security and became familiar with the Indians—eating, drinking, and sleeping amongst them." The attack was led by Opechancanough, Powhatan's brother, and the Indians pretended to come as friends, bringing gifts of food, and in the end, used the English settlers' tools to kill them. A third of the settlers were killed—men, women, and children. Following the attack, the colonists moved to the fort and other defensive areas; however, because they had also lost crops and supplies, the settlers were forced to trade with the Indians in the winter of 1622–1623. Many Jamestown residents died of malnutrition, putting the settlement in even more dire straits.[14]

The English vowed to retaliate by killing Indians whenever they could. As a consequence of the 1622 attack and other signs of mismanagement, however, the Virginia Company was dissolved in 1624, and Virginia was made a royal colony. The relationship between the Indians and settlers continued to deteriorate, however, and Opechancanough led another attack in 1644, killing almost 500 settlers.

Settlers in New England, New York, and Pennsylvania encountered a different group of Indians, the five tribes of the Iroquois League, or as they referred to themselves, the people of the Longhouse. The five nations–the Mohawks, the Oneidas, the Onondagas, the Cayugas, and the Senecas (joined by a sixth nation, the Tuscaroras, in the eighteenth century)—spoke related languages and lived in what is now referred to as upstate New York. They had a geographical advantage in that they lived inland and away from the initial settlements of Europeans; thus the diseases brought by white explorers, colonists, and missionaries did not affect them immediately. At the same time, their geographic location set them between competing European powers and trade routes—the French along the St. Lawrence, and the Dutch, then English along the Hudson River—which permitted the Iroquois to negotiate the most advantageous alliances by playing the Europeans against each other.[15]

Eventually, European diseases and encroachment affected the tribes of the Five Nations. They "replaced" the members lost to disease and war through taking captives and adopting them. These "mourning wars" were part of an elaborate ritual used to assuage grief over the loss of a family member, as well as ensuring that the individual's name, social position, and spiritual power would live on within the community. By the use of "Requickening" ceremonies, Iroquois families transferred the name and position of a dead individual to someone else. Often these successors were captives taken during war raids.[16]

For the Iroquois, mourning was a highly ritualized process. The rituals served as a means of redirecting the grief of mourners, who might otherwise harm themselves or other members of their tribe. For ten days, members of the household of the dead individual were in "deep mourning." They were excused from all of their duties, and they showed their despair by cutting their hair and smearing their faces with dirt. A less intense mourning period continued for a year after that. During the mourning period, members of other kin groups took over their duties, gave gifts, provided feasts, and tried to ease the grief of the mourners.[17]

It was the women of a mourning household who decided whether they needed a raid to gain captives. Young warriors who lived in other long-houses but who were connected by marriage to the female mourners carried out the raid. If they did not agree to do so, they faced public humiliation by the women. Upon their return with captives, the elder women decided whether they wanted to adopt the captives as replacements for lost family members, or whether they wanted to execute them. Women and children captives were less likely to be executed.

Adult males who were scheduled to be executed were still "adopted" into a family. They were addressed respectfully as "uncle" or "nephew," and given a death feast. At the execution, men, women, and children used blazing sticks and other smoldering objects to burn the captive, who was expected to endure his suffering without complaint. He was then scalped. His torture finally ended when someone stabbed him with a knife or cut his neck with a hatchet. The women then cut up his body, cooked it, and served it to the whole village. Most likely this was a religious ritual that transferred the captive's spiritual power to his adoptive family.[18]

By 1620, the diseases carried by Europeans, such as smallpox, began to reach the Iroquois. Through a series of epidemics, the population of the Five Nations was cut in half. In addition, because in affected villages the young adults who did most of the work were ill or dead, there were no men and women available to do the hunting, farming, gathering of plants and firewood, or to take care of the children and elderly. As thousands of Iroquois died, the surviving women demanded mourning wars, and the Iroquois began to attack the Huron, destroying their villages and taking captives. The wars "soon merged into a single conflict that pitted the Five Nations against virtually every Indian people in the Northeast."[19]

The Iroquois took captives in the raids. On the journeys back to their villages, the warriors stripped the captives and forced them to endure physical hardships and even torture. Although women and children were not usually injured, they did have to watch their male kin suffer. Once the war party and captives reached the attackers' village, the captives had to endure more severe torture before a decision was made whether to adopt them or not. Those who were chosen for adoption then received tender treatment from their new female family members. Because European captives, unlike Native Americans, were unprepared for the experience of captivity, they were not as easily assimilated. Many Indian captives, however, did adapt and became comfortable with their new lives.[20]

Although a male adoptee might have to prove his loyalty to his new family by participating in an attack on his former tribe, women usually only had to perform the tasks assigned to them and act appropriately to their new kin. In 1636, one female prisoner who was given to the French to "requicken" slain colonists seemed sad at first. After being told that the French were honorable, she declared that "she was now of their [French] nation; that she did not fear they would do her any harm; that if she were commanded to marry she would obey."[21]

In contrast to the Iroquois, Wabanaki warfare did not include the rituals of the mourning war. Wabanaki means "People of the Dawnland," and the term includes the Abenaki, Penobscot, Passamaquoddy, Maliseet, and Mi'kmaq (or Micmac), which were tribes that share linguistic and cultural traits of the eastern Algonquian-speaking peoples. They lived in the area that now includes Maine, Nova Scotia, New Brunswick, and southeastern Quebec.[22]

Taking captives was never a primary motive for going to war for the Wabanaki. From about 1500 to 1620, taking captives was more of an afterthought in warfare. After this period, as more Europeans settled on their land and changed their situation, the taking of captives evolved, as well. For example, English captives could be exchanged for their own people being held prisoner, or the English captives could be ransomed for cash or goods. The Wabanaki generally took captives during raids, and then distributed them according to need. Sometimes Wabanaki families adopted captives, usually young children, but this was not a usual practice.[23]

Surviving evidence suggests that indigenous women who were taken captive by the Wabanaki were considered to be sexually available to their captives. Englishwomen, however, were not considered sexually available. As one scholar explains:

> The adoption of adult women taken captive could be an indigenous practice that predates the early contact period, but the evidence suggests that it was uncommon at best. Captive women were readily incorporated into households as slaves or concubines, and the fact that they were not kin gave their captors a certain freedom that might include harsh treatment, physical abuse, and forced sexual intimacy.... But captive women could also be incorporated into the kin group through marriage, sometimes as a second or third wife, and apparently this was a common practice.[24]

As more Englishwomen were taken captive, new patterns developed, such as adopting women as sisters. This made them sexually unavailable, but involved them in reciprocal duties and obligations.

Of course, not all female captives were adopted. In fact, the Wabanaki were particular about whom they adopted, and even adopted captives might be ransomed. As slaves, however, English captives were often valued for the skills they might have, such as the ability to knit (as Mary Rowlandson discovered) or the ability to write.[25]

Throughout the seventeenth century, Anglo-Americans continued to have numerous clashes with Native Americans, but they fought with each other as well. In these conflicts, women of all races were witnesses, victims, captives, and in a few instances, warriors or leaders. For example, in 1675, a string of attacks between settlers in New England and the Native American population took place. Metacom's Rebellion (also known as King Philip's War) began in Plymouth Colony, spread to Connecticut, and eventually led to clashes in Maine. Metacom, called King Philip by the English, led a confederation of Wampanoag, Narragansett, Abenaki, and Nipmuck. Between 1675 and 1676, Indians attacked fifty towns out of ninety in the region and destroyed twelve of them. The colonial economy was in ruins, as well. Of even more significance, nearly everyone in New England was affected by the war. One in sixteen men of fighting age was killed in the conflict or died as a result of it, and many other men, women, and children were taken captive. In August 1676, Metacom was killed, and other Indian leaders and their families were killed or sold as slaves.[26]

Native Americans already touched by war were further torn apart in its aftermath as they saw family members sold as servants and slaves. Plymouth Colony ruled that all male Indian captives over age fourteen should be sold and removed from the colony. The wives of these men could choose to stay in Plymouth or go with their husbands as slaves. Authorities reported that one woman said, "She is willing to goe with her husband if to King Charles his Countrey [an English colony]." Officials in Massachusetts Bay, Rhode Island, and Plymouth distributed Indians to masters in New England, as well as to those in other colonies. Sometimes the bondage was for a temporary period of time, five or ten years. Sometimes, however, they were slaves for life. Children, as well as adults, were bound out. In August 1676, magistrates in Massachusetts Bay bound out thirty-one Indian children ranging in age from four to sixteen years old. Most of these children had lost one or both parents.[27]

In a few cases, "friendly" Indians were sold by mistake. John Nemasitt, an Indian man who had fought for the English, only narrowly managed to get his wife and baby back after they were sold as part of a group of captives because someone had discovered it was an error. His family was put in the prison in Boston for safekeeping. Fortunately, the magistrate agreed that the family should be reunited.[28]

Although Metacom's death ended the war in southern New England, it continued for two more years in Maine and in skirmishes along the coast of New England. The records of the First Church of Salem reported in July 1677 that "The Lord having given a commission to the Indians to take no less that thirteen of the Fishing Ketches of Salem and captivate the men (though divers of them cleared themselves and came home,) it struck a great consternation into all the people here."[29] The "great consternation" extended to people throughout New England. As Thomas

Goffe Rallying the Men of Hadley, 1883. Indians attacked many New England towns during the seventeenth century, sometimes taking captives. According to legend, General William Goffe thwarted an attack on the town of Hadley, Massachusetts, where he was hiding from English officials during King Philip's War. Goffe was a fugitive due to his role in the execution of King Charles I. Courtesy of Library of Congress.

Hutchinson explained in a later history of Massachusetts, "Every person, almost in the two colonies [Plymouth and Massachusetts], had lost a relation or near friend, and the people in general were exasperated."[30]

Having experienced the fighting of Metacom's Rebellion and the taking of the Salem ships, the residents of nearby Marblehead were tense and anxious in July 1677 when a ship sailed into the harbor with two captive Indians aboard. According to one of the sailors, Robert Roules, the townspeople demanded to know why the crew had not killed the Indians. The men replied that they hoped to get something from them to cover their losses. They had intended to give the Indians to the constable, who would deliver them to the court in Boston. However, the people of the town surrounded the Indians and began to insult them

> and soon after, the women surrounded them, drove us by force from them, (we escaping at no little peril,) and laid violent hands upon the captives, some stoning us in the meantime, because we would protect them, others seizing them by the hair, got full possession of them, nor was there any way left by which we could rescue them. Then with stones, billets of wood, and what else they might, they made an end of these Indians. We were kept at such distance that we could not see them till they were dead, and then we found them with their heads off and gone, and their flesh in manner pulled from their bones. And such was the tumultation these women made, that for my life I could not tell who these women were, or the names of any of them.[31]

One historian argued that the behavior of the Marblehead women drew on the English tradition of "disorderly women." Between the seventeenth and the early nineteenth centuries, English women participated in riots and other acts of political disobedience. The disorderly woman or "virago" was fierce, and her rage could not be controlled. When the Marblehead women murdered the Indians, "they symbolically restored the potency of a frightened and desperate community." In doing so, they also freed men from having to take responsibility, as the women "suffered neither constable nor mandrake, nor any other person to come near them, until they had finished their bloody purpose."[32]

Anglo-Americans did not doubt the power of women. Although women might be "the weaker sex," they were also "daughters of Eve" with her ability to seduce and tempt. Women could beguile with words, hence the fear of women like Anne Hutchinson. They were easily seduced by Satan, and then could tempt others to evil. Women also had the capacity to do violence—it was how and when they used this violence that was important. The women of Marblehead murdered the Indians, but they were, in a sense, acting for the community, and they were not punished for their actions.

Following the war, New Englanders tried to make sense of the destruction surrounding them. To the Puritans, it seemed that God was using the Indians to chastise them because they had betrayed their covenant with Him. New Englanders were becoming too interested in worldly goods and pursuits and less interested in examining their own souls. Perhaps because of this need to find meaning in the devastation around them, the Puritans were ready for heroes. One of the earliest heroines in American history emerged from the literature written about the Metacom's Rebellion. Mary Rowlandson wrote about her captivity in a narrative that was published in 1682. (Her narrative as a literary work is discussed in Chapter 7.) She was born in England in 1637. In 1638, she arrived in Salem, Massachusetts, with her parents, Joan and John White. In 1653, the Whites moved farther into the frontier to the town of Lancaster, and at age nineteen, Mary White married the town's minister, Joseph Rowlandson. In the Indian attack of February 10, 1675–1676, a group of Indians burned the town and took Mary Rowlandson, her three children, and several other people captive. At the time of the attack, Joseph Rowlandson was on his way to Boston trying to get help in defending the town.[33]

Mary Rowlandson stayed with the Indians for almost three months, until she was finally reunited with her husband in May 1676; two of her children, Joseph and Mary, were released shortly afterwards. Her youngest child, Sarah, who was six when they were captured, died in captivity of wounds she received during the initial assault. The Rowlandsons lived in Boston for a year, and then moved to Wethersfield, Connecticut. Joseph Rowlandson died in 1678. Mary Rowlandson married Samuel Talcott the following year. She outlived her second husband by twenty years, and died in 1710–1711.[34]

In her narrative, Mary Rowlandson is revealed as a sturdy New England good wife. She survives her captivity through her faith in God and her superior skills as a housewife. Yet Mary Rowlandson was not the only seventeenth-century woman to be captured by Indians in New England. Throughout Metacom's Rebellion and subsequent conflicts, Indians took captives either to ransom them or to adopt them. The risk of New

The Captivity of Mrs. Rowlandson, 1857. Courtesy of Library of Congress.

Englanders being captured by Indians continued well into the eighteenth century.

In the wars of empire fought by England and France, Indians were very much involved as the two nations battled over territory in North America. King Philip's War was followed by King William's War (1689–1698) then by Queen Anne's War (1703–1713).[35] During each war, combinations of Indians and Frenchmen attacked frontier settlements in northern New England and New York. Historians have estimated that 270 men, women, and children were taken from northern New England to Canada between 1689 and 1730. One hundred twenty-eight of these captives were women and girls, and 142 were men and boys.[36] Women who were married at the time they were captured were more likely to return to their homes in New England after being held captive. Neighbors and officials admired their courage and the knowledge they acquired about the Indians during their captivity. In testimony before the governor and council of Massachusetts in 1695, Grace Higiman even offered military advice, noting "That if the yearly supply from France to St. John's could be intercepted they would be greatly distressed and forced to draw off."[37]

Young, single women were more likely to remain in Canada than older women or men. Because women in European cultures usually assume the background and status of their husbands, it would be somewhat easier for a female captive to become a French or Indian wife than it might have been for a male captive to become a French or Indian husband. As well, in the growing frontier society of New France, women would have been particularly welcomed as wives. Furthermore, the parents of these young women were far away and unable to restrain them from marrying an ardent, but unsuitable, suitor.[38]

Indian attacks and captivity played an important role in the Salem witchcraft crisis of 1692. Historians have information about twenty-one of the twenty-four unmarried women who were over sixteen years old at the time of the witchcraft outbreak. Of these, seventeen had lost one or both parents, mainly as a result of Indian attacks. As orphans living as servants in the homes of strangers, these young women probably saw little hope for their futures. Although some of them lived with relatives, they were still servants without financial prospects. It was common for young, single women to live with other families as servants during this time, but for these women, there was not much of a chance that their futures would improve, since the land and estates of their fathers were gone or greatly diminished because of the Indian attacks, and most men did not want to marry a woman without a dowry.[39]

Indeed, the future was glum for many of these women. Economic conditions in New England made marriage uncertain for many young women at this time, a fact recognized by the Massachusetts General Court, which passed a law stating that single young women should be permitted to "any lawful trade or employment for a livelihood ... any law, usage or custom to the contrary notwithstanding."[40] Most likely this law was intended to help the families who were supporting these women, since the law also restated that single people needed to live within a household. The situation of the possessed women was generally worse than it was for other women. Those who did marry tended to do so at a later age, and they and their husbands were not as prosperous as they probably would have been had the women not lost parents and property to the Indian raids. The case of Mary Watkins is probably the most extreme. After accusing her wealthy mistress of being a witch, Mary was threatened with punishment by authorities. She then accused herself of being a witch and was placed in the jail in Boston for several months. Her remaining family members would not help her, and she could not pay her jail fees. Desperate, she finally asked to be sold as a servant in Virginia.[41]

Some of the young women accusers returned to live in New England after suffering traumatic experiences during captivity. Mercy Short, for example, had been captured by Wabanakis during a raid of her town in March 1689–1690. Her parents and some of her siblings were killed during this raid. Mercy and the other captives were forced on a difficult journey to Canada. Along the way, they witnessed several violent deaths. One of the captives killed was Robert Rogers. After he had tried unsuccessfully to escape, the Wabanakis stripped his clothing from him, tied him to a stake, and partially burned him. Then while he was still alive, they cut chunks of flesh from his body and threw them in his face until he finally died. Other captives, including children, were also chopped up in front of the other witnesses as a warning to behave. Mercy was redeemed in Quebec and returned to Boston, where she was most likely taken in by Margaret Thacher.[42] (See Chapter 5 for more on witches and the connection to religion.)

Although she was not charged, Margaret Thacher was later suspected of being a witch. The mistresses of alleged witchcraft victims were frequently assumed to be witches. Margaret Thacher was a wealthy and pious widow. Her first husband, Henry Webb, had been a merchant with business connections and property in Maine. Her second husband, the Reverend Thomas Thacher, had been the minister of Old South Church in Boston. On a day in May 1692, it is possible that she sent her servant, Mercy Short, to the jail in Boston to bring food or other gifts to one of the prisoners being held there, Mistress Mary English, who was the wife of a wealthy Salem merchant. Mercy encountered the suspect witch Sarah Good at the jail, and she was taken with fits.[43]

In subsequent testimony, Mercy describes specters and torments that closely resembled people and events that she would have seen or experienced while she was a captive. According to Cotton Mather's account, Mercy described the devil as "A Short and a Black Man" but "not of a Negro, but of a Tawney, or an Indian colour." There were other specters with him who resembled people she knew or at least knew of. They wanted her to sign the devil's book, and when she refused, they tortured her in several ways; "But Burning seem'd the cruellest of all her tortures," Mather noted in his account. When the specters left her to attend meetings with witches, they kept her chained. Then when they all gathered around her, she saw "French Canadiens and Indian Sagamores among them, divers of whom shee knew, and particularly Nam'd them." In addition, these specters consulted Catholic devotional literature.[44]

Mercy Short was not the only former captive to combine in her witchcraft testimony elements of her captivity experience with torture carried out by the devil or his minions. Others in Essex County had witnessed similar horrors, or they had heard gossip about such things. Cotton Mather called the Wabanakis "Devils." With fear of Indians so prevalent in the area, it is not surprising that torture by Indians and torture by the Devil became one and the same, especially in the minds of people already traumatized by attacks on themselves or loved ones.[45]

With the constant fear of Indian attacks, it is not a surprise that those who fought Indians would be celebrated as heroes. The Marblehead women exacted a sort of biblical revenge on the Indian captives they killed, but their actions did not prevent additional attacks. By the last quarter of the seventeenth century, New Englanders had been devastated by Indian attacks, faced a decline in Puritan zeal, weathered political instability and a new charter, and lived through the Salem witchcraft crisis. When Hannah Duston was taken captive in 1697 and fought and killed her Indian attackers, New Englanders were ready to declare her a hero. Because she was a woman, in fact, a woman who had just recently given birth, it seemed clear that God must have been working through her for her to have endured such a difficult journey through the woods, then killed her captors and escaped.

Hannah Duston had given birth just five days before, when the Indians attacked Haverhill, Massachusetts, early in the morning in March 1697. They captured her and her nurse, Mary Neff, along with ten others from the town. The Indians killed her newborn infant and burned the town before they departed. Hannah's husband, Thomas, managed to save the couple's seven other children, but he was unable to rescue Hannah or the others. About two weeks later, after marching for one hundred miles into the wilderness, Hannah Duston, Mary Neff, and a boy named Samuel Lennardson killed the Indians while they were sleeping. As proof of the deed, they brought home ten scalps, for which the General Assembly awarded them each a scalp bounty.[46]

Hannah Duston visited Boston in April 1697. She was feted and inter-viewed, and Cotton Mather preached a sermon in her honor. In 1702, Mather further honored her in his *Magnalia Christi Americana*, where he compared her to the Biblical Jael, who slew her enemy, Sisera, after lulling him to sleep. In his text, Mather first stressed Hannah Duston's feminin-ity by mentioning her sighs and fear. Then he explained how she was forced by necessity to perform the brutal act of killing her captors, despite being a frail woman. In Mather's hands, Hannah Duston became a mythi-cal heroine, though in reality she came from a family filled with its own share of violent behavior. Years before, her father had been summoned to court for abusing her sister, Elizabeth Emerson, and Elizabeth herself was executed for infanticide in 1693. (Elizabeth Emerson is discussed in Chapter 4.) The real-life Hannah Duston thus belonged to both a culture and family permeated by violence.[47]

The image of a woman committing acts of violence can be seen (and heard) in the number of Anglo-American ballads from the seventeenth century that featured "warrior women." In these ballads, women typically dressed as soldiers or sailors to follow a lover or revenge his death. The ballads originated in England, and then crossed the Atlantic to the colo-nies. *Mary Ambree* was one of the most popular ballads of the seven-teenth century. In this ballad, Mary Ambree dresses as a soldier after "the brave Sir John Major was slaine in her sight, / Who was her true lover, her joy, and delight." The ballad describes how she dresses for battle, gathers the troops, and leads them into combat, slaying more and more soldiers. Eventually, her enemies capture her, and it is revealed that the brave captain is a woman.[48]

Cross-dressing heroines also appear in the literature and theater of the seventeenth century. (Literature is discussed in more detail in Chapter 7.) For example, the Widow Ranter, the title character of Aphra Behn's play *The Widow Ranter; or the History of Bacon in Virginia* (ca. 1690) dresses as a soldier to fight during Bacon's Rebellion in 1676. In reality, some women did actually dress as men to become soldiers or sailors, or to have experiences they could not have as women. Thomas/Thomasine Hall, dis-cussed in Chapter 4, dressed as a man, both to fight in Europe and make her situation easier as an indentured servant, while Joanna Delony, dis-cussed in Chapter 2, fantasized about dressing as a man to teach her hus-band's lover a lesson. There are probably many other women whose cross-dressing went undiscovered, and who are therefore absent from the historical record.[49]

The motif of the cross-dressing warrior woman provided seventeenth-century Anglo-Americans with a romantic and heroic view of women. They were women who only stepped into men's roles temporarily, how-ever, because they needed to act for or revenge the death of their lovers.

Presumably once the crisis was over, or it was discovered that she was a woman, the cross-dressing warrior woman once again donned both her female attire and her female role. In real life, however, most people found cross-dressing women threatening because they neither appeared nor behaved as proper seventeenth-century women, and it was uncertain that they would indeed step back into a feminine role. By acting as men, they demonstrated that they were not under the control of their husbands or fathers, and thus, they were dangerous. Without controls or regulation, a woman was likely to behave licentiously and immodestly, breaking apart families and disrupting society. Women were weak and easily tempted to fall into evil ways, but even worse, they might seduce others into following them.

Cross-dressing concerned seventeenth-century Anglo-Americans, but it was not a common occurrence. Much more common, and therefore, a more likely threat, were outspoken, or "brabbling women." For instance, a woman such as Anne Hutchinson who spoke in public was dangerous because she appeared to be unrestrained by her husband as she spread subversive ideas to both men and women, and consequently, her actions undermined the hierarchical structure of both family and society. During wars and times of crisis, however, outspoken women were considered even more dangerous because their dissident ideas might incite others to rebellion.

Such was the case in Virginia during Bacon's Rebellion (1676) when commentators on both sides blamed the disorderly speech of women for inciting tempers and creating both domestic and political instability. Disorderly women did not cause the rebellion; however, their words added to the brew of dissatisfaction simmering in the colony. There was widespread discontent over low tobacco prices, high taxes, and decreased opportunities for freed servants. Newcomers and recently freed servants who were looking for land had to move farther and farther into frontier areas. For about two decades before the start of the rebellion, Virginia had endured threats to its political stability from religious dissenters, disorderly women, rebellious servants and slaves, and discontented newcomers. Moreover, those who lived along the frontier engaged in frequent skirmishes with Indians and believed that the wealthy planter leaders of the colony had abandoned them. They were less willing to follow the colony's elite.

During the English Civil War, many royalists immigrated to Virginia. As aristocrats, they sought land and positions commensurate with their status and formed connections through family relationships and marriage. When Governor Berkeley was restored to power in 1660, he gave the most influential positions to members of this elite group. Yet during this same period, members of radical sects, such as the Quakers, also fled to Virginia, causing authorities to fear the disruption of social order. They were especially eager to restrain the speech of Quaker women, and Governor Berkeley passed a proclamation in 1661 threatening imprisonment for Quaker women who held meetings and spoke publicly. (See Chapter 5.)[50]

All of these simmering tensions boiled over in July 1675, when a dispute over hogs arose between Thomas Mathew and Doeg Indians. After Mathew killed one of the Doegs, and they retaliated, troops marched out and mistakenly killed a number of friendly Susquehannahs. The Susquehannahs then retaliated in a series of attacks during the fall and winter of that year.

Planters, several of whom had had servants and overseers killed in Indian raids, urged Governor Berkeley to fight the Indians. The governor refused to do so. Instead he put restrictions on trade with the Indians and called for forts to be built, which would require a tax increase and only served to anger people more. At this point, Nathaniel Bacon, Jr., who was a recent immigrant to Virginia and who was related to the governor's wife, emerged as the leader of mostly poorer planters who pleaded with the governor to send out troops against the Indians.

Bacon came from a prominent family in England, but as a recent arrival to Virginia, he was not a part of the Anglo-Virginia aristocracy that included Governor Berkeley. Nevertheless, the governor and his wife welcomed Bacon and his wife when they first arrived in Virginia, and Governor Berkeley even made Bacon a member of his council. Yet, Bacon never became a part of Berkeley's elite inner circle.[51]

Although the governor refused to grant a commission to Bacon, Bacon led troops anyway, and they destroyed an Occaneechee village. In May 1676, Governor Berkeley declared Nathaniel Bacon a traitor; however, voters in Henrico County elected Bacon to the Assembly. In June, the governor pardoned Bacon, after Bacon's supporters staged a demonstration demanding that the governor give Bacon his commission. Yet this did not end the conflict. Bacon continued to gather disgruntled poor planters, servants, and slaves, and they continued clashing with Indians and looting the homes of those loyal to the governor. Unfortunately for the rebels, Nathaniel Bacon died in October 1676, ending the rebellion. Governor Berkeley then seized the estates of the rebels, and signed the orders to execute twenty-three of them.[52]

A number of contemporary accounts blamed the governor's wife, Lady Frances Berkeley, for many of the problems that occurred during Bacon's Rebellion or that led to the rebellion. Lady Berkeley was a thirty-six-year-old widow when she married William Berkeley, who was thirty-three years her senior. She was wealthy, well connected, and politically outspoken. According to one petition from a colonist in Maryland to the king,

Governor Berkeley became a fool and initiated foolish policies because he was too busy trying to satisfy his young wife sexually. Moreover, the document implied that Lady Berkeley knew her husband's policies were thoughtless and could lead to rebellion, but continued to lead him into a weak course of action.

More significant, however, is the way in which Lady Berkeley expressed her opinions to authorities and political rivals of her husband's directly and without fear. In May 1676, Governor Berkeley removed Nathaniel Bacon from the council. A few days later, Bacon wrote a letter to the governor and complained that Lady Berkeley had spread gossip about him, saying that he was poor. Lady Berkeley then went on the offense. In a public accounting, and naming her informants, she noted that several planters had told her that Bacon could not pay his debt. Among the men she named were friends and acquaintances of Bacon's. Thus, she explained that she was only repeating what they told her, and "If they have done him wrong, Hee may disprove them." In the seventeenth century, men's reputations could be harmed by accusations of indebtedness, just as women's were affected by accusations of sexual looseness. Yet, accusations about a man's worth or untrustworthiness were normally voiced by men against other men.[53]

As one historian has noted, Lady Berkeley's account demonstrated her astute political skills. She hinted that Bacon had lied about his worth and misled his followers. She also objected to Bacon's comment that she had said he was supporter of the Parliamentary side during the English Civil War, a serious charge in royalist Virginia. Although Lady Berkeley surely did know that one of Bacon's relatives had been a supporter of the Parliamentary side, she simply denied having made the remark. After this, Lady Berkeley moved back to the feminine realm, accusing him of "ingratitude," saying that he had "rent" her heart, and asking how she could "deserve so mean an affront."[54]

When the king sent commissioners to investigate the rebellion, Lady Berkeley was equally outspoken with them. She attempted to both defend her husband and attack those who spoke against him; however, Berkeley was recalled to England for his mismanagement of the rebellion. After Berkeley died in 1677, Lady Berkeley married another powerful man, Philip Ludwell.[55] Although Lady Berkeley's public forays into the political arena sparked volleys from her opponents, she managed to emerge unscathed.

The public speech of the rebel women was more of a threat to domestic and social disorder because it helped to incite treasonous action. Since Bacon was a rebel and without funds, he relied upon individual men and women to spread the word about what he was doing. Women were particularly effective in broadcasting news of Bacon's activities.[56] According to Governor Berkeley, "Mrs. Sarah Grendon (once Mrs. Stegg) told hundreds ... that I was a greater friend to the Indians than to the English." He noted that her news was "personally spread through the whole country," stirring up the "rabble" to attack the "better sort of people."[57] Sarah Drummond, who was the wife of William Drummond, one of Bacon's chief lieutenants, publicly spread word of her husband's activities. When he wrote her an open letter that urged people to take up arms, she publicized his words. She also shared her own treasonous thoughts in public, noting that the "power of England" was no more than the stick she broke, and she further declared, "the child that is unborn shall have cause to rejoice for the good that will come by the rising of the country."[58] William Drummond was hanged for treason and his estate was seized. Although other rebels had their estates returned to them, Sarah Drummond's was not. She petitioned for the return of her estate, and as most petitioners did, she attempted to minimize her involvement. Instead, Sarah Drummond characterized herself as a poor widow and a victim of the governor's injustice. Her petition stated that the governor not only "took away" the life of her husband and "caused his small Plantation to be seized," but that she "with her five poor children" had to "fly from their habitation, and wander in the Deserts and Woods, till they were ready to starve."[59]

The words of the rebel women were seen as dangerous because they could seduce men into insurgency. In contrast, contemporaries seldom discussed the words of most of the male rebels, other than those of Nathaniel Bacon. Instead they vilified them by claiming they were immoral and dissolute. Those writing about the rebels claimed that they were overly fond of "wenches," a term denoting lower class women and African slave women. Loyalists also insulted female rebels' reputations, which dishonored their husbands. Governor Berkeley called Lydia Chisman a whore when she attempted to plead for her husband's life by claiming that she had led him to rebel. Her husband, Edmund, was the son of Mary Chisman, who held Quaker meetings with her ex-slaves. (See Chapter 5.)[60]

In contrast to the female rebels, contemporaries portrayed loyalist women as virtuous and pure. This is particularly evident in an episode of the rebellion referred to as the "white aprons" episode. During the rebellion, Bacon ordered a group of loyalist wives to be brought to stand on some dirt ramparts outside of Jamestown. The rebels jeered at the loyalist troops. The governor's troops were forced to leave Jamestown to the rebels, who then burned the town. The loyalist women were known as "white aprons" because their white aprons set them apart from the lower status white women and female slaves who worked in the tobacco fields and wore rougher garments. The loyalist women were the "innocent and harmless wives" of "prime gentlemen." As they stood silently in their

white aprons, they became the symbol of virtuous wives, a tribute to do-
mesticity, while Bacon and his followers represented the evil destroyers of
homes and families.[61]

The list of women who were made victims by Bacon and his followers
even extended to the Indian queen of the Pamunkeys, Cockacoeske.
Cockacoeske became the leader of the Pamunkeys in 1656 after the death
of her husband, Totopotomoy. Totopotomoy was killed in battle while
fighting for the English against hostile Indians. When Bacon's Rebellion
began, Bacon and his followers fought and killed Pamunkeys, despite their
status as friendly Indians. The Virginia Council asked Cockacoeske to
supply Indian warriors to help fight Bacon. Cockacoeske "with grave
courtlike gestures and a majestic air in her face," appeared before the
committee attended by her son and an interpreter, even though she probably did understand English. She spoke passionately about the death of
her husband and the other warriors as they fought for the English, and
how she had never received any compensation for the deaths. After being
treated rudely by the chairman of the committee, she grudgingly agreed
to supply twelve warriors.[62]

After the rebellion, the royal commissioners wanted to restore a good
relationship with the Pamunkey. They explained that when Nathaniel Bacon fought the Pamunkeys, it was not at the command of the king. The
commissioners placed Cockacoeske's name at the top of the list of people
who were to be compensated for losses they sustained during Bacon's
Rebellion. Cockacoeske refused to speak English and remained aloof, as she
had previously when she had appeared before the Assembly. Nevertheless,
she did manage to gain some influence and power from the peace settlement negotiated by the commissioners (the Treaty of Middle Plantation,
1677), which placed several Indian tribes under her power and ensured
peace for a time between Native Americans and white settlers in Virginia.[63]

Yet war would continue to affect the lives of women in the British
North American colonies. As white settlers moved farther into western
frontier areas, they fought the Indians protecting their homelands and
their own way of life. In the eighteenth century, as European nations continued their quest for global domination in the Seven Years War, fighting
raged across the British colonies in its American counterpart known as
the French and Indian War. Finally, women of all classes and races would
be both closely involved and affected as the American colonies sought independence from England during the American Revolution.

NOTES

1. Francis J. Bremer, *The Puritan Experiment: New England Society from
Bradford to Edwards* (New York: St. Martin's Press, 1976), 108–12; David Cressy,

Coming Over: Migration and Communication between England and New England in the Seventeenth Century (New York: Cambridge University Press, 1987), 199.

2. Mary Beth Norton, *Founding Mothers and Fathers: Gendered Power and the Forming of American Society* (New York: Vintage Books, 1996), 282–83.

3. William Hand Browne, ed. Archives of Maryland, 72 vols. (Baltimore: Maryland Historical Society, 1883–1972), 1:238–39, quoted in Debra Meyers, *Common Whores, Vertuous Women, and Loveing Wives: Free Will Christian Women in Colonial Maryland* (Bloomington: Indiana University Press, 2003), 25.

4. Mary Beth Norton makes this point in *Founding Mothers and Fathers*, 287.

5. David William Voorhees, "The 'Fervent Zeale' of Jacob Leislet," *William and Mary Quarterly* 51 (July 1994): 465.

6. For more details on the Long Swede and the possible plot to retake New Sweden, see Evan Haefeli, "The Revolt of the Long Swede: Transatlantic Hopes and Fears on the Delaware, 1669," *Pennsylvania Magazine of History and Biography* 130 (April 2006): 137–80.

7. A brief biography of Armegot Printz can be found in Susan E. Klepp, "Encounter and Experiment: The Colonial Period," in *Pennsylvania: A History of the Commonwealth*, ed. Randall M. Miller and William Pencak (University Park, PA: Penn State University Press, 2002), 60.

8. Edmund B. O'Callaghan and Berthold Fernow, eds., *Documents Relative to the Colonial History of the State of New York*, 15 vols. (Albany, NY, 1853–1887), 12: 465–467, 469, 472, quoted in Haefeli, "The Revolt of the Long Swede," 143, 165.

9. Kathleen M. Brown, *Good Wives, Nasty Wenches, and Anxious Patriarchs: Gender, Race, and Power in Colonial Virginia* (Chapel Hill: North Carolina Press, 1996), 106.

10. Ibid., 56, 61.

11. Ibid., 62; Kathleen M. Brown, "Women in Early Jamestown," Interpretive Essays. Available at: Virtual Jamestown, Virginia Center for Digital History, University of Virginia, http://www.virtualjamestown.org/essays/brown_essay.html.

12. Helen C. Rountree, *The Powhatan Indians of Virginia: Their Traditional Culture* (Norman: University of Oklahoma Press, 1989), 148–49, 120–21, 84–85.

13. J. Frederick Fausz and John Kukla, "A Letter of Advice to the Governor of Virginia, 1624," *William and Mary Quarterly* 34 (January 1977): 108.

14. "Robert Beverley's Description of the 1622 Indian Attack." Available at: Virtual Jamestown, Virginia Center for Digital History, University of Virginia. http://www.virtualjamestown.org/1622attk.html.

15. Daniel K. Richter, *The Ordeal of the Longhouse: The Peoples of the Iroquois League in the Era of European Colonization* (Chapel Hill: University of North Carolina Press, 1992), 1–3.

16. Ibid., 32–33.

17. Ibid., 33.

18. This description comes from Daniel Richter's insightful book, *Ordeal of the Longhouse*, 35–36. As he notes, it is difficult to know exactly what the rituals of the Iroquois meant to them because they come to us through European observers.

19. Richter, *Ordeal of the Longhouse*, 58–62.

20. Ibid., 64–74.

21. Reuben Gold Thwaites, ed., *The Jesuit Relations and Allied Documents: Travels and Explorations of the Jesuit Missionaries in New France, 1610–1791*, 73 vols. (Cleveland, OH, 1896–1901), 9: 265–69, quoted in Richter, *Ordeal of the Longhouse*, 71.

22. This information comes from Alice Nash, "'None of the Women Were Abused': Indigenous Contexts for the Treatment of Women Captives in the Northeast," in *Sex without Consent: Rape and Sexual Coercion in America*, ed. Merril D. Smith (New York: New York University Press, 2001), 11–12.

23. Ibid., 13.

24. Ibid., 21.

25. Ibid., 22–23.

26. Richard Slotkin and James K. Folsom, eds., *So Dreadful a Judgment: Puritan Responses to King Philip's War, 1676–1677* (Hanover, NH: Wesleyan University Press, 1978), 3–4.

27. Ann Marie Plane, *Colonial Intimacies: Indian Marriages in Early New England* (Ithaca, NY: Cornell University Press, 2000), 100–101.

28. Ibid., 100.

29. "Indians Taking Salem Fishing Vessels," First Church of Salem Record, Essex Institute Historical Collections, vol. 2, 1860, p. 104. Available at: http://www.hawthorne insalem.org/images/fullpageimage.php?name=MMD1129.

30. Thomas Hutchinson, *The History of the Colony of Massachusetts-Bay* (Boston, 1764), 307, quoted in James Axtell, "The Vengeful Women of Marblehead: Robert Roules's Deposition of 1677," *William and Mary Quarterly* 31, no. 4 (October 1974): 648.

31. Axtell, "Robert Roules's Deposition," 652.

32. Laurel Thatcher Ulrich, *Good Wives: Image and Reality in the Lives of Women in Northern New England, 1650–1750* (New York: Oxford University Press, 1982), 194–95; Axtell, "Robert Roules's Deposition," 652.

33. Ulrich, *Good Wives*, 173; Steven Neuwirth, "Her Master's Voice: Gender, Speech, and Gendered Speech in the Narrative of the Captivity of Mary White Rowlandson," in *Sex and Sexuality in Early America*, ed. Merril D. Smith (New York: New York University Press, 1998), 56.

34. Neuwirth, "Her Master's Voice," 56.

35. For an analysis of Iroquois involvement and an extensive bibliography, see Jon Parmenter, "After the Mourning Wars: The Iroquois as Allies in Colonial North American Campaigns, 1676–1760," *William and Mary Quarterly* 64 (January 2007): 39–82.

36. Ulrich, *Good Wives*, 203.

37. "Statements of Grace Higiman and Others in Relation to Being Taken Captive by the Indians," *New England Historical and Genealogical Register* 18 (1864): 161–163, quoted in Ulrich, *Good Wives*, 207.

38. Ulrich, *Good Wives*, 177, 209.

39. Carol F. Karlsen, *The Devil in the Shape of a Woman: Witchcraft in Colonial New England* (New York: Vintage Books, 1987), 226–27.

40. Ibid., 229.

41. Ibid., 228–29.

42. Mary Beth Norton, *In the Devil's Snare: The Salem Witchcraft Crisis of 1692* (New York: Knopf, 2002), 135, 176–82.

43. Ibid., 176–79.

44. George Lincoln Burr, ed., *Narratives of the Witchcraft Cases, 1648–1706* (New York, 1914), 261–63, 266–67, 282, quoted in Norton, *In the Devil's Snare*, 180.

45. Norton, *In the Devil's Snare*, 135–36.

46. Ulrich, *Good Wives*, 167–68. Ulrich writes that Hannah Duston was awarded a scalp bounty of 25 pounds. Other sources report sums of forty to fifty pounds, or that Hannah shared a sum of fifty pounds with her cocaptives. Robert D. Arner,

"The Story of Hannah Duston: Cotton Mather to Thoreau," *American Transcendental Quarterly* 18 (1973): 19–23. Available at: http://www.hawthorneinsalem.org/page/11874.

47. Ulrich, *Good Wives*, 168–72, 185–201; Else Hambleton, *Daughters of Eve: Pregnant Brides and Unwed Mothers in Seventeenth-Century Massachusetts* (New York: Routledge, 2004), 135–36.

48. Laura Browder, *Her Best Shot: Women and Guns in America* (Chapel Hill: University of North Carolina Press, 2006), 22, 25–26; Dianne Dugaw, *Warrior Women and Popular Balladry, 1650–1850* (Chicago: University of Chicago Press, 1996) 43. Dianne Dugaw performs Mary Ambree and other songs about warrior women on her CD, *Dangerous Examples: Fighting and Sailing Women in Song* (2001); "Mary Ambree," Arthur Quiller-Couch, ed. *The Oxford Book of Ballads* (1910), Ballad 165. Available at: http://www.bartleby.com/243/165.html.

49. Terri L. Snyder, *Brabbling Women: Disorderly Speech and the Law in Early Virginia* (Ithaca, NY: Cornell University Press, 2003), 11–15; 85–86.

50. Brown, *Good Wives, Nasty Wenches*, 139–44.

51. Ibid., 160–61.

52. Snyder, *Brabbling Women*, 25–26.

53. Snyder, *Brabbling Women*, 28–29; Lady Frances Berkeley to [unknown], [n.d.], Coventry Papers of the Marquess of Bath at Longleaf House, microfilm, Library of Congress, vol. 77, f. 41, quoted in Snyder, *Brabbling Women*, 29.

54. Lady Frances Berkeley to [unknown], [n.d.], Coventry Papers, vol. 77, f. 41, quoted in Snyder, *Brabbling Women*, 30.

55. Snyder, *Brabbling Women*, 24, 31–32.

56. Brown, *Good Wives, Nasty Wenches*, 162–63.

57. Sir William Berkeley to [T. Ludwell], 1 July 1676, Coventry Papers, vol. 77, f. 144, quoted in Snyder, *Brabbling Women*, 34.

58. Herbert R. Paschal, ed. "George Bancroft's 'Lost Notes' on the General Courts of Virginia," *Virginia Magazine of History and Biography* 91 (July 1983): 355–58, quoted in Snyder, *Brabbling Women*, 35.

59. Snyder, *Brabbling Women*, 36; Wilcomb E. Washburn, "The Humble Petition of Sarah Drummond," *William and Mary Quarterly* 13 (July 1956): 356.

60. Snyder, *Brabbling Women*, 35; Brown, *Good Wives, Nasty Women*, 174–75.

61. Snyder, *Brabbling Women*, 37; Brown, *Good Wives, Nasty Women*, 165–66.

62. Martha W. McCartney, "Cockacoeske, Queen of the Pamunkey, Diplomat and Suzeraine," in *Powhatan's Mantle: Indians in the Colonial Southeast*, ed. Gregory A. Waslkov, Peter H. Wood, and M. Thomas Hatley (Lincoln: University of Nebraska Press, 2006), 243, 247–48; "The Beginning, Progress, and Conclusion of Bacon's Rebellion in Virginia, in the Years 1675 and 1676," First Hand Accounts of Virginia, 1575–1705. Available at: Virtual Jamestown, Virginia Center for Digital History, University of Virginia, http://etext.lib.virginia.edu/etcbin/jamestown-browse?id=J1057.

63. Brown, *Good Wives, Nasty Wenches*, 168; McCartney, "Cockacoeske," 248, 251.

SUGGESTED READING

Brown, Kathleen M. *Good Wives, Nasty Wenches, and Anxious Patriarchs: Gender, Race, and Power in Colonial Virginia.* Chapel Hill: University of North Carolina Press, 1996.

Dugaw, Dianne. *Warrior Women and Popular Balladry, 1650–1850.* Chicago: University of Chicago Press, 1996.

Karlsen, Carol F. *The Devil in the Shape of a Woman: Witchcraft in Colonial New England.* New York: Vintage Books, 1987.

Nash, Alice. "'None of the Women were Abused': Indigenous Contexts for the Treatment of Women Captives in the Northeast." In *Sex without Consent: Rape and Sexual Coercion in America,* edited by Merril D. Smith, 10–16. New York: New York University Press, 2001.

Norton, Mary Beth. *In the Devil's Snare: The Salem Witchcraft Crisis of 1692.* New York: Knopf, 2002.

Richter, Daniel K. *The Ordeal of the Longhouse: The Peoples of the Iroquois League in the Era of European Colonization.* Chapel Hill: University of North Carolina Press, 1992.

Rountree, Helen C. *The Powhatan Indians of Virginia: Their Traditional Culture.* Norman: University of Oklahoma Press, 1989.

Snyder, Terri L. *Brabbling Women: Disorderly Speech and the Law in Early Virginia.* Ithaca, NY: Cornell University Press, 2003.

Ulrich, Laurel Thatcher. *Good Wives: Image and Reality in the Lives of Women in Northern New England, 1650–1750.* New York: Oxford University Press, 1982.

7

⟶ ∞∞∞ ⟵

Women and Education, Literature, and Recreation

In early modern Europe, most people did not know how to read and write, and very few children attended schools. Yet both boys and girls received instruction or training suitable to their status and future plans. In some cases, this involved formal apprenticeships, but in other instances, parents taught their offspring or sent them to live in the homes of others. All female children were trained in the domestic arts, as even wellborn women had to know how to run a household and do fine needlework. Scholars and theologians, however, debated whether girls should be taught to read and write. Many believed that women who were taught to read became sexually promiscuous, especially if they were taught Latin, Greek, or Hebrew. Nevertheless, some girls did receive educations that went beyond domestic skills and needlework. In Italy, for example, at least some Jewish girls were instructed in reading and sometimes in other subjects, as well. This education ranged from barely learning to read Italian to learning both Italian and Hebrew. A few of these educated Jewish women even became scholars and wrote their own books. Some rabbis believed that it was beneficial for a Jewish woman to have some basic literacy skills to help run her household and assist with a family business, and "to serve as a decorative ornament that enhanced the public prestige and honor of the entire family."[1] In the seventeenth century, many young women in Europe also received sophisticated musical training from well-known composers, such as Antonio Vivaldi in Italy and Henry Purcell in England, who taught music in schools, in addition to writing and performing their own works. Thus, literate and accomplished women were not unknown in seventeenth-century Europe, and at least some acceptance in the belief that women should be educated carried over to the British North American colonies.[2]

With the Protestant Reformation came increased attention to literacy throughout Europe, as Protestants believed it was important for men and women to be able to read the Bible. For Puritans in England, education became an issue of extreme importance. Before the Civil War, Puritans had complained that many among the clergy were lacking in scholarship of the scriptures, as well as in general knowledge. Moreover, some of the clergy were actually neglectful of their parishioners, or even disreputable. Thus, Puritans in England often held their own meetings to pray and study scripture. They also circulated information about educated ministers who were pious and respectable. Many of these dedicated clergymen were graduates of Cambridge who were critical of the established Anglican Church.[3]

Puritans believed that both men and women should be able to read so that they could understand and interpret the Bible for themselves, rather than relying on an intermediary priest. Yet most people lacked the formal education necessary to comprehend the complexities of biblical text. Although they believed each individual experienced his or her own personal relationship with God, demonstrated most clearly in the conversion experience, and each individual was responsible for this relationship with God, he or she could seek advice and guidance from learned clergymen. Because women were not permitted to attend universities or to become ministers, it was especially important for them to be able to consult educated ministers, so that their reading and contemplation did not lead them to wicked and heretical beliefs. (See Chapter 5 for more on women and religion.)

Despite the warning of some men that too much learning could make a woman become unbalanced, and the concerns of others that highly educated women posed a threat to religious orthodoxy, Puritan women were encouraged to read, or at least to read the Bible. In fact, reading was one of the activities virtuous women engaged in, according to the ministerial literature of the late seventeenth century. Both men and women were encouraged to read the Bible through once a year. Published eulogies laud the virtuous women who read the Bible through more than once a year and who spent time reading other religious works, although most likely they were only a small percentage of the population—often the wives, daughters, and mothers of educated men.[4]

It is difficult to determine literacy rates in colonial America. Scholars have examined legal documents such as wills from seventeenth- and eighteenth-century New England to see how often men and women actually signed their names, as compared to how many merely marked them. Although the numbers vary, these studies indicate that well into the eighteenth century women were less likely than men to be able to sign their names. This does not mean, however, that the women could not read. In fact, many New England women probably could read, even though they could not write.[5]

In the seventeenth century, Massachusetts, Connecticut, New Haven, Plymouth, New York, and Pennsylvania passed laws requiring the teaching of reading. Massachusetts was the first colony to pass such a law in 1642. Under this law, the select men in every town were asked to "have a vigilant eye over their brethren & neighbors" to make sure that all children and apprentices learn enough "to inable them perfectly to read the english tongue, & knowledge of the Capital Lawes." Children and apprentices were also supposed to learn the catechism, which the selectmen could ask them to recite. Parents or masters who did not teach their children or servants to read could be fined, and the children might even be removed from their homes and placed elsewhere.[6] Several Massachusetts towns, such as Dorchester, Salem, and Watertown, carried out inspections and found families in which the children were illiterate. In general, these children came from poor families.[7]

Although the Massachusetts law required that children be taught to read, it did not mention writing until the subsequent version passed in 1703. This version stated that masters should provide "for the instructing of children so bound out, to read and write, if they be capable." A 1710 amendment clarified this law and called for "males to read and write, females to read." It is clear that lawmakers considered writing to be a necessary skill for boys, but not for girls.[8]

Writing was a specialized skill that was usually taught only by men. As well as designating an educated man, the ability to write was essential for boys who wanted to enter business, as clerks, for example. Yet it was just as necessary for farmers and shopkeepers to be able write to keep accurate accounts. Early Americans perceived writing as a job-related skill, and something boys needed to know. Susanna Anthony Roberts, a free African in New Amsterdam, recognized the importance of reading and writing. Although she could not write, as guardian for her brother, she made sure that his apprenticeship agreement included that he be taught to read and write. Girls, however, did not need to be able to write because they were being trained to be wives and mothers. For them, sewing was a necessary skill. This way of thinking can be seen clearly in one 1656 Hartford Court ruling. In an examination of Thomas Gridley's estate, the court ordered "the sons shall have learning to write plainly and read distinctly in the Bible, and the daughters to read and sew sufficient for the making of their ordinary linen."[9]

In contrast to writing, seventeenth-century Anglo-Americans considered reading to be a skill that was easy to learn and important for both boys and girls to know. Reading was taught orally, and therefore, it was not necessary to know how to write to teach reading. Basic reading skills were usually taught by women, either mothers, mistresses, or teachers in "dame schools," informal schools held in women's homes. (See Chapter 4 for more on women as teachers.) The Reverend Increase Mather's mother, a "very Holy praying woman," taught him to read; however, it became quite common early in the seventeenth century for children of both sexes to attend a privately funded dame school. Children started there at about age three or four. Boys could then go on to attend grammar schools, where they learned writing, Latin, and other subjects from schoolmasters. Girls were seldom admitted to these schools, and women did not teach in them.[10]

Other Protestant sects also considered Bible reading to be important. During his journey through New York, the Dutch traveler Jasper Danckaerts met an Indian woman who told him and his companion the story of how she became a Christian. The woman became alienated from her own mother because of her desire to embrace Christianity, and she went to live with a Dutch woman who

> taught her to read and write and do various handiwork, in which she advanced so greatly that everybody was astonished. She had especially a great desire to learn to read, and applied herself to that end day and night, and asked others, who were near her, to the vexation and annoyance of the other maids, who lived with her, who could sometimes with difficulty keep her back. But that did not restrain her; she felt such an eagerness and desire to learn that she could not be withheld, particularly when she began to understand the Dutch language, and what was expressed in the New Testament, where her whole heart was. In a short time, therefore, she understood more about it than the other girls with whom she conversed, and who had first instructed her, and, particularly, was sensible in her heart of its truth. She had lived with different people, and had very much improved; she spoke of it with heart-felt delight. Finally, she made her profession, and was baptized.[11]

According to Danckaerts' account, no one seemed surprised that the woman who took in the Indian woman also taught her to read and write, and he did not seem surprised either. The woman's desire to learn in order to read the Bible is similar to the stories told by Puritan ministers of virtuous Puritan women.

The Puritans' commitment to education led to the founding of Harvard College. A bequest from John Harvard permitted the school to open in 1638. Modeled on the English universities at Oxford and Cambridge, the curriculum of Harvard added the study of Hebrew and Aramaic in order for its scholars to better understand the scriptures. Nevertheless, less than half of its graduates actually became ministers.[12]

Although only men were permitted to attend Harvard, it was a woman who established the first scholarship there. Ann Radcliffe, Lady Mowlson, created a scholarship to assist a poor scholar in 1643. Ann Radcliffe was born in 1576. She married Thomas Mowlson in 1600, and they had two children who died at a young age. Her husband left her with half of his estate when he died in 1658. She managed it so well that she was able to loan money to Parliament and support Puritan causes. She died in 1661. The women's college connected to Harvard was named after her in 1894. Radcliffe College is now a part of Harvard University.[13]

Much of the instructional material for schools and scholars came from England. Hornbooks, for example, usually a child's first introduction to reading, were imported. Hornbooks consisted of one page attached to a paddle. A thin, transparent layer of cow's horn protected the paper or parchment. The page contained a listing of the alphabet, a guide to pronouncing vowel sounds, and The Lord's Prayer. The noted diarist Samuel Sewall recorded the first time his almost three-year-old son, Joseph, went off to a dame school. In his diary entry for April 27, 1691, Sewall wrote Joseph was off "to Capt. Townsend's Mother's." His cousin, Jane, went with him and carried his hornbook.[14]

Although nearly all books had to be brought from across the sea in the early years of settlement, New England Puritans purchased books whenever they could afford to do so. In one comparison of inventories from Jamaica and Suffolk County, Massachusetts, probated between 1670 and 1700, it can be seen that in most Jamaican homes there were Bibles, but usually not many more books. The Suffolk County inventories, however, "disclose a good many sizeable libraries, generally of a very sober taste."[15] Usually, the books they bought were religious books. Almost every home had a Bible, but Puritans also bought published sermons, religious tracts, and other religious works. Wealthier Puritan households were more likely to own books; however, even those without much money owned some books. For instance, the widow Emme Mason, who was not a wealthy woman, owned fourteen books, including a Bible and a book of sermons.[16]

Books became more generally available toward the end of the seventeenth century. This availability can be viewed in a more ominous light in the records of the Salem Witchcraft crisis. Two decades before the events in Salem, Elizabeth Knapp was the first woman in New England to describe signing the Devil's book, rather than a piece of paper. The account of her affliction was published widely, and people in Salem would have been familiar with her story. A striking number of the afflicted victims and the confessed witches in Salem described signing or being asked to sign the Devil's book. Historians believe that this obsession with books in Salem arose from books of all sorts suddenly becoming available after the mid-1680s. For many years, the only printing press in the British North American colonies was one in Massachusetts. This press only printed religious works and official documents, but toward the end of the seventeenth century, presses in New England and the Middle Colonies started to print almanacs and primers. Salem residents may also have been exposed to books on occult topics such as astrology that were being imported by booksellers.[17]

Wealthier women, of course, were more likely both to own more books and to be better educated. Women from wealthy families received writing instruction from private writing masters, but this was more likely to happen in Boston and other cities, rather in rural areas, because there were more men who could teach writing in urban areas. When men such as Cotton Mather praised the writing of virtuous women, the women they praised were nearly all women of high social status, and often the sisters, daughters, or wives of ministers. Such women took notes on church sermons and left pious reflections for their families when facing death. Often, the male eulogizer took care to mention that the woman did not neglect her needle or other duties in order to write.[18]

Nevertheless, sometimes circumstances forced a woman to step out of her domestic role and take on what would normally be the duties of a man. This was particularly true of women living in frontier areas. During wars, for example, women often had to take over the responsibilities of absent husbands, or even become "warrior women," as described in Chapter 6. On at least a few occasions, Indians made use of and valued the writing skills of female captives. During Metacom's Rebellion, the Abenakis captured Elizabeth Hammon. After spending a year with them, she wrote and delivered a letter to the English that described possible settlement terms. Cotton Mather described a similar occurrence in 1691 after some captives had been redeemed. He noted that the Indians had not wanted Mistress Hull to leave them "because being able to Write Well, they made her serve them in the Quality of a Secretary."[19]

In contrast, Mary Rowlandson used her skill at writing to produce a book about her captivity experience. Published in 1682, six years after her release from captivity, *The Sovereignty & Goodness of God, Together, with the Faithfulness of His Promises Displayed* is the only extant record of the 1675–1676 Indian raid of Lancaster, Massachusetts. Moreover, it is one of the few published works written by a seventeenth-century American woman. (See Chapter 6 for details on Mary Rowlandson's life.)[20]

Although colored by a seventeenth-century Puritan perception of Indians as cruel, brutish heathens, Mary Rowlandson's narrative is deeply moving, especially as she describes such events as the death of her daughter, who had been wounded when they were captured.[21] Mary Rowlandson's faith in God sustained her throughout her captivity. Indeed, her identity as a Puritan woman provided her with a framework in which she attempted to make sense of her experience in captivity. Because she was a Puritan, she believed that humans were naturally corrupted and easily led astray. As the wife of a minister and a member of the church, she could believe that she was one of the elect, while acknowledging that it was only through God's mercy. During her captivity, she read a Bible given to her by an Indian visitor, and that comforted her in moments of despair.

Nevertheless, the Mary Rowlandson who emerges from the narrative is "more housewife than saint." For example, she used her skill with sewing and knitting needles to barter for food. In addition, Mary Rowlandson understood what it meant to live in a hierarchical society. In her own society, she held a prominent rank as the wife of a minister, but in captivity, she became a slave, especially to Wetamoo, the wife of her master Quinnapin.[22]

Because seventeenth-century Anglo-American women were rarely permitted to voice their opinions in public, the well-known minister Increase Mather provided a preface to Mary Rowlandson's narrative asserting her humility and desire only to help others by publicizing her story. As he states: "this gentlewoman's modesty would thrust it into the press, yet her gratitude unto God made her not hardly persuadable to let it pass, that God might have his due glory, and others benefit by it as well as herself."[23] The title page asserts that the book was "Written by Her Own Hand for Her Private Use, and Now Made Public at the Earnest Desire of Some Friends, and for the Benefit of the Afflicted."[24]

Similarly, Massachusetts Puritan Anne Bradstreet's first published book of poetry, *The Tenth Muse Lately Sprung Up in America* (1650), contained an introduction by her brother-in-law, Reverend John Woodbridge, to assure readers of the author's modesty and decorum. He noted that he "presumed to bring to publick view, what she resolved in such a manner should never see the Sun." Reverend Woodbridge further assured readers that she was not neglecting her duties as a wife and mother: "[T]hese Poems are the fruit but of some few houres, curtailed from her sleep and other refreshments."[25] Although published several decades before Mary Rowlandson's narrative, both books shared a similar understanding that women who stepped out of the private roles of wives and mothers and into the public forums of men were immediately suspected of being immoral and dissolute—unless it could be demonstrated that they did so out of necessity or because they had been convinced to do so by honorable men in order to benefit the general public.

Anne Bradstreet was eighteen when she arrived in Massachusetts in April 1630 with her husband, Simon Bradstreet, and her parents, Thomas and Dorothy Dudley. She had lived a comfortable life in England. Her

Title page of *The Tenth Muse* by Anne Bradstreet,
1650. Courtesy of The Granger Collection, New York.

father was the steward of the Puritan Earl of Lincoln, and her husband
was her father's assistant. Her father taught her Greek, Latin, French, and
Hebrew, and she had access to the earl's vast library. Although her
husband had not attended a university, he was well educated.[26]

Thomas Dudley and Simon Bradstreet were among the founders of the
Massachusetts Bay Company. The two families sailed to Massachusetts
with John Winthrop and other Puritans on the *Arbella*. Yet life was difficult in Salem, Massachusetts, and the Dudley and Bradstreet families
shared a cramped house that was bitterly cold in the winter. After several
moves, the Bradstreets and the Dudleys finally settled in Ipswich in 1635,
and Anne Bradstreet began writing the poems that would eventually
appear in *The Tenth Muse*. Although the Bradstreets had four children by
1640, and Simon Bradstreet was often away on business as a member of
the Court of Assistants, Anne Bradstreet continued to write and to have

children, despite her constant ill health. The Bradstreets had eight children in all, and moved several more times.[27]

Anne Bradstreet wrote a number of love poems to her husband. Many of them were written during his frequent absences. The often-quoted opening lines from her poem "To My Dear and Loving Husband" clearly express the love she had for her husband:

> If ever two were one, then surely we.
> If ever man were lov'd by wife, then thee.
> If ever wife was happy in a man,
> Compare with me, ye women, if you can.[28]

Puritans believed that husbands and wives should love one another—but not so much that it eclipsed their love of God. Similarly, Puritan parents were expected to love their children, but again, not too deeply. Anne Bradstreet's poems often reflect the conflict she felt between her love for her husband and children and her duty to God. Many of these deeply personal poems appeared in the second edition of *The Tenth Muse*, published in 1678, six years after Anne Bradstreet's death.

One of these poems was written in 1669 after the death of one of her grandchildren.

> With troubled heart & trembling hand I write,
> The Heavens have chang'd to sorrow my delight
> How oft with disappointment have I met,
> When I on fading things my hopes have set?
> . . . .
> I knew she was but as a withering flour,
> That's here to day, perhaps gone in an hour;
> Like as a bubble, or the brittle glass,
> Or like a shadow turning as it was.
> More fool then I to look on what was lent,
> As if mine own, when thus impermanent.[29]

Although Anne Bradstreet attempted to be a proper Puritan wife and mother, she also wanted recognition as a poet. In her early poems, many of them published in *The Tenth Muse*, she portrayed herself as meek and not worthy of inclusion in the company of male poets. Nevertheless, she clearly wanted to be considered as good a poet as any man.[30]

Anne Bradstreet was not being unduly cautious in her approach to literary achievement. Women who ventured into the male world of literature often found themselves labeled as dangerous to themselves and to others. In 1645, John Winthrop, governor of Massachusetts, recorded in his journal that Anne Hopkins, wife of Connecticut's governor, had lost "her understanding and reason, which had been growing upon her divers years, by occasion of her giving herself wholly to reading and writing, and had written many books." Winthrop continued, noting that her husband had failed to see that he should have disciplined her before it was too late, and made sure that she confined herself to "her household affairs."[31]

The lesson to be cautious in speaking out hit even closer to home for Anne Bradstreet. In 1646, her younger sister, Sarah, was excommunicated from the church in Boston for preaching and "Prophesying in mixt Assemblies." As a result, Sarah Keayne's husband divorced her, and her father disinherited her.[32]

Yet it was probably the excommunication and exile of Anne Hutchinson that most clearly demonstrated the dangers women faced if they chose to speak or write in public. (For more on Anne Hutchinson and religion, see Chapter 5.) Anne Bradstreet and Anne Hutchinson came from very similar backgrounds, and they had both been members of John Cotton's congregation in England, and supported him in Massachusetts. They came from families in which education was valued and where they were exposed to intellectual discussion. Both women were intelligent and longed to express themselves. Anne Bradstreet did it through poetry. Anne Hutchinson did it through speech. By all accounts, she was a gifted speaker, but it was this gift that angered and disturbed the authorities. John Winthrop wrote that she inspired her followers in such a way that

> the influence was speedily felt in the serious disturbance, first of domestic happiness, and then of public peace. The matrons of Boston were transformed into a synod of slanderous praters, whose inquisitional deliberations and audacious decrees, instilled their venom into the innermost recesses of society; and the spirits of a great majority of the citizens being in that combustible state in which a feeble spark will suffice to kindle a formidable conflagration, the whole Colony was inflamed and distracted by the incontinence of female spleen and presumption.[33]

In contrast, Anne Bradstreet managed not to step outside of her role as wife and mother; even as she wrote poetry, she took care of her household and eight children. Although a few times she did come close to challenging authorities in her works, she was careful never to go too far. Since her husband and father were among the men who prosecuted Anne Hutchinson, Anne Bradstreet must have been aware of what awaited women who spoke in public or who dared to challenge authorities.[34]

Although there were only a few seventeenth-century women who were published authors, other women did write, either for themselves in journals and notes on religious matters, or for others in letters or on business matters. Letters were especially important as a method of keeping informed about one's families and friends. As one historian has noted, "Letters provided an emotional lifeline, a cord of communication, that stretched across the wide ocean to inform, comfort, or persuade kinsmen and friends on the other side."[35]

The well to do and educated were more likely to send letters. In fact, it was expected that they would do so. Just as modern-day American parents remind their college-bound sons and daughters to call home or to send them an email, John Winthrop reminded his son Fitz-John before he left for England in 1658 to write letters to his family. "Your mother will also be much troubled that most others that have relations here have written to their friends, and she cannot hear of any from you. You should write by every way that offers."[36]

Yet even poorer people and those who were illiterate might send a letter if they had a pressing need or desire to do so. For example, Francis Chapple, an illiterate fisherman in Marblehead asked his neighbor, James Mander, to write several letters. Francis Chapple was trying to convince his sweetheart in England, Mary Litten, to come to Massachusetts and marry him. Chapple also sent Mary Litten some tokens of his affection with some friends who were returning to England.[37]

Letters were also used in attempts to reconcile married couples. Although some men immigrated to New England, and then brought their wives and families over later, other couples used "separation by ocean" as a form of self-divorce. When John Leech of Salem was brought before the Essex County Court in 1649 because he and his wife were not living together, he stated that "he often sent and wrote to her, but she was unwilling to come, and he was not able to live in old England."[38]

Women who could write letters used this skill to keep in touch with their husbands and children. When they did not hear from loved ones, however, they wrote letters to others asking for news about spouses or offspring. Ann Hoskins, for example, wrote to her kinsman John Winthrop asking about her son. "I pray if my son be living let him write me a letter."[39] In contrast, John Hall, who was born in Massachusetts, but returned to England, kept up a correspondence with his mother, Rebecca Symonds, who lived in New England, for nearly two decades. As he wrote to her in 1666, "The only way by which at a distance I can discourse with you is by letters." In addition to the letters, John Hall often sent his mother items of clothing and accessories that were currently in fashion in London and gave her advice on the latest styles.[40]

Dipping a pen in ink and writing a legible letter took some skill and practice. Sometimes an illness, weakness, or old age made the task impossible to complete. Those who could not write because they were too sick, weak, or injured asked for help from family members of friends. For example, in the 1680s when Dorothy Rider, Samuel Sewall's aunt in

England, could not write because of a weakness in her hand, his cousin Sarah took over the letter writing.[41]

To write a letter, colonists required pen, paper, and ink. Paper was expensive, because it had to be imported, but many people made their own ink. There were many recipes for ink, which could be made from many different substances. One recipe in a 1611 book used wine as its base:

> To make common Inke of wine take a quart
> Two ounces of Gumme let that be a part,
> Fiue ounces of Gals, of Copres take three,
> Long standing doth make it the better to be.
> If wine ye do want, raine water is best,
> And then as much stuffe as aboue at the least.
> If Inke be too thicke, put vineger in:
> For water doth make the colour more dim.[42]

In addition to the pen, ink, and paper, letter writers usually used wax to seal the letter, and often used powder to dry the ink. Adequate light and a level writing surface were useful, but sometimes difficult to find. In writing to the Countess of Lincoln in 1631, Thomas Dudley reported that "having yet no table, nor other room to write in than by the fireside upon my knee, in this sharp winter; to which my family must have need to resort, though they break good manners, and make me so many times forget what I would say, and what I would not."[43]

Like books, writing paper, and many other goods, colonists brought the educational practices and curriculum over from England. In New England, the education of both laity and clergy assumed even more importance because settlers were in the wilderness surrounded by heathen Indians and Catholic French who might tempt them or their children and lead them into wickedness. To uphold their covenant with God, Puritans needed to know and understand his word. Moreover, Puritans intended New England to serve as an example of a godly society to the rest of the world.

Settlers in other colonies may not have felt this sense of mission, but many of them did believe that education was important. In the Chesapeake colonies, formal education and books were not a high priority for most people in the early part of the seventeenth century when most of the population consisted of young, single, indentured servants. As a native born white population became established, education became more important, as parents wanted to ensure that their children would have the skills to improve their situations. By the close of the seventeenth century, for instance, white children usually received very gender-specific educations. This is clearly revealed in the indentures for white children. The indentures for a girl might state that she be taught to read, but they almost always noted that she be taught sewing, spinning, and other "household work." On the other hand, boys' indentures specified that they be taught to read and write, and that they learn the skills of a particular trade. Implicit in these indentures was the idea that neither white girls nor boys would have to perform agricultural work.[44]

In all of the colonies, as in England, sewing was a skill that nearly every girl learned as part of her education. In the recommendations for the fifty-seven young women who sailed to Virginia in 1621 to become wives several mention their domestic skills. Of these, five were reported to be good with thread or needle; one could make bone lace; others were able to sew, knit, spin, weave, or make buttons. Ann Tanner could "Spinn and sewe in blackworke . . . brue, and bake, make butter and cheese, and doe housewifery."[45] Although some aristocratic seventeenth-century girls learned to do fine needlework and to embroider, it was a pastime more suited to the "pretty gentlewomen" of the eighteenth century than the "good wives" and indentured servants of the seventeenth century. In frontier settlements, it was more important to be able to sew and repair clothing than it was to embroider.[46] As mentioned previously, Mary Rowlandson's skill with a needle enabled her to survive her captivity.

Yet the first American-made sampler comes from Plymouth Colony. Loara Standish, born sometime after 1627, was the daughter of the May-flower passengers Myles and Barbara Standish. She stitched the sampler in silk thread on fine linen in a variety of colors. The sampler contains a signed verse, indicating that someone must have taught her the alphabet, as well as skilled embroidery.[47]

Wealthier and educated parents in the Chesapeake also believed in the importance of educating their children. Beginning in 1667, a few Maryland girls were able to attend a Jesuit boarding school in Newton, Maryland, but most girls were educated at home by their mothers. Because there were few Anglican or Catholic priests in the colony, mothers were generally in charge of religious educations for their children, as well as teaching them the basics of reading, and perhaps writing. Signatures on land transfer documents and court records indicate that some Maryland women were able to write, and therefore, they may have been able to teach their children some rudimentary skills. If parents did not depend on their children's labor, they sent them for some formal schooling for a year or two in a school taught by either a clergyman or a female teacher. This happened at about age twelve—after children had received some instruction from their mothers.[48]

As in New England, however, Maryland authorities sometimes considered educated women to be immoral or dissolute, especially if they spoke in public or "flaunted" their knowledge. Father William Hunter, for

Loara Standish sampler. Courtesy of Pilgrim Society, Pilgrim Hall Museum.

example, complained that women in the colony were involved in "licentious discourses, indiscreet libertiys, immodest looks, dangerous curiositys, readings, conversation, and diversions unbecoming a [Christian], excesses against temperance, & a soft & sensual life." Father Hunter's sermon against women who spent time reading and who engaged in discussions outside of their homes indicates that there must have been at least some women who did engage in such activities.[49]

In fact, there were elite women in the Chesapeake colonies who wrote letters and discussed political and social matters with men and women. Margaret Brent, for example, appeared in court numerous times, served as executrix for Governor Leonard Calvert, and was the attorney for Lord

Baltimore. Lady Francis Berkeley wrote letters to officials, friends, and relatives, and she engaged in public discourse before, during, and after Bacon's Rebellion in 1676.

Although women such as Anne Hutchinson got into trouble for expressing opinions to men and women in public meetings, it should be noted that the culture of seventeenth-century America was very much an oral culture. Likewise, the line between public and private was not always distinct. Letters from family and friends were passed around, and many books and pamphlets were read aloud. It is likely that women heard news that their husbands and fathers told other men, and then they passed the news along to other women.

In New England, reading aloud to others was a popular recreational activity. Courting couples sometimes even held reading parties. Of course, in seventeenth-century New England, people generally read published sermons and other religious works. The published sermons were usually about twenty to thirty pages long and not filled with overly complex arguments. They were written to be entertaining, as well as instructive, and sometimes they even contained material that was meant to titillate.

One historian has noted that the style of the of these religious pamphlets tended to be

> allusive but not usually elusive. Puritan language contained puffs of smoke, sudden storms, pieces of food laden with symbolic meanings; and it contained raw, direct, descriptive prose befitting people who prided themselves on having the courage to confront the world head-on with its sinfulness. Anecdote, folklore, hearsay, and overstatement coursed through their writings. Imps, demons, witches, voices in the night, infernal trumpets blaring were among the parts of the invisible world that Puritan writers tried to make visible to their readers.[50]

In small Puritan towns, especially during the cold winter months, hearing someone read these religious works filled with all sorts of incredible beings and situations must have been very entertaining.

In Puritan towns and in frontier areas, in particular, entertainment opportunities were limited. Singing and dancing were not strictly prohibited. Men and women sang madrigals, and they played instruments such as flutes and violins. Puritans even sang hymns during services, but without accompaniment. People sang the words to the tunes of ballads with which they were familiar. Singing itself was not considered to be immoral, but it was not supposed to be done to show off or to be done in a wanton way.[51]

Similarly, dancing itself was not necessarily considered immoral, and some Puritans pointed out that even Oliver Cromwell, Lord Protector of England, enjoyed dancing. It was considered by some to be good exercise, but others were afraid it would lead to sin, especially when women and

The Dances at Their Great Feasts. Engraving by Theodor de Bry, 1590, after a watercolor by John White. Courtesy of Library of Congress.

men danced together. Some towns did prohibit dancing in public, so that all dancing had to be done at home. In 1684, Increase Mather wrote *An Arrow Against Profance & Promiscuous Dancing Drawn out of the Quiver of the Scriptures.* Mather wrote this work to try to prevent a dancing school from opening in Boston. He believed that dancing itself was not bad, but that it could lead to lewd and lascivious behavior between men and women. Nevertheless, when Massachusetts became a royal colony in 1692, Governor Sir William Phips sponsored some formal balls that became very popular with the elite of Boston.[52]

Many Native Americans also enjoyed dancing. The Powhatans believed dancing was an essential part of life, and they took pleasure in dancing "almost as frequent[ly] . . . as their meat and drinck."[53] Fires were made in the evening, and anyone who wanted to dance could do so. Men and women both danced, and frequently they danced together in a circle with someone or something in the center. As well, they danced to honor visitors. For example, in 1608, thirty young women danced for the English visitors waiting to meet with Powhatan.[54] Although a few English observers remarked on the similarities between Indian dances and music and

English dances and music, most believed them to be savage and crude, as they did about most aspects of Native American culture.

When combined with deliberately lewd behavior and Indian "savages," dancing became dangerous and untenable to Massachusetts Puritans. In 1626, Thomas Morton took over Wollaston plantation just outside of Plymouth Colony and renamed it Merry Mount. Morton and his followers set up a maypole, and as Governor William Bradford recorded, "drinking and dancing about it for many days together, inviting the Indian women for their consorts, dancing and frisking together." Although Morton declared that the activities were just "harmless mirth," the colonists of Plymouth viewed the behavior of Morton and the others as degenerate and pagan. It was this type of immoral activity that they had hoped to leave behind in England.[55]

Much of the culture of old England, however, did follow men and women to New England and the rest of British North America. In 1660, the court in New Haven complained about young men and women who gathered together "debauching themselves" and singing and dancing. Sometimes the young people met for such illicit pursuits under cover of officially sanctioned activities such as husking corn. Yet women had to be particularly careful of their reputations. In 1674, the Massachusetts General Court ordered that no "single woman or wife in the absence of her husband" be permitted to "entertain or lodge any inmate or sojourner," unless she first received permission from the town authorities.[56]

In Massachusetts, authorities tried to keep the values of the first generation of settlers alive, but by the 1670s, Boston was a growing city with citizens who were eager to display their wealth. One way they did this is through portraits of themselves or their families. Although there are no known professional female artists from the seventeenth century, a few women did sit for portraits. One of these women was Elizabeth Freake, whose portrait with her infant daughter, Mary, is one of the few portraits of seventeenth-century American women in existence. The portrait was started around 1671. Elizabeth Freake was married to a wealthy Boston merchant, John Freake, who had his portrait painted by the same anonymous artist. Both Freakes have the almond-shaped eyes that were this artist's trademark. The paintings display the Freakes in expensive finery with elegant furniture and backgrounds. The Freakes were Puritans, but not as austere as previous generations.[57]

Women in seventeenth-century America had a number of different roles, and for much of the century they had little time to devote to cultural pursuits. Yet that does not mean that they were not interested. Colonial women had varying degrees of education and interest in books, but few African or African-American women were taught to read, especially in the South. Although many white women in New England knew how to read, nearly all of them were thoroughly educated in domestic skills. Most women,

Elizabeth Clarke Freake (Mrs. John Freake) and Baby Mary. Courtesy of Worcester Art Museum, Worcester, Massachusetts, Gift of
Mr. and Mrs. Albert W. Rice.

however, probably had little time to spend in reading or writing, unless they
had servants or older daughters who could take over some domestic chores.
Nevertheless, many of them did find the time to instruct their children in
the basics of reading. Moreover, even in Puritan New England, some
women took pleasure in listening to works read aloud or occasionally
enjoyed singing a ballad, or tapping their feet to an old English tune.

NOTES

1. Howard Edelman, "The Literacy of Jewish Women in Early Modern Italy," in
Women's Education in Early Modern Europe, 1500–1800, ed. Barbara J. Whitehead
(New York: Routledge, 1999), 134.

2. For an overview of women's education in early modern Europe, see Meg Lota
Brown and Kari Boyd McBride, *Women's Roles in the Renaissance* (Westport, CT:
Greenwood Press, 2005), chap. 1.

3. Marilyn J. Westerkamp, *Women and Religion in Early America, 1600–1850: The Puritan and Evangelical Traditions* (New York: Routledge, 1999), 12; Francis J. Bremer, *The Puritan Experiment: New England Society from Bradford to Edwards* (New York: St. Martin's Press, 1976), 26.

4. Laurel Thatcher Ulrich, "Vertuous Women Found: New England Ministerial Literature, 1668–1735," in *A Heritage of Her Own: Towards a New Social History of American Women*, ed. Nancy F. Cott and Elizabeth H. Pleck (New York: Simon and Schuster, 1979), 58–61.

5. E. Jennifer Monaghan, "Literacy Instruction and Gender in Colonial New England," in *Reading in America: Literature and Social History*, ed. Cathy N. Davidson (Baltimore: Johns Hopkins University Press, 1989), 53–54.

6. Massachusetts Bay School Law (1642). Available at: http://personal.pitne.net/primarysources/schoollaw1642.html.

7. Monaghan, "Literacy Instruction," 62–63.

8. Quoted in Monaghan, "Literacy Instruction," 63.

9. Joyce D. Goodfriend, "The Souls of African American Children: New Amsterdam," *Common-Place* 3, no. 4 (July 2003). Available at: http://www.common-place.org; Walter H. Small, "Girls in Colonial Schools," *Education* 22 (1902): 534, quoted in Monaghan, "Literacy Instruction," 64.

10. Monaghan, "Literacy Instruction," 58, 68–70. Quote is from *The Autobiography of Increase Mather*, ed. M. G. Hall (Worcester, MA, 1962), 278.

11. Bartlett Burleigh James and J. Franklin James, eds., *Journal of Jasper Danckaerts, 1679–1680* (New York: C. Scribner's Sons, 1913), 204.

12. Bremer, *The Puritan Experiment*, 182–83.

13. "A Collection Related to Ann Radcliffe, 1894–1977: A Finding Aid," Radcliffe College Archives, Arthur and Elizabeth Schlesinger Library on the History of Women in America, July 2007.

14. Monaghan, "Literacy Instruction," 54.

15. Richard S. Dunn, *Sugar and Slaves: The Rise of the Planter Class in the English West Indies, 1624–1714* (New York: W. W. Norton, 1972), 270–71.

16. Virginia DeJohn Anderson, *New England's Generation: The Great Migration and the Formation of Society and Culture in the Seventeenth Century* (Cambridge: Cambridge University Press, 1993), 173–75.

17. Mary Beth Norton, *In the Devil's Snare: The Salem Witchcraft Crisis of 1692* (New York: Knopf, 2002), 52.

18. Ulrich, "Vertuous Women," 62.

19. Cotton Mather, *Decennium Luctuosum* (Boston, 1699), 227, quoted in Laurel Thatcher Ulrich, *Good Wives: Image and Reality in the Lives of Women in Northern New England, 1650–1750* (New York: Oxford University Press, 1982), 207.

20. Steven Neuwirth, "Her Masters's Voice: Gender, Speech, and Gendered Speech in the Narrative of the Captivity of Mary White Rowlandson," in *Sex and Sexuality in Early America*, ed. Merril D. Smith (New York: New York University Press, 1998), 81, n. 11.

21. Mary Rowlandson's narrative has been published in several editions. Some are available online; see "Narrative of the Captivity of Mrs. Mary Rowlandson, 1682," in *Narratives of the Indian Wars, 1675–1699*, ed. Charles H. Lincoln (New York: C. Scribner's Sons, 1913). Available at: http://www.mith2.umd.edu/eada/html/display.php?docs=rowlandson_narrative.xml&action=show.

22. Ulrich, *Good Wives*, 227–28.

23. Richard Slotkin and James K. Folsom, *So Dreadful a Judgment: Puritan Responses to King Philip's War, 1676–1677* (Middletown, CT: Wesleyan University Press, 1978), 320, quoted in Neuwirth, "Her Master's Voice," 59.

24. Neuwirth, "Her Master's Voice," 60.

25. John Harvard Ellis, ed., *The Works of Anne Bradstreet in Prose and Verse* (Charlestown, MA: Abram E. Cutter, 1867), 84, quoted in Wendy Martin, *An American Triptych: Anne Bradstreet, Emily Dickinson, Adrienne Rich* (Chapel Hill: University of North Carolina Press, 1984), 37.

26. Martin, *American Triptych*, 20–22.

27. Ibid., 24–26.

28. Anne Bradstreet, "To My Dear and Loving Husband," in *Works of Anne Bradstreet in Prose and Verse*, ed. John Harvard Ellis (Charlestown, MA: A. E. Cutter, 1867). Available at: http://www.mith2.umd.edu/eada/html/display.php?docs=bradstreet_tomydear.xml&action=show.

29. Ellis, *Works*, 405–406, quoted in Martin, *American Triptych*, 70.

30. Martin, *American Triptych*, 30–32.

31. John Winthrop, *Winthrop's Journal: History of New England, 1630–1649*, ed. James Kendall Hosmer, 2 vols. (New York: Charles Scribner's Sons, 1908), 2: 225, quoted in Martin, *American Triptych*, 58.

32. Martin, *American Triptych*, 59.

33. John Winthrop, *A Short History of the Rise, Reign, and Ruine of the Antinomians, Familists, and Libertines, That Infected the Churches of New England* (London: R. Smith, 1644), reprinted in *Antinomianism in the Colony of Massachusetts Bay*, ed. Charles Francis Adams (Boston: The Prince Society, 1894), 83, quoted in Martin, *American Triptych*, 63.

34. Martin, *American Tritych*, 63–65.

35. David Cressy, *Coming Over: Migration and Communication between England and New England in the Seventeenth Century* (New York: Cambridge University Press, 1987), 213.

36. Everett Emerson, ed., *Letters from New England: The Massachusetts Bay Colony, 1609–1638* (Amherst, MA, 1976), 139–40, quoted in Cressy, *Coming Over*, 214.

37. Cressy, *Coming Over*, 220.

38. Essex Courts, vol. 1, 159, 173; vol. 5, 65–67; quoted in Cressy, *Coming Over*, 267.

39. *The Winthrop Papers* (Boston, 1931–1947), 4: 7–8, quoted in Cressy, *Coming Over*, 271.

40. "Letters of John Hall," May 21, 1666, Manuscripts, American Antiquarian Society, Worcester, MA, quoted in Cressy, *Coming Over*, 230.

41. Cressy, *Coming Over*, 220.

42. The recipe is from "Rules Made by E. B. for Children to Write By," in *A New Booke, Containing All Sort of Hands* (1611) in Elisabeth Leedham-Green, "Early Modern Handwriting: An Introduction." Available at: http://www.english.cam.ac.uk/ceres/ehoc/intro.html.

43. "Dudley's Letter to the Countess of Lincoln," in *Chronicles of the First Planters of the Colony of Massachusetts Bay, from 1623 to 1636*, ed. Alexander Young (Boston, 1846; reprinted, Williamstown, MA, 1978), 303, 305, quoted in Cressy, *Coming Over*, 221.

44. Kathleen M. Brown, *Good Wives, Nasty Wenches, and Anxious Patriarchs: Gender, Race, and Power in Colonial Virginia* (Chapel Hill: University of North Carolina Press, 1996), 295.

45. David R. Ransome, "Wives for Virginia, 1621," *William and Mary Quarterly* 48 (January 1991): 15.

46. Ulrich, *Good Wives*, 77, 116–17, 228.

47. "The 17th Century: Loara Standish." Available at: Pilgrim Hall Museum, http://www.pilgrimhall.org/samplers2.htm.

48. Debra Meyers, *Common Whores, Vertuous Women, and Loveing Wives: Free Will Christian Women in Colonial Maryland* (Bloomington: Indiana University Press, 2003), 5, 106–107.

49. Ibid., 119.

50. Bruce C. Daniels, *Puritans at Play: Leisure and Recreation in Colonial New England* (New York: Palgrave MacMillan, 1995), 31–32.

51. Ibid., 54–56.

52. Ibid., 109–11.

53. William Strachey, *The Historie of Travell into Virginia Britania* (1612), ed. Louis B. Wright and Virginia Freund, Hakluyt Society Publications, 2nd ser., 103 (Cambridge, 1953), 86, quoted in Helen C. Rountree, *The Powhatan Indians of Virginia: Their Traditional Culture* (Norman: University of Oklahoma Press, 1989), 98.

54. Rountree, *The Powhatan Indians*, 97–98.

55. Quoted in Richard Godbeer, *Sexual Revolution in Early America* (Baltimore: Johns Hopkins University Press, 2002), 164–65.

56. Godbeer, *Sexual Revolution*, 28–31, 101.

57. Elisabeth L. Roark, *Artists of Colonial America* (Westport, CT: Greenwood Press, 2003), 42–43, 50.

SUGGESTED READING

Cressy, David. *Coming Over: Migration and Communication between England and New England in the Seventeenth Century*. New York: Cambridge University Press, 1987.

Daniels, Bruce C. *Puritans at Play: Leisure and Recreation in Colonial New England*. New York: Palgrave MacMillan, 1995.

Martin, Wendy. *An American Triptych: Anne Bradstreet, Emily Dickinson, Adrienne Rich*. Chapel Hill: University of North Carolina Press, 1984.

Meyers, Debra. *Common Whores, Vertuous Women, and Loveing Wives: Free Will Christian Women in Colonial Maryland*. Bloomington: Indiana University Press, 2003.

Monaghan, E. Jennifer. "Literacy Instruction and Gender in Colonial New England." In *Reading in America: Literature and Social History*, edited by Cathy N. Davidson. Baltimore: Johns Hopkins University Press, 1989.

Rountree, Helen C. *The Powhatan Indians of Virginia: Their Traditional Culture*. Norman: University of Oklahoma Press, 1989.

Ulrich, Laurel Thatcher. *Good Wives: Image and Reality in the Lives of Women in Northern New England, 1650–1750*. New York: Oxford University Press, 1982.

Selected Bibliography
and Resources

BOOKS AND ARTICLES

Amussen, Susan D. *An Ordered Society: Gender and Class in Early Modern England.* Oxford: Basil Blackwell, 1988.

Anderson, Virginia DeJohn. "Animals into the Wilderness: The Development of Livestock Husbandry in the Seventeenth-Century Chesapeake." *William and Mary Quarterly* 59 (April 2002): 377–408.

———. *New England's Generation: The Great Migration and the Formation of Society and Culture in the Seventeenth Century.* Cambridge: Cambridge University Press, 1993.

Archer, Richard. "New England Mosaic: A Demographic Analysis for the Seventeenth Century." *William and Mary Quarterly* 47 (October 1990): 477–502.

Berkin, Carol. *First Generations: Women in Colonial America.* New York: Hill and Wang, 1996.

Boyer, Paul, and Stephen Nissenbaum. *Salem Possessed: The Social Origins of Witchcraft.* Cambridge, MA: Harvard University Press, 1974.

Bremer, Francis J. *The Puritan Experiment: New England Society from Bradford to Edwards.* New York: St. Martin's Press, 1976.

Brown, Kathleen M. *Good Wives, Nasty Wenches, and Anxious Patriarchs: Gender, Race, and Power in Colonial Virginia.* Chapel Hill: University of North Carolina Press, 1996.

Brown, Meg Lota, and Kari Boyd McBride. *Women's Roles in the Renaissance.* Westport, CT: Greenwood Press, 2005.

Bullough, Vern L., and Bonnie Bullough. *Cross-Dressing, Sex, and Gender.* Philadelphia: University of Pennsylvania Press, 1993.

Carr, Lois Green, and Lorena S. Walsh. "Economic Diversification and Labor Organization in the Chesapeake, 1650–1820." In *Work and Labor in Early America,* edited by Stephen Innes, 144–88. Chapel Hill: University of North Carolina Press, 1988.

——. "The Planter's Wife: The Experience of White Women in Seventeenth-Century Maryland." In *A Heritage of Her Own: Toward a New Social History of American Women*, edited by Nancy F. Cott and Elizabeth H. Pleck, 25–57. New York: Simon and Schuster, 1979.

Cavallo, Sandra, and Lyndan Warner, eds. *Widowhood in Medieval and Early Modern Europe*. New York: Longman, 1999.

Crane, Elaine Forman. *Ebb Tide in New England: Women, Seaports, and Social Change, 1630–1800*. Boston: Northeastern University Press, 1998.

Crawford, Patricia M., and Laura Gowing, eds. *Women's Worlds in Seventeenth-Century England: A Sourcebook*. New York: Routledge, 1999.

Cressy, David. *Coming Over: Migration and Communication between England and New England in the Seventeenth Century*. New York: Cambridge University Press, 1987.

Daniels, Bruce C. *Puritans at Play: Leisure and Recreation in Colonial New England*. New York: Palgrave Macmillan, 1995.

Demos, John Putnam. *Entertaining Satan: Witchcraft and the Culture of New England*. New York: Oxford University Press, 1982.

——. *A Little Commonwealth: Family Life in Plymouth Colony*. New York: Oxford University Press, 1970.

Diner, Hasia R., and Beryl Lieff Benderly. *Her Works Praise Her: A History of Jewish Women in America from Colonial Times to the Present*. New York: Basic Books, 2002.

Dugaw, Dianne. *Warrior Women and Popular Balladry, 1650–1850*. Chicago: University of Chicago Press, 1996.

Foster, Thomas A. "Deficient Husbands: Manhood, Sexual Incapacity, and Male Marital Sexuality in Seventeenth-Century New England." *William and Mary Quarterly* 56 (October 1999): 723–44.

Foyster, Elizabeth. *Manhood in Early Modern England: Honour, Sex, and Marriage*. London: Longman, 1999.

Frost, J. William. *The Quaker Family in Colonial America: A Portrait of the Society of Friends*. New York: St. Martin's Press, 1973.

Gaunt, Peter. *The English Civil War: The Essential Readings*. Oxford: Blackwell, 2001.

Godbeer, Richard. *Sexual Revolution in Early America*. Baltimore: Johns Hopkins University Press, 2002.

Graham, Willie, Carter L. Hudgins, Carl R. Lounsbury, Fraser D. Neiman, and James P. Whittenburg. "Adaptation and Innovation: Archaeological and Architectural Perspectives on the Seventeenth-Century Chesapeake." *William and Mary Quarterly* 64 (July 2007): 451–522.

Hambleton, Else L. *Daughters of Eve: Pregnant Brides and Unwed Mothers in Seventeenth-Century Massachusetts*. New York: Routledge, 2004.

Hughes, Ann. *The Causes of the English Civil War*. 2nd ed. New York: St. Martin's Press, 1998.

Karlsen, Carol F. *The Devil in the Shape of a Woman: Witchcraft in Colonial New England*. New York: Vintage Books, 1987.

Klein, Herbert S., Stanley L. Engerman, Robin Haines, and Ralph Shlomoiwitz. "Transoceanic Mortality: The Slave Trade in Comparative Perspective." *William and Mary Quarterly* 58 (January 2001): 93–117.

Lang, Sabine. *Men as Women, Women as Men: Changing Gender in Native American Cultures*. Austin: University of Texas Press, 1998.

Levy, Barry. *Quakers and the American Family: British Settlement in the Delaware Valley*. New York: Oxford University Press, 1988.

Main, Gloria L. *Peoples of a Spacious Nation: Families and Cultures in Colonial New England*. Cambridge, MA: Harvard University Press, 2001.

Martin, Wendy. *An American Triptych: Anne Bradstreet, Emily Dickinson, Adrienne Rich*. Chapel Hill: University of North Carolina Press, 1984.

Meyers, Debra. *Common Whores, Vertuous Women, and Loveing Wives: Free Will Christian Women in Colonial Maryland*. Bloomington: Indiana University Press, 2003.

Monaghan, E. Jennifer. "Literacy Instruction and Gender in Colonial New England." In *Reading in America: Literature and Social History*, edited by Cathy N. Davidson, 53–80. Baltimore: Johns Hopkins University Press, 1989.

Morgan, Edmund S. *The Puritan Family: Religion and Domestic Relations in Seventeenth-Century New England*. New York: Harper Torchbooks, 1966.

Nash, Alice. "'None of the Women Were Abused': Indigenous Contexts for the Treatment of Women Captives in the Northeast." In *Sex without Consent: Rape and Sexual Coercion in America*, edited by Merril D. Smith, 10–26. New York: New York University Press, 2001.

Norton, Mary Beth. *Founding Mothers and Fathers: Gendered Power and the Forming of American Society*. New York: Vintage Books, 1996.

———. *In the Devil's Snare: The Salem Witchcraft Crisis of 1692*. New York: Knopf, 2002.

Pagan, John Ruston. *Anne Orthwood's Bastard: Sex and Law in Early Virginia*. New York: Oxford University Press, 2003.

Parmenter, Jon. "After the Mourning Wars: The Iroquois as Allies in Colonial North American Campaigns, 1676–1760." *William and Mary Quarterly* 64 (January 2007): 39–82.

Pettigrew, William A. "Free to Enslave: Politics and the Escalation of Britain's Transatlantic Slave Trade, 1688–1714." *William and Mary Quarterly* 64 (January 2007): 3–38.

Plane, Ann Marie. *Colonial Intimacies: Indian Marriage in Early New England*. Ithaca, NY: Cornell University Press, 2000.

Ransome, David R. "Wives for Virginia, 1621." *William and Mary Quarterly* 48 (January 1991): 3–18.

Reis, Elizabeth. *Damned Women: Sinners and Witches in Puritan New England*. Ithaca, NY: Cornell University Press, 1997.

Richter, Daniel K. *The Ordeal of the Longhouse: The Peoples of the Iroquois League in the Era of European Colonization*. Chapel Hill: University of North Carolina Press, 1992.

Roark, Elisabeth L. *Artists of Colonial America*. Westport, CT: Greenwood Press, 2003.

Rountree, Helen C. *The Powhatan Indians of Virginia: Their Traditional Culture*. Norman: University of Oklahoma Press, 1989.

Rutman, Darrett B., and Anita H. Rutman. "Of Agues and Fevers: Malaria in the Early Chesapeake." *William and Mary Quarterly* 33 (January 1976): 31–60.

Rutz-Robbins, Kristi. "'Divers Debts': Women's Participation in the Local Economy, Albemarle, North Carolina, 1663–1729." *Early American Studies* 4 (Fall 2006): 425–41.

Salmon, Marylynn. "The Cultural Significance of Breastfeeding and Infant Care in Early Modern England and America." *Journal of Social History* 28 (Winter 1994): 247–69.

Scott, Donald M., and Bernard Wishy, eds. *America's Families: A Documentary History.* New York: Harper and Row, 1982.

Sievers, Julie. "Drowned Pens and Shaking Hands: Sea Providence Narratives in Seventeenth-Century New England." *William and Mary Quarterly* 63 (October 2006): 743–77.

Smith, Merril D., ed. *Sex and Sexuality in Early America.* New York: New York University Press, 1998.

———. *Sex without Consent: Rape and Sexual Coercion in America.* New York: New York University Press, 2001.

Snyder, Terri L. *Brabbling Women: Disorderly Speech and the Law in Early Virginia.* Ithaca, NY: Cornell University Press, 2003.

Soderlund, Jean R. "Women's Authority in Pennsylvania and New Jersey Quaker Meetings, 1680–1760." *William and Mary Quarterly* 44 (October 1987): 722–49.

Thornton, John. "Cannibals, Witches, and Slave Traders in the Atlantic World." *William and Mary Quarterly* 60 (April 2003): 273–94.

Tomlins, Christopher L., and Bruce H. Mann. *The Many Legalities of Early America.* Chapel Hill: University of North Carolina Press, 2001.

Trexler, Richard. *Sex and Conquest: Gendered Violence, Political Order, and the European Conquest of the Americas.* Ithaca, NY: Cornell University Press, 1995.

Ulrich, Laurel Thatcher. "Big Dig, Little Dig, Hidden Worlds: Boston." *Common-Place* 3, no. 4 (July 2003). Available at http://www.common-place.org.

———. *Good Wives: Image and Reality in the Lives of Women in Northern New England, 1650–1750.* New York: Oxford University Press, 1982.

———. *A Midwife's Tale: The Life of Martha Ballard Based on Her Diary, 1725–1812.* New York: Knopf, 1990.

———. "Vertuous Women Found: New England Ministerial Literature, 1668–1735." In *A Heritage of Her Own: Toward a New Social History of American Women,* edited by Nancy F. Cott and Elizabeth H. Pleck, 58–61. New York: Simon and Schuster, 1979.

Vaughan, Alden T., and Francis J. Bremer, eds. *Puritan New England: Essays on Religion, Society, and Culture.* New York: St. Martin's Press, 1977.

Walsh, Lorena S. "The Chesapeake Slave Trade: Regional Patterns, African Origins, and Some Implications." *William and Mary Quarterly* 58 (January 2001): 139–70.

Weisberg, D. Kelly. "'Under Greet Temptation': Women and Divorce in Puritan Massachusetts." *Feminist Studies* 2, no. 2/3 (1975): 183–93.

Westerkamp, Marilyn J. *Women and Religion in Early America, 1600–1850: The Puritan and Evangelical Traditions.* New York: Routledge, 1999.

Wiesner, Merry E. *Christianity and Sexuality in the Early Modern World: Regulating Desire, Reforming Practice.* New York: Routledge, 2000.

Winthrop, John. *Winthrop's Journal, History of New England, 1630–1649.* Edited by James Kendall Hosmer. New York: Charles Scribner's Sons, 1908.

FILMS

The Crucible (1996), directed by Nicholas Hytner. Adapted by Arthur Miller from his stage play, this movie starring Daniel Day-Lewis as John Proctor uses the Salem witchcraft crises to warn of the dangers of political and religious extremism.

The New World (2005), directed by Terence Malick. The establishment of Jamestown by the English is the subject of this movie, as well as the encounters between the Englishmen John Smith and John Rolfe and the Powhatan maiden Pocahontas.

Stage Beauty (2004), directed by Richard Eyre. Based on Jeffrey Hatcher's play, *Complete Female Stage Beauty*, the story is about Edward "Ned" Kynaston (Billy Crudup), the actor who was famous for playing female roles during the reign of Charles II. When the king decrees that women are permitted to act on public stages, Kynaston's career is naturally threatened.

Three Sovereigns for Sarah (1985), directed by Philip Leacock. Vanessa Redgrave stars as Sarah Cloyce, one of the women accused of being a witch during the Salem witchcraft crisis in 1692. The film was shot of location and includes some material from the actual trial transcripts.

WEB SITES

Common-Place, http://www.common-place.org.
   An online history journal with essays covering early American history and culture, as well as reviews, and other topics of interest for historians, scholars, and teachers.

The Costumer's Manifesto: Seventeenth Century Fashion Links Page, http://www.costumes.org/history/100pages/17thlinks.htm#1665-1700.
   This is a fun and useful site for those who are interested in clothing and costumes.

Early Americas Digital Archive, http://www.mith2.umd.edu/eada.
   A collection of electronic texts covering c. 1492–1820, the site is supported by the Maryland Institute for Technology in the Humanities. It also includes a search engine that searches other web sites.

History Matters, http://www.history-matters.com.
   This site covers U.S. history. It includes primary documents, how historians use primary sources, and links to other web sites, teaching assignments, and syllabi.

The Library of Congress: American Memory, http://lcweb2.loc.gov/amhome.html.
   A section of the Library of Congress site with online historical documents, prints, manuscripts, and more.

New Netherland Institute, http://www.nnp.org/index.shtml.
   This site has links to the New Netherland Institute and the New Netherland Project. It includes a virtual tour of New Netherland, maps, documents, and other resources.

Salem Witch Trials: Documentary Archive and Transcription Project, http://etext.virginia.edu/salem/witchcraft/home.html.
   Everything you ever wanted to know about the Salem witchcraft crises. The site includes links to the transcribed documents and other court records, maps, other primary sources, and links to Danvers (formerly Salem Village).

Virtual Jamestown, http://www.virtualjamestown.org/page2.html.
   This site contains primary sources, maps, and interpretive essays. More material continues to be added.

Index

About the Author

MERRIL D. SMITH is an independent scholar and editor of *Encyclopedia of Rape* (Greenwood, 2004) and other titles.